blue
rider
press

THE CEO PAY MACHINE

THE CEO
PAY MACHINE

HOW IT TRASHES AMERICA AND HOW TO STOP IT

Steven Clifford

BLUE RIDER PRESS   *New York*

blue
rider
press

An imprint of Penguin Random House LLC
375 Hudson Street
New York, New York 10014

Library of Congress Cataloging-in-Publication Data

Names: Clifford, Steven, author.
Title: The CEO pay machine : how it trashes America and how to stop it / Steven Clifford.
Description: New York : Blue Rider Press, 2017.
Identifiers: LCCN 2016052097 (print) | LCCN 2017014632 (ebook) | ISBN 9780735212404 (Ebook) | ISBN 9780735212398 (hardback)
Subjects: LCSH: Executives—Salaries, etc.—United States | BISAC: BUSINESS & ECONOMICS / Business Ethics. | BUSINESS & ECONOMICS / Corporate Finance.
Classification: LCC HD4965.5.U6 (ebook) | LCC HD4965.5.U6 C55 2017 (print) | DDC 331.2/81658400973—dc23
LC record available at https://lccn.loc.gov/2016052097
p.   cm.

Printed in the United States of America
10 9 8 7 6 5 4 3 2 1

BOOK DESIGN BY NICOLE LAROCHE

CONTENTS

THE CEO PAY MACHINE

CHAPTER ONE

Heresy

I started to question the standard CEO pay system in 2012 while I was a board member of a large family-owned business. The board accepted that CEO compensation must have three components: salary, short-term bonus, and long-term incentive. No board member asked why this trinity was holy. It would have been like asking why we worked in an office building or had an accounting department. It was how things were done.

The board was following a pay structure that expert compensation consultants had established ten years previously, along with a host of other pay practices, including peer groups, percentile ranking, compensation targets, performance measures, bonus targets, bonus ranges, and equity awards. The consultants argued that this system achieved "pay for performance" by linking CEO pay to the achievement of measurable goals. By 2012, virtually all large American companies used it to determine CEO pay.*

The CEO pay process starts with the compensation ("comp")

---

* I use "large company" to refer to the Fortune 500 or the nearly identical S&P 500 or representative samples of either. The first ranks companies by revenues, the second by market capitalization.

committee of the board. At this family company, the comp committee established annual performance measures and goals for
both the short-term bonus and the long-term incentive and measured the CEO's performance against them. Two-thirds of his
bonus was based on financial measures and one-third on the
achievement of nonfinancial goals.

I began to find annual nonfinancial goals problematic because
important initiatives rarely fell neatly into a calendar year. If
turning around a money-losing subsidiary was going to be a
three-year struggle, what should be the measurable achievement
for the first year? Hiring a new president for the subsidiary?
Achieving a smaller loss? Drafting a good turnaround plan?
When another board member actually proposed this, I objected.
"I can draft a good turnaround plan right now. My plan is to stop
losing money. Do I get a bonus?" The response was, "Okay, wise
guy, how would you measure the first year's progress on a three-
year turnaround?" I had no good answer.

For the company's most important goals, what could be clearly
defined and measured within a year was neither important nor
revealing. One year, a major goal for the CEO was to hire a new
chief financial officer (CFO). Offered a bonus for this achievement, should he get one for hiring his dog Buster as CFO? To prevent this, the board could specify that he get a bonus only if he
hires a first-rate CFO, prompting the question: What is a first-rate
CFO, and how can we tell if we have hired one?

Aggravating this lack of specificity, bonus measures were established before the start of the New Year, then often became obsolete
after January 1 as the company faced unexpected opportunities or
threats. One year, bonus goals were geared toward growth, but we
suddenly had the chance to sell a large subsidiary at a great price

and pay the shareholders a special dividend. The bonus goals now pushed in the wrong direction. Should we change goals? Perhaps, but unexpected events always happen. Should the company change bonus plans monthly? Daily?

I tried to imagine what would happen if the Pentagon drafted bonus plans in September 1942 for achievements in 1943. General George S. Patton's bonus might have depended on capturing particular towns in North Africa, while General Douglas MacArthur might have gotten one for protecting Australia from invasion. If we assume that bonuses influence behavior, MacArthur diverts resources from island-hopping to defending Australia, while Patton stays in North Africa and ignores the opportunity in Sicily. Or imagine structuring a set of bonus bogeys for General Dwight D. Eisenhower to motivate him to take the right actions when he was the Supreme Allied Commander.

If generals got bonuses for winning battles, they might be encouraged to fight easy, meaningless battles. To correct this, the military could award generals a bonus only after capturing at least a thousand enemy soldiers, but then generals might have an incentive to end the battle as soon as a thousand soldiers were captured, because they wouldn't get any extra pay for capturing more. But modifying the bonus criteria to remove these perverse incentives would inevitably introduce more unintended consequences.

"This is a ridiculous analogy," you may think. "Eisenhower was trying to win a war. He was concerned with soldiers' lives, not money. He would do the right thing regardless of any bonus."

You are probably correct. But then why have a bonus system? A bonus system makes sense only if it changes people's actions, decisions, and behavior. A bonus system that does not change behavior is a complete waste of money.

We recognize the absurdity of an annual bonus system for generals, but generals and CEOs face many of the same challenges. They command but must also lead and persuade. They face enemies (competitors), battle over territories (markets), introduce new weapons (products), coordinate their divisions, and make strategic decisions under conditions of uncertainty. Then why are annual bonuses absurd for a general but necessary for a CEO? Perhaps because the military trusts its officers, and in a strange way, corporations do not.

"Duty, honor, country," MacArthur told the Corps of Cadets at West Point, "those three hallowed words reverently dictate what you ought to be, what you can be, what you will be." The military believes that the strength of this commitment will guide officers to make the right decisions and take the proper actions without the financial reinforcement of duty bonuses, honor bonuses, and country bonuses. Corporate America implicitly fears that if CEOs are paid only a salary, they will neglect their responsibilities to shareholders. Therefore, a bonus system is necessary to animate CEOs actions, decisions, and behavior.

Remember that bonus systems are indefensible unless they change people's actions. A company cannot justify a bonus for actions that would have occurred without it. The great irony is that CEO bonuses do change actions and decisions: they make CEOs more selfish and less aligned with the interests of the shareholders.

Corporate directors would bristle at the suggestion that they don't trust their CEOs and argue that they are "paying for performance" and therefore "aligning the CEO and shareholders." But paying for performance assumes that the performance bonus will cause the CEO to act differently. In crude terms, the board holds that the CEO will make the shareholders more money only if he pockets his share of the loot. To get him to do the right thing, the board must bribe him. This does not exhibit a high level of trust.

While I was always happy to pocket one, an annual cash bonus is a dumb idea and almost always counterproductive. A cash bonus—money—is a powerful tool. Too powerful. I've seen CEOs neglect what I thought were more important issues to achieve their bonus goals. I can't blame them. When a board specifies certain goals as deserving a bonus, the CEO will naturally pursue these even if it means neglecting other initiatives. This is what the bonus system inevitably produces as the CEO rationalizes that he is pursuing the board's priorities.

In 2012, the board chair of the family company asked me to join the comp committee and help negotiate a new compensation plan with our CEO. This was something of a demotion. I had been chairing the audit committee, and in the corporate hierarchy, the saying goes that the second dumbest director chairs audit. The dumbest gets comp.

The comp committee comprised three independent directors, meaning that they did no business with the company and were not large shareholders. No member of the committee was an expert in executive compensation. This is normal in corporate America, where directors are usually generalists.

At that time (and this continues today), the newspapers overflowed with outrage, as the pay for CEOs running large companies in 2012 had increased 12.7 percent over 2011 and 37.4 percent since 2009. *The New York Times* asked, "Is any C.E.O. worth $1 million a day?" and ran stories about shareholder revolts over CEO compensation at Citigroup, Barclays, Chesapeake Energy, Morgan Stanley, Bank of America, and elsewhere.

This reporting encouraged me to pursue heretical thoughts.

According to compensation consultants, our CEO pay system was well designed and effective. But the CEO always did better than the shareholders. The shareholders had mostly good years, but some bad years. The CEO had only good years. Year after year, he surpassed his goals and made more than 100 percent of his target bonus.

I could not blame the CEO, whom I will call Brad. He was honorable, hardworking, and very effective. He acted precisely as the system told him to act. He focused on the tasks the board designated as the most important when they attached a bonus to them.

I had no problem with Brad's total compensation, which was orders of magnitude below that of Fortune 500 CEOs, but I concluded that the bonus system was misguided: It encouraged him to concentrate on short-term objectives that could be accomplished within a calendar year and to pay less attention to creative innovations and unexpected opportunities.

It seemed to me that either we were doing a bad job of applying the pay-for-performance model or there was something profoundly wrong with it, so I did some research. After reading academic studies on performance pay and surveying the business press, I reached a stunning conclusion: The emperor had no clothes. No matter how one defined pay for performance, no company had figured out how to make it work well. It always seemed to make things worse.

Brad had done an outstanding job. The board wanted him to stay for seven more years, until he retired. He was agreeable but wanted a fair contract. As a comp committee member, I wanted a pay plan that would keep him both satisfied and focused on what was truly important. The plan would also need to be explained to the satisfaction of the four hundred family members who were shareholders.

Brad did not need a bonus to be motivated. The compensation system needed only to channel this motivation. It would do so ineffectively if we offered a bonus for specific achievements such as increasing next year's earnings, gaining market share in one product line, or improving customer satisfaction at a subsidiary.

The company was best served if his motivation was directed toward his own satisfaction in a job well done with an economic incentive to always act in the long-term best interests of the shareholders.

This produced a radical proposal: THE CEO SHOULD RECEIVE ONLY SALARY AND RESTRICTED STOCK, NEITHER OF WHICH SHOULD BE SUBJECT TO ANY PERFORMANCE CRITERIA.* The only exception was that he would forfeit a portion of the restricted stock when he retired if the shareholders had not achieved a satisfactory return over the entire period of his contract. If appreciation of shares plus dividends had not exceeded a fixed rate of return, the CEO would forfeit a large part of his restricted share grants.

The dean of one of America's better business schools chaired our comp committee. Like me, he had become disillusioned with the standard CEO pay system, which produced insane pay levels and dysfunctional incentives, and was tired of reading about the outrage at CEO pay. "Why does everyone use this convoluted pay process?" he asked me one day on the phone, and then answered

---

* Restricted stock cannot be sold until certain conditions are met. For CEOs, restricted stock usually becomes unrestricted over time. For example, restrictions on a grant of stock might lapse 20 percent each year over five. This means that the CEO is free to trade 20 percent of the grant after year one, 40 percent after year two, and so on.

his own question. "They do it because everyone else does it. I'm ready to try something new."

He liked my idea of jettisoning the annual bonus and relying only on restricted stock. "If we want him to think like a shareholder, we need to make him a shareholder." He suggested I meet with Brad to see if we could reach an agreement on the principles of my proposal.

Like most business executives, Brad valued money and understood that more was better than less. While he saw some advantages in this proposal, he raised practical concerns: What is the salary? What about future salary increases? How many shares of restricted stock would be granted each year? What portion of these would be subject to forfeit? How would a target for a fair shareholder return be established?

I told him I would talk with the committee, the board chair, and the other directors. If they agreed, Brad and I could negotiate the numbers. Most of this group, including the chair, a woman who was elected recently, were family members. She wanted a large portion of restricted stock subject to forfeit. But I argued that a significant amount should not be subject to forfeit. First, I was sure that Brad would not agree to have nearly everything at risk. Second, I wanted him to be a shareholder and think like one. In good times and bad, his economic interests should be aligned with the shareholders. If he received a fixed number of restricted shares each year, the best way for him to increase his wealth was to constantly increase the share price. However, if too large a portion was subject to forfeit and he was running below the return target, he might take large risks in his last years to beat the target.

Moreover, the portion subject to forfeit would depend on the ease or difficulty of hitting the seven-year return target. The lower the target, the higher the forfeit Brad would accept. So the board chair, the comp chair, and I agreed on the lowest acceptable return target; then I could negotiate for a higher forfeit and a higher target, trading off one against the other.

The comp committee then sent a memo to the board that said the following:

We have a simple proposal for Brad's compensation: Salary plus restricted stock. There will be no annual bonus and no performance measures save this one: Brad will forfeit a significant amount of his restricted stock if over the seven-year period shareholders receive less than a satisfactory return.

Our reasoning is:

The compensation system is not needed to motivate Brad. Brad is already highly motivated. The comp system should precisely align his interests with those of the shareholders. The only way to do this is to make him a shareholder and eschew additional bonuses beyond restricted stock that dilute this alignment.

Our current compensation system is too complex. It inevitably incorporates counterproductive incentives. For example, if we set return targets on investments and ignore leverage, the CEO will have an incentive to borrow too much. However, if we adjust for leverage, the CEO will have an incentive to borrow too little.

The CEO knows more about the company than the board. He will always have an advantage when negotiating bonus structures, goals, and payouts.

We and other boards cannot design methods to effectively measure and reward CEO performance.

All pay-for-performance systems cause more harm than good. They generate perverse incentives, undeserved and often absurdly high bonuses, and damage the companies that use them.

Salary plus restricted stock is simple and effective. We know that Brad is a highly capable executive with unquestioned integrity. We should pay him fairly and rid ourselves of the complexities and perversities of our present system.

We have discussed these ideas with Brad. He is amenable in principle, but of course, he wants to see the hard numbers.

We then suggested floors and ceilings for the variables to be negotiated, including:

1. Salary
2. Future salary increases
3. Number of shares of restricted stock granted each year
4. The portion of these shares subject to forfeit
5. The target for an adequate shareholder return

(As I am bound by a confidentiality agreement, I cannot disclose these or any of the numbers discussed and agreed on in these negotiations.)

After three negotiating sessions, Brad and I reached an agreement and signed a memorandum of understanding that we sent to our lawyers. The lawyers then did what they always do. "What happens if it rains frogs?" they asked. After three drafts, they reached an agreement on this point, and then turned to the question of whether a rain of tadpoles is the same as a rain of frogs. Once they had billed enough hours to satisfy their professional standards for minimum care, we had an agreement.

Our new CEO pay plan worked very well. Long-term value creation became the economic goal of both Brad and the shareholders. He is happier and more focused, and has remarked that the new system influenced his behavior and decision-making.* The board is happy. The shareholders are happy. Happiest of all is the comp committee. They don't have to revisit the issues of CEO compensation or retain compensation consultants or deal with lawyers for seven years.

While our pay system worked well, the clamor over CEO pay grew more intense. Among the reports in 2014 alone:

- *AFL-CIO Executive Paywatch* trumpeted, "CEO Pay Hits 'Insane Level.'"
- Former secretary of labor Robert Reich found that the "growing divergence between CEO pay and that of the

---

* Again, I cannot provide examples without breaching a confidentiality agreement.

typical American worker isn't just wildly unfair. It's also bad for the economy."

- A report from the Institute for Policy Studies, a Washington think tank, stated: "An alarming number of CEOs are not adding exceptional value to [the US] economy. They are extracting vast sums from it." The president of the Economic Policy Institute stated, "The escalation in CEO pay was not accompanied by a corresponding increase in output. They didn't make the pie bigger but they are taking a bigger piece of it. What that means is that everyone else has a smaller piece."

- Headlines in *The New York Times* blared, "For the Highest-Paid C.E.O.s, the Party Goes On," "How Much Is Too Much? CEO Pay Laid Bare," and "Outrage Over Wall St. Pay."

- The *Times* ran articles on the eye-popping CEO pay packages at Microsoft, Blackstone, Morgan Stanley, General Motors, Bank of America, Time Warner, Yahoo, Disney, JPMorgan Chase, and many others.

The result of all this was that nothing changed: CEO pay increased by 15.6 percent from the previous year in 2014. According to the Economic Policy Institute, since 1978, CEO pay (inflation adjusted) had risen tenfold. Over the same time period, a typical worker's wages grew from $48,000 in 1978 to just $53,200 in 2014, an increase of less than half of 1 percent per year. Since 1978, CEO pay has grown 90 times faster than the pay of a typical worker.

By 2014, depending on the method of calculation, large-company CEOs got paid an average of $13.5 million or $22.6

million or $30 million-plus in 2014.* That was somewhere be-
tween 300 and 700 times more than the average worker made. (I
lean toward the higher number.) Such outsize CEO pay is a relatively recent phenomenon. As recently as 1978, the average large-
company CEO was paid only 26 times more than the average
worker.

In 2015, CEO pay increased only modestly. Average CEO pay
rose 2.0 percent to $12.6 million, while median CEO pay received
a 4.5 percent increase to $10.8 million at S&P 500 companies for
CEOs who served two full consecutive fiscal years.

That year, *The New York Times* selected the 200 largest companies, ranked by revenue, and compared them with a similarly prepared list from 2014. Median pay in this group rose 5 percent to
$16.6 million in 2015. However, the average pay for these 200 CEOs
decreased from $22.6 million in 2014 to $19.3 million in 2015.

The seeming contradiction can be explained by the absence of
$100-million-plus CEO paydays in 2015. There were two CEOs
above $100 million in 2014. This absence lowered average pay
among the top 200 even while median pay increased and both
median and average pay rose in the larger group of S&P CEOs.

A large part of the decrease in average pay reported by the

---

* These numbers vary because, first, there are different definitions of "large company." The AFL-CIO arrived at $13.5 million by surveying 472 companies in the
S&P 500 where valid employee and CEO pay was available. Equilar, an executive
compensation firm, averaged the 200 highest-paid public companies' CEOs to
arrive at $22.6 million. Second, there are two different ways of calculating CEO
pay. The major difference is that one includes and the other excludes gains on the
exercise of stock options awarded in prior years. This is explained in some detail
in chapter 9. When William Lazonick included realized appreciation on both
stock options and stock awards, he arrived at the $30.3 million figure. William
Lazonick, "Taking Stock: Why Executive Pay Results in an Unstable and Inequitable Economy," Roosevelt Institute, June 5, 2014, http://rooseveltinstitute.net
/taking-stock-executive-pay.

Times is an artifact of how one man, media mogul John Malone, whom we will meet later, determines CEO rewards in the companies he controls. He decreased compensation for David Zaslav, CEO of Discovery Communications, from $154.3 million in 2014 to $32.4 million in 2015. Most of Zaslav's 2014 pay was really a signing bonus for a five-year contract, and thus did not recur in 2015. Two other Malone companies similarly paid their CEOs extraordinary amounts in 2014 but not in 2015. Michael T. Fries, CEO of Liberty Global, made $111.9 million in 2014 and $27.7 million in 2015, and Gregory B. Maffei of Liberty Media and Liberty Interactive made $73.8 million in 2014 and $26.7 million in 2015. Malone's idiosyncratic practices should not be mistaken for a national trend toward CEO pay restraint.

Why has CEO pay continued to escalate in the face of public outrage? Because nobody understands the roots of the problem. A lot of angry people think the explosion in CEO pay is a consequence of globalization and greed. But other advanced economies function without bestowing vast wealth on CEOs. In Japan, the ratio of CEO-to-average-worker pay is 16 to 1. It's 48 to 1 in Denmark and 84 to 1 in the UK.

Why is America such an outlier? Can American CEOs really be 20 to 60 times better than Japanese CEOs?

Unrestrained greed does not explain gargantuan CEO pay. Undoubtedly, many CEOs are greedy. They are not hired by the Little Sisters of the Poor to comfort the impoverished; they are hired by corporations to make money.

But if American CEOs are greedy, did their greed triple in intensity around 2000, just when my classmates from Harvard Business School and I were retiring? I don't think so. I would stack up my classmates against anyone on the Greed-o-Meter. These are guys who fondly remember the psychedelic 1960s as the decade when the Dow Jones industrial average rose 42 percent. Is there no greed in Europe and Asia? Are Danish and Japanese CEOs altruists?

No one planned the CEO pay explosion, though many CEOs welcomed it and exploited it, while many boards were, and remain, quiescent. How this occurred is far more complex than most people understand, particularly those who want to fix the problem with more regulations and procedures that would only exacerbate it.

Like the family company I worked with, corporate America has adopted pay procedures and practices that may have seemed reasonable, but they have collectively ensured a dizzying upward spiral in CEO compensation. I call this the CEO Pay Machine. Mechanically and inexorably, the Machine made CEO pay escalation a mathematical certainty.

Boards and government overseers never understood how the Machine functions, dooming all attempted reforms. As CEO pay escalated, efforts to reform the system and control the increases, both those mandated by the government and initiated by the companies, compounded the problem by introducing warped incentives and unanticipated consequences. These interventions enabled the Pay Machine to push CEO pay beyond the dreams of avarice.

Before stumbling further, corporate boards, government regulators, shareholders, politicians, and editorial writers need to understand how the sausage is made—how the Pay Machine actually works, how its parts interact, and how every step in the process pushes CEO pay to higher and higher levels.

I decided to write a book about it. "I've got some great stuff about CEO pay," I told a friend in publishing.

"Everybody knows CEO pay is unconscionable," he responded. "Nobody wants to read about it."

"But I can explain how it happened and why it happened," I said.

"Nobody cares."

"But the CEO pay system is both crazy and corrupt."

"So what if CEOs are showered with riches? A lot of people, including rock stars, baseball players, and movie producers, make a lot of money. Why pick on CEOs?"

"Rock stars, baseball players, and movie producers make money in a free market. CEO pay has nothing to do with a free market," I said. "CEO compensation is as market-driven as were the salaries of Soviet commissars. Both pay systems are corrupt, not market-driven, and administered by those who captured power."

"So the system is corrupt. Everyone over the age of ten suspects this. Why buy a book about it?"

"But I've got a solution."

"Big deal. Their lawyers will find a way around it."

"What if I could show that colossal CEO pay harmed all large American companies, impeded economic growth, and threatened the foundations of democracy?"

"That might sell," he said, "especially if you could lead with how this affects the Kardashians."

I was a CEO for fourteen years before retiring at age fifty-seven. Since then, I've served on many corporate boards. I've seen the CEO Pay Machine work. I've even had a hand on the controls. As a CEO, I was overpaid, but not enough. As a director of a dozen companies, I was overpaid, but not enough. I now bite the hand that fed me for many years.

I'll start with a fairy tale to illustrate how a board of directors figures out how much to pay its CEO. To make it simple, I ask you to imagine a company that's not calculating what to pay its CEO, but what to pay an average employee, perhaps someone like you.

CHAPTER TWO

You Get Paid Like a CEO: A Fairy Tale

You have a job, but you need more money. Your $75,000 salary as a loan officer at the Midwest Bank isn't enough, so you ask your fairy godmother to intervene.

You say, "I can't get by on my salary, Fairy Godmother. Can you help me get a promotion?"

"I can do better than that," she answers. "I will get you more money for the same job."

The next day, your phone rings. It's the chairman of the board calling. "We're trying a new experiment here at the bank, and you've been chosen to participate," he says. "You probably know that Midwest Bank employs an equitable, objective, and effective system for determining CEO compensation. We now want to apply those same compensation practices to other employees. We think this will produce spectacular results. Tomorrow, please meet with Charles Bunge, who chairs the board's compensation committee, to discuss your new pay package."

The next day you meet Mr. Bunge, a distinguished-looking, silver-haired gentleman.

"Our CEO pay process motivates and rewards performance. It enables us to attract and retain the best executives," Bunge tells you. "Now we want to apply this system to your compensation."

He explains that your new plan will be performance-based, just like the CEO's. "If you achieve your goals, you will be rewarded. Once we prove how well this works, we'll move all bank employees to pay for performance. How does that sound to you?"

"It sounds good to me. It's the American way. I benefit when the company benefits. What's not to like?"

"Nothing, except that the details of the plan are complicated." Mr. Bunge advises you to retain, at the company's expense, a compensation consultant to help you draft your plan. He explains, "The use of a third-party consultant will ensure that your compensation plan is unbiased, is based on objective data, and has the approval of an independent expert. We ask you to work with your selected consultant and propose to us the appropriate structure and dollar amounts for your new compensation plan."

Later you ask your fairy godmother for advice. "Who should I hire as a compensation consultant?"

"Any of the big human resources consulting firms will do. Towers Watson, Mercer, or Williams Wilson. Find one that already has a big contract at Midwest Bank, for example, administering its health plans. Hint that you have some influence with Midwest's health plans. And make sure they understand that their contract to advise you will be renewed annually, so long as you're satisfied with the results."

You call a friend at headquarters and find out that Midwest

Bank retains Williams Wilson to administer its employee health care plan. So you hire them.

A few days later, you meet with Sarah Burke, one of their compensation consultants. "The first thing we have to do," she says, "is establish your peer group."

"What's that?"

"A peer group is a group of companies comparable to Midwest. We'll survey them and find out what they pay people with jobs similar to yours."

That sounds reasonable. "What companies should be in the peer group?"

She thinks about it for a minute. "We should start with Goldman Sachs and add Morgan Stanley, JPMorgan Chase, and Wells Fargo."

"Wow. Those are really big banks, much bigger than Midwest. Are they really comparable?"

"Your job is to make loans to builders and developers for construction projects, right? All these bigger banks have people who do exactly what you do. Their job descriptions are exactly the same as yours. They have the same duties and responsibilities you have. What difference should it make that their loans have a couple of extra zeros?"

Six weeks later, Sarah presents her survey of your peer group. "For your position," she says, "your peer group companies have a median salary of $150,000."

"Wow, that's great. That's double what I'm making now. You've done a great job. I really appreciate it."

"Well, thank you, but this is just the beginning. I just told you the peer group's median salary for your position. That means that half your peer group companies have a higher salary and half have a lower salary. I'm sure the Midwest board won't be comfortable paying you the median salary. That would say, 'We're a mediocre bank that employs mediocre people.' I'm going to recommend that they benchmark your salary at the 75th percentile, where you'd be making more than 75 percent of your peers. You're better than average, and Midwest is a better-than-average bank, so your salary should be higher than average. It should be around $200,000."

Is this great, or what? You can't wait to thank your fairy godmother. "Can you believe it?" you tell her that evening. "Williams Wilson is recommending raising my salary to $200,000. I never imagined I could earn that much! How can I ever thank you enough?"

"You moron. You're going to be paid like a CEO. Salary is small potatoes. It's just the beginning. Go back to Sarah and ask about Midwest's short-term bonus and long-term incentive plans. That's where the big bucks are."

You do exactly that at your next meeting with Sarah.

She explains, "Your annual cash bonus should be targeted at two times your salary, or $400,000. That's the 75th percentile of your peer group. One-quarter of the peer group received a higher cash bonus last year and three-quarters got less. The market is very competitive. If Midwest wants to attract, motivate, and retain the best people, they know they have to pay above average."

It may seem unbelievable, but it's true. You can make another $400,000 in a cash bonus.

While you're almost fainting with joy, Sarah continues. "Four hundred thousand is only your target bonus. You can make as much as $1.2 million in a cash bonus. If you achieve your bonus target—they call it a bonus bogey—you'll get the $400,000, but if you surpass your bogey, you can get much more. In fact, you can earn up to three times your target bonus. That would be $1.2 million."

"And what are my bogeys?"

"To start the process, we'll submit our suggestions."

You feel dizzy. "Let me get this straight. I can negotiate my own bonus bogeys?"

"Absolutely. What would you like for bonus bogeys?"

Does this require a lot of thought? No. You're beginning to get the idea. You say, "Something that will allow me to make three times my target bonus."

"Your job is to loan money for building construction. What was the total value of loans you made last year?"

"Eighty million dollars."

"Suggest tying your cash bonus to the increase in your loans. If you increase loans by 10 percent—that would be $88 million—you'll get your target bonus of $400,000. If you increase loans by 20 percent, you'll get an $800,000 bonus, that's double your target. If you increase loans by 30 percent, you'll get a $1.2 million bonus, that's three times your target."

"But wouldn't that give me an incentive to make bad loans?"

"None of your new loans will go bad next year," Sarah answers, quite reasonably, "so your bonus is safe. Don't worry. No one on the compensation committee knows much about construction lending or even banking. Just tell them that volume of loans is the standard measure of performance in construction lending."

"But, Sarah, I'm worried that some of the loans could go bad after a year, and it's my job to make good loans, not bad ones."

"You should worry about that," Sarah says, nodding emphatically. "That's why Midwest will give you a long-term incentive plan, which will compensate you for thinking about the long-term financial health of Midwest. As you'll see, the bank has carefully designed its CEO compensation package to balance short-term gains against long-term interests."

"How does the long-term incentive work?"

"The company gives you stock options and restricted stock."

"What's a stock option?"

"A stock option is the right to buy Midwest stock at a fixed price. Under its stock option plan, Midwest would give you the right to purchase a share of its stock from the company at today's market price of $30 a share. You can exercise this option anytime over the next ten years. If, for example, the price has increased to $50, you can buy a share at $30 from Midwest, and then turn around and sell it immediately on the open market for $50, and pocket a $20 gain."

"Big deal," you say. "I wait ten years to get twenty lousy dollars."

"No, no. You get $20 for each option. Suppose they grant you 100,000 options this year. If the stock goes up to $50 a share, you'd make a total profit of $2 million. If it goes higher, you'd make more, and you don't buy or sell it until the price is right."

"So I could get 100,000 options this year?"

"No, not exactly. You're being paid like a CEO. You get them only if the company hits its performance bogey for the year."

"So what's the company's performance bogey?"

"The bogey is a 7 percent increase in earnings per share.* That's

---

* Earnings per share (EPS) is the company's net earnings divided by the number of common shares outstanding, which is simply the amount that each share earned. EPS is seen as a better measure of performance than earnings alone because a company could increase earnings by issuing new shares and profitably investing the proceeds. This could reduce EPS if the relative increase in shares is greater than the increase in earnings.

what the CEO negotiated with the board. If he manages the company to a 7 percent increase, he gets 600,000 options."

"Will he hit 7 percent?"

"It's a very low hurdle," Sarah says, with a mysterious smile. "He negotiated it himself. My guess is that the company will actually hit 14 percent, and the CEO will get 1.2 million options."

"Do you mean he could double the stock options the same way I could double my cash bonus?"

"Correct. And if he doubles his options, you double your options, since you're both on the same plan. And both of you would also double your number of shares of restricted stock."

"Restricted stock? What's restricted stock?"

"Those are shares the company gives you, but you can't sell the stock until the shares vest. They will vest over four years. Once they vest, you own the shares outright and may do whatever you want with them."

"That sounds okay, but what does 'vest' mean?"

"Vesting means they give them to you, but it takes a while before you really own them. Your restricted stock will vest over four years. That means that after the first year, one-quarter of your restricted shares will become unrestricted, and you can hold them or sell them. That pattern will be repeated annually."

When you tell your fairy godmother about these bonuses, you can't help but express your excitement over how much more money you'll be making. You'll have more than salary. You'll have a pay package worth millions. "I'll receive riches beyond my fondest dreams. We're talking a $200,000 salary, a cash bonus up to $1.2 million, and millions more in options and restricted stock."

"Why are all my godchildren idiots? You're going to be paid like a CEO and you forgot about perks? Go back and ask about perks."

"What are perks?"

"Perks are goodies that every CEO gets: a company car and driver, free personal use of the corporate jet, country club dues, life insurance, that sort of thing. And since the company's going to pay you all this money in all these different forms and from so many different sources, it should provide you with a personal financial planner. It does that for the CEO, so the company should do it for you. I think you can easily see that these perks are necessities for a person in your position."

Sheepish, you call Sarah the next day and ask about perks.

"We can ask for the things that everybody gets. That would be a company car and driver, free personal use of the corporate jet, country club dues, life insurance, and financial planning assistance. Next year we'll start asking for art consultants and curators for our CEOs who collect art."

"That's all?" says your fairy godmother. "What about retirement, deferred income plans, death benefit, and spousal benefits? And don't forget a golden parachute triggered by a change of control."

"What about retirement, deferred income plans, death benefit, and spousal benefits?" you ask Sarah. "And don't forget a golden parachute triggered by a change of control."

"We might as well ask for them. The worst they can do is say no."

A few weeks after Sarah submits a fifty-five-page proposal to the compensation committee, Charles Bunge calls you to set up an informal lunch to discuss the plan.

"Due to all the publicity and outrage over CEO pay, my committee is subject to great scrutiny these days," the committee chairman solemnly explains. "As fiduciaries, we have a duty to ensure that all compensation decisions are in the shareholders' best interest. Applying this rule, we find certain elements of your proposal problematic."

You see all your hard-earned riches evaporating in the blazing heat of public outrage. The clock is striking midnight. Your long-term incentive will become a pumpkin.

"I don't see how we can go along with free use of the corporate jet," Charles says. "Even directors don't get that. And we think you've been a little too aggressive on the golden parachute. We can't go above $10 million."

You wait, but the other shoe doesn't drop. That's it. You control your emotions. You too are solemn. You look Charles in the eye and say, "I'm disappointed, but I understand the pressure you're under. I don't want to make life more difficult for you or the company. I can live with this."

"Deal!" he says. You shake hands enthusiastically.

For eight months, you worked hard to close construction loans. By August, you'd hit $104 million in new loans, a 30 percent increase over the previous year. This ensured your maximum cash bonus of $1.2 million, so you spent the rest of the year working on your golf game—your fairy godmother had advised you not to establish a higher base for next year's bonus.

Most of your loans were less creditworthy than those you'd made in the past, but you rationalized that this was what the bank wanted. It gave you powerful guidance in the form of incentives, and you responded to them. It offered you a bonus to lend more money, so you lent more money.

Meanwhile, the CEO increased earnings per share (EPS) by 14 percent, thereby doubling everyone's stock options and restricted stock awards. The bank could have shown a 21 percent increase, but the CEO used accounting tricks to push excess earnings into the next year. Since he would receive nothing for exceeding 14 percent, he would save those excess earnings for the calculations of next year's bonus. The board was oblivious to the earnings he had banked for the following year.

Including bonuses, your compensation for the year was salary $200,000, cash bonus $1,200,000, perks $95,000, 200,000 options, and 3,000 shares of restricted stock. Four years later, when your options and stock became fully vested, you cashed them in for $4,350,000.

Applying CEO pay practices and procedures had increased your compensation from $75,000 to $5,845,000.

Because the price of Midwest stock increased by 50 percent over the same four years, the board called the compensation experiment a spectacular success. Academics agreed. They generated reams of studies, formulas, and statistics demonstrating that your bonuses were strongly correlated with the price of Midwest stock. The board congratulated itself on the courage it showed in experimenting with cutting-edge compensation policies. Business gurus proclaimed a new paradigm of employee compensation. It was included in most lists of the Ten Best New Business Paradigms of the Year.

One business reporter discovered that regional banks the same size had done even better than Midwest, averaging stock price increases over 70 percent. But since she published this finding in a newspaper, nobody read it.

Everyone lived happily ever after.

ALL FAIRY TALES have a point. This one introduces the parts, processes, and functions of the Pay Machine with as little pain as possible. The Pay Machine *does* begin with a carefully selected "peer group" of highly paid CEOs. The board *does* "benchmark" its CEO, usually near the 75th percentile. These two actions *do* produce compensation targets for cash and equity bonuses. The comp committee *does* establish performance measures, bonus bogeys, and bonus ranges that allow CEOs to earn multiples of their target bonuses. The board *does* make enormous stock options grants to the CEO, often with no performance hurdle, and then supplements this with lavish perks and retirement benefits. We will later examine each of these steps in detail.

In real life, people don't have fairy godmothers. Only CEOs live in the fairy-tale world where all of them are above average and receive a bonus for showing up. Our fairy tale seems absurd because the system it illustrates is both absurd and harmful. The CEO Pay Machine damages all the companies that use it. This includes virtually every large, publicly traded company in America. If you're a shareholder, it hurts you. If you own a broad index or mutual fund, you probably indirectly own stock in companies that overpay their CEOs to the tune of hundreds of millions of dollars a year.

CHAPTER THREE

How the Pay Machine Harms Companies and Shareholders

Why should you care how much CEOs make? Because, as I told my publishing friend, colossal CEO pay harms American industry, curbs economic growth, and undermines democracy. Later we will examine the four CEOs named the highest paid in 2011 through 2014: Stephen Hemsley of UnitedHealth Group, who made $102 million, John Hammergren of McKesson, who made $145 million, Charif Souki of Cheniere Energy, who made $142 million, and David Zaslav of Discovery Communications, who made $156 million or $224 million, depending on how you count.*

---

* *Forbes* named Hemsley and Hammergren the highest-paid CEO in 2011 and 2012, respectively. However, *Forbes* used data from a prior year. In Hemsley's case, it was data from 2009. For Hammergren, it was from McKesson's fiscal year that ended March 30, 2011. *Forbes* also named Hammergren as the highest paid for 2014. However, Zaslav was paid more than Hammergren no matter how one measures compensation. Moreover, I found it interesting to add a fourth company to analyze.

But these companies could have paid their CEOs 90 percent less and gotten exactly the same performance from them, and no other company would have offered them a higher-paying job.

The immense cost of top management compensation makes American companies less competitive internationally, since they compete against foreign companies that are not wasting millions on their CEOs. In addition to this direct waste, outsize CEO pay generates huge hidden costs. It costs the companies when CEOs accept excessive risks because the stock options—the bulk of their pay—give them a big upside but no downside. It hurts companies when CEOs concentrate on goals that can earn them a bonus and ignore everything else. If potential gains encourage CEOs to manipulate earnings, or suppress bad news when unloading their own stock, or use inside information to time the buying and selling of shares, they benefit, but the company and shareholders lose.

Even more costly are the effects on employee morale. The CEO Pay Machine embodies the principle of external equity—the idea that CEO compensation should be based on what other CEOs make—rather than on internal equity—how the CEO's pay compares with that of everyone else in the organization.

This is a tough sell to employees. I have yet to meet an employee who cared how her CEO's pay compared to that of other CEOs. Perhaps I haven't looked hard enough, but I've found most employees to be very parochial. They care about how their own pay compares with their CEO's, and they like the gap to be smaller rather than larger.

Many studies have concluded that high CEO-to-worker-pay ratios lower morale and company performance. To me, this is as surprising as studies that reveal that the Pacific Ocean is actually *full of water.* Will news that the boss made $102 million raise or lower morale with UnitedHealth Group employees? Will McKesson employees be more or less motivated upon learning that their CEO made $145 million? You don't need a PhD to answer correctly.

In any case, academic studies have found that a high CEO-to-worker-pay ratio:

- Hurts employee morale and productivity.
- Can cause high employee turnover and lower job satisfaction. Given the costs of recruiting and training employees, replacing them is expensive and, at least initially, lowers performance.
- Tends to produce high turnover and low employee morale because the high CEO pay makes other employees feel undervalued.
- Can result in a lower-quality product. Why care about quality when the boss is reaping all the benefits?

Employees who distrust their bosses are unlikely to be highly productive. It doesn't help when the boss makes 300 to 700 times more than you. The American Psychological Association's 2014 Survey of American workers revealed that nearly one-quarter distrust their employer and only about one-half believe their employer is open and up-front with them.

The Pay Machine causes more economic harm by encouraging companies to buy back their own stock. Since it loads them with stock options and restricted stock, CEOs want to keep their share price high. They also have a tool to legally manipulate the price of their stock—stock buybacks.

Many companies today buy back their own stock on the open market. In theory, they should do this when (1) their stock is cheap and below its intrinsic value, (2) they have excess cash, and (3) they lack attractive internal investment opportunities.

In practice, companies do not buy back stock when the price is low. They buy it when the price is high in an attempt to keep the price high. In the long run, buying your own stock when it is expensive is idiotic and self-defeating. But as John Maynard Keynes noted, in the long run we are all dead. Living CEOs therefore enjoy maintaining a high stock price by buying back their own stock. This also enables them to get top dollar when they cash in their stock options and restricted stock.

Buybacks are so high that corporate America is using the stock market not as a source of capital for new investments but to decapitalize. In 2015, buybacks and dividends by American public companies exceeded net income by 16 percent. Kimberly-Clark, Home Depot, Lowe's, AT&T, Cisco, and Time Warner all devoted over 170 percent of net income to buybacks and dividends.

Cisco's stock repurchases exceeded its net income during the entire ten-year period of 2003–2012. In May 2014, Cisco CEO John Chambers sold more than $50 million of his own Cisco stock on the open market. In the twelve-month period ending June 30, 2014, Cisco repurchased $8 billion of its own stock, providing some nice support for Mr. Chambers's sales.

From 2009 through 2014, Qualcomm, a maker of digital devices, repurchased 238 million shares at a cost of $13.6 billion. Amazingly, this did not reduce the number of shares outstanding. In fact, shares outstanding increased by 2 percent. How did this happen? The company granted a superabundance of stock and option awards to its executives.

Cisco and Qualcomm are not alone. April 2015 was a record month for buyback announcements—$141 billion. That month Apple and General Electric announced $50 billion programs. Between 2003 and 2012, Microsoft, IBM, Procter & Gamble, Hewlett-Packard, Intel, and Pfizer all spent more than 70 percent of their net income on stock buybacks. The effect of buybacks on earnings per share is substantial. Deutsche Bank calculated that in recent years about a quarter of the growth in EPS resulted from buybacks that reduced the number of shares outstanding.

In the twelve-month period ending in March 2016, operating earnings of the S&P 500 decreased 14 percent, but this did not curtail buybacks. Buybacks rose 9 percent to $589 billion over $538 billion in the same prior period. These CEOs kept their stock prices high, but at what cost to the future of both their companies and America? From 2001 to 2013, stock buybacks by the S&P 500 totaled $3.6 billion, 50 percent more than they paid out in dividends. This is $3.6 billion that could have been invested in research and development, new technology, or productive assets. To the detriment of the American economy, the Pay Machine motivated CEOs and their boards to use this $3.6 billion to decapitalize and disinvest.

While companies are buying back their own stock, they are cutting back on research and development. By one measure, corporate R&D has fallen by two-thirds between 1980 and 2007.* This is like eating the seed corn. A company cannot grow and

---

* It is not possible to determine how much companies spend on R&D. Therefore, Ashish Arora, Sharon Belenzon, and Andrea Patacconi used the share of publicly traded companies whose scientists publish in academic journals as a proxy for R&D expenditures. They found that this measure fell from 18 percent in 1980 to 6 percent in 2007, as reported in their paper "Killing the Golden Goose? The Decline of Science in Corporate R&D," NBER Working Paper No. 20902, January 2015.

prosper for long without innovation and R&D. But because the average tenure of Fortune 500 CEOs is only 4.6 years, the seed corn becomes mighty tasty.

A recurring theme in CEO pay is how government actions have fueled the pay explosion. In the 1970s, the Securities and Exchange Commission (SEC) proposed rules to impede corporations from manipulating their own stock, but the reforms were discarded in the Reagan administration. In 1982, the SEC adopted Rule 10b-18, which effectively legalized the use of buybacks to manipulate stock prices. Today, companies do not even need to announce when they are buying back stock, and this is a significant help to the companies' efforts to support CEO option sales.* This seems logical. Stock manipulations will not work well if they are publicly disclosed.

Buybacks provide only a onetime EPS boost by reducing the number of shares outstanding. Sound investments can generate decades of gains. Between 2008 and 2015, McDonald's allocated about $18 billion to stock buybacks. The reduction in shares outstanding generated a 4.4 percent increase in EPS. However, had McDonald's invested this amount at a measly 2.3 percent annual return, its EPS would have increased more.

These CEO "job creators" really know how to create jobs: Invest the company's money neither in research nor innovative

---

* In 1981, President Reagan appointed John Shad, vice chairman of the stock brokerage firm E. F. Hutton, to head the SEC. In 1982, in line with the Reagan free market, deregulatory philosophy, the SEC changed the rules of stock buybacks, allowing companies to make stock purchases for which they previously would have been charged with stock manipulation. According to *The Wall Street Journal*, Shad hoped that stock buybacks would increase stock prices and benefit the shareholders. Richard L. Hudson, "SEC Eases Way for Repurchase of Firms' Stock," *Wall Street Journal*, November 10, 1982.

technology nor production facilities. Instead, goose your company's stock price by buying your stock. Then sell the stock and use your millions to buy art, thus creating more jobs for art auctioneers at Christie's and Sotheby's.

Some might contend that it's impossible for major American companies to engage in a costly folly such as overpaying their CEOs. Economists would reason that efficient markets preclude the persistence of such profligacy. Competitors would adopt saner pay practices and drive the imprudent ones out of business. (I hope some boards will consider this approach.)

Why do companies use the CEO Pay Machine that costs them so much money? For the same reason that French aristocrats danced the minuet, doctors bled patients, and intellectuals in the fifties accepted Freud's theories as scientific truth. Because everybody else does it. Everybody does CEO compensation this way, and after all, this is what the experts—the pay consultants—prescribe. The really smart guys who sit on the boards of JPMorgan, McKesson, Discovery, and UnitedHealth Group do it this way. They must know what they're doing. And board members can escape punishment for failing, so long as they fail conventionally. On the other hand, acting unconventionally and failing is perhaps the only way a director can be fired.

CHAPTER FOUR

How the CEO Pay Machine Curtails Economic Growth and Weakens Democracy

Since the excessive CEO Pay Machine harms virtually every large company in America, it can't be doing the economy much good. The billions it wastes directly and indirectly slow economic growth.

In addition, CEO pay and corporate buybacks could precipitate the next market crash. "Corporate CEOs are keeping stock prices at insanely high levels by buying back their own stock and then getting rich when they cash in stock options," one canny investor recently told me. "This has caused the market to become extremely overvalued. A huge correction is coming." American companies last set a twelve-month buyback record in December 2007. Eighteen months later, the stock market had lost half its value.

Historically, the two best indicators of an overvalued stock market are (1) the ratio of the market value of stocks to GDP, and (2) the Shiller PE ratio, the price/earnings ratio based on average inflation-adjusted earnings from the previous ten years. Warren Buffett labeled the first "the best single measure of where valuations stand at any given moment." Severe downturns followed its peaks in 1969, 1987, 2000, and 2007. As of March 2017, it was 31 percent above its historical average. The Shiller PE also peaked in 1969, 1987, 2000, and 2007. It was 75 percent above its historical average as of March 2017, indicating that stocks are overvalued and awaiting a correction.

But in the long term, the indirect effect of the Pay Machine—the increase in income inequality—is economically more injurious than the erosion of company earnings or a stock market downturn.

Income inequality in America has risen sharply since 1976. Economists and pundits point to multiple causes—globalization and competition from low-wage countries; growing educational disparities that particularly affect men and minorities; technological changes that reward the highly skilled; decline of labor unions; changes in corporate culture that place stock price and earnings above employees; free market philosophy and the rise of winner-take-all economics; households with high-income couples; lower rates of marriage and of intact families; high incarceration levels; immigration of low-skilled individuals; income tax and capital gains tax cuts and other conservative economic and tax policies; deregulation; and decreased welfare and antipoverty spending coupled with redistribution programs that disproportionately benefit the elderly.

All of the above may contribute to inequality. However, the proximate cause is quite simple. The jump in inequality is due to a small number of people, mostly business executives, who make huge amounts of money. They are the Mega Rich, the top

0.1 percent in income, who averaged $6.1 million in income in 2014. The Merely Rich are the rest of the 1 percent. It's the Mega Rich, not the Merely Rich, who drive inequality. (I'm a member of the Merely Rich, so don't blame me.)

As shown in the graph on the following page, between 1980 and 2014 the average real income of the Mega Rich has nearly quadrupled, increasing by 381 percent.* Over the same period, the Merely Rich doubled their income while the bottom 90 percent lost ground, suffering a 3 percent decline.

The Mega Rich captured most of the national income gains during the last four decades as their share of income increased from 3.4 percent in 1980 to 10.3 percent in 2014. The share of the Merely Rich rose from 6.6 percent to 11.0 percent over the same period. Thus the Mega Rich snared over three-fifths of the income growth of the 1 percent and nearly 40 percent of all income growth. In the tepid recovery from 2010 to 2012, the 1 percent took virtually all of the income gains. The Mega Rich again got the lion's share: their average income increased 49 percent in this three-year period.

The Mega Rich are getting mega richer. Their average household made 113 times as much as the typical American household in 2014. In 1980, this number was 47. In 2014, the 115,000 Mega Rich households had as much wealth as the bottom 90 percent. They now hold 22 percent of the nation's wealth, nearly double their 1995 share.

Since Fortune 500 CEOs can account for only 500 of the

---

* Data from Facundo Alvaredo, Anthony B. Atkinson, Thomas Piketty, Emmanuel Saez, and Gabriel Zucman, The World Wealth and Income Database, April 5, 2016, http://www.wid.world.

AVERAGE U.S. ANNUAL INCOME
(INCLUDING CAPITAL GAINS)

—■— Top 0.1%   —•— Top 1-0.1%   —•— Bottom 90%

Data from Facundo Alvaredo, Anthony B. Atkinson, Thomas Piketty, Emmanuel Saez, and Gabriel Zucman, *The World Wealth and Income Database*, http://www.wid.world, April 5, 2016.

115,000 Mega Rich, you might be surprised to learn that the majority of the Mega Rich are business executives. CEOs and other business executives constitute the largest high-income group in America. Not the old families with their inherited wealth. Not the sports heroes with their jaw-dropping contracts. Not the movie stars at $20 million per blockbuster movie. Executives, managers, supervisors, and financial professionals constitute three-fifths of the top 0.1 percent. Moreover, they accounted for about 70 percent of the increase in income going to the top 0.1 percent from 1979 to 2005. As Nobel Prize–winning economist Paul Krugman puts it, "Basically, the top 0.1 percent is the corporate suits, with a few token sports and film stars thrown in."

In *Capital in the Twenty-First Century*, Thomas Piketty, after analyzing enormous amounts of data, wrote:

The vast majority (60 to 70%, depending on what definitions one chooses) of the top 0.1% of the income hierarchy in 2000–2010 consists of top managers. By comparison, athletes, actors, and artists of all kinds make up less than 5% of this group. In this sense, the new US inequality has much more to do with the advent of "supermanagers" than with "superstars."

Piketty asserts that increasing income inequality is caused not by investment income but by high wages driven by "the emergence of extremely high remunerations at the summit of the wage hierarchy, particularly among top managers of large firms."

Furthermore, "CEOs use their own power not only to increase their own salaries, but also those of their subordinates," one study determined. As a result, the majority of "supermanagers" are either CEOs or executives whose compensation is heavily influenced by their pay—private company CEOs, other senior corporate executives, and the professionals who advise them. There are more than 5,000 publicly traded companies and 5.7 million private companies with employees.

The graph on the following page shows that the annual income of the Mega Rich and the ratio of CEO to average worker pay are highly correlated—the two lines look almost identical. While correlation does not prove causation, I find it easier to believe that runaway CEO pay caused the income of the Mega Rich to skyrocket rather than the other way around.

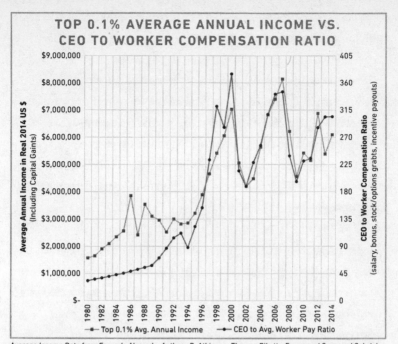

TOP 0.1% AVERAGE ANNUAL INCOME VS. CEO TO WORKER COMPENSATION RATIO

Average Income Data from Facundo Alvaredo, Anthony B. Atkinson, Thomas Piketty, Emmanuel Saez, and Gabriel Zucman, The World Wealth and Income Database, http://www.wid.world, April 5, 2016. Compensation Ratio Data from Mishel, Lawrence, and Alyssa Davis. "Top CEOs make 300 Times More than Typical Workers: Pay Growth Surpasses Stock Gains and Wage Growth of Top 0.1 Percent." Economic Policy Institute. June 21, 2015. Accessed May 16, 2016.

Keep this graph in mind as we analyze how growing inequality curbs economic growth. Every time you see the phrase "increasing inequality" or "income inequality," you could substitute "rising CEO pay."

"There's been class warfare going on for the last twenty years," said Warren Buffett, "and my class has won." Some celebrate this result in the belief that free markets have justly rewarded talent, hard work, and initiative. Others bemoan the division of America into the Mega Rich who pluck the fruits of economic growth and the 99 percent who stagnate.

I side with the bemoaners, but others have examined the moral and social reasons why income inequality is bad far better than I can.* I will examine the economic damage. Americans may differ about politics, religion, and sports teams, but all applaud economic growth. They may argue how to best divide the pie, but they agree that a bigger pie beats a smaller one and that economic growth is preferable to its alternative—a recession. Whether increasing inequality helps or hurts the economy is the wrong question. The right question (and an easier one) is, "Given where America is today, will greater or lesser income inequality spur economic growth?"

From 1949 to 1979, while the ratio of CEO-to-average-worker pay was relatively constant, the US economy grew 2.56 percent annually. When this ratio surged from 1981 to 2014, economic growth dropped to 1.71 percent a year.† The difference may sound small, but over half a century, the higher growth rate results in an economy that is 50 percent larger. That's a big difference.

This correlation doesn't prove that income inequality slowed economic growth, but it suggests that overpaying CEOs has not done much to help. Economist Richard Freeman draws an inequality curve in the form of an inverted U as shown on the next page. The vertical axis shows the level of inequality. The horizontal

---

* See Timothy Noah, *The Great Divergence: America's Growing Inequality Crisis and What We Can Do About It* (New York: Bloomsbury, 2012); Richard Wilkinson and Kate Pickett, *The Spirit Level: Why Greater Equality Makes Societies Stronger* (New York: Bloomsbury, 2009); Joseph Stiglitz, *The Price of Inequality: How Today's Divided Society Endangers Our Future* (New York: W. W. Norton, 2012); Chuck Collins, *99 to 1: How Wealth Inequality Is Wrecking the World and What We Can Do About It* (San Francisco: Berrett-Koehler, 2012).

† My measure of the economy is per capita US real gross domestic product (GDP), which is the value of all goods and services produced. I use the real per capita measure, since it removes the effect of population growth and inflation. A GDP increase driven only by population growth or inflation, on average, helps no one.

axis depicts total economic output or GDP. At Point A on the left, there is perfect equality; everyone gets the same amount of money regardless of talent and effort. Therefore, no one has a financial incentive to work and economic output is zero. From this point, increases in inequality are good for the economy, for a while. At some point, more inequality begins to stifle growth. At the right end of the curve, one person gets all the money, and again, no one has an incentive to work. At the top of this curve, between total equality and total inequality, economic output is maximized at Point I.*

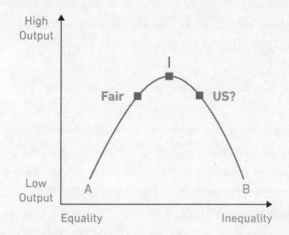

* Freeman explains that "Increases in inequality raise output if economy is to the left of I*. Decreases in inequality raise output if economy is to the right of I*. The peak output I* does not necessarily reflect the ideal point. Societies may choose to trade off total output for more preferable distributions of output, for instance, by preferring inequality at Fair (because, say, the politically dominant majority gains more from lower inequality than they lose from lower output). Or a society may prefer inequality above I* (because, say, a wealthy politically dominant minority gains more from higher inequality than they lose from lower output). Society pays for this in the form of lower output."

Plotting the curve from evidence is difficult, but we were almost certainly nearer the optimum output point (I*) between 1949 and 1979 than we are today.

Leading economists who argue that increasing income inequality hampers economic growth include Nobel laureates Krugman and Joseph Stiglitz, Piketty, Alan Krueger (former chairman of the White House Council of Economic Advisers), and Raghuram Rajan (former chief economist at the International Monetary Fund).

In a 2014 report, the ratings agency Standard & Poor's says that current inequality levels are hindering US economic growth and the firm has cut its growth forecast. Its report states, "We've reduced our 10-year U.S. growth forecast to a 2.5 percent rate. We expected 2.8 percent five years ago."

SUSTAINED ECONOMIC GROWTH

Even the poorest of countries can produce growth spurts for a few years, but sustained growth, such as the United States and western European countries enjoyed from the end of World War II through the mid-seventies, is rare because it's much easier to ignite growth than to sustain it.

The International Monetary Fund (IMF) demonstrated that relatively equal income distribution was required for sustained economic growth. "A 10% decrease in inequality increases the expected length of a growth spell by 50%. The effect is large, but is the sort of improvement that a number of countries have experienced during growth spells." Relative income equality showed a stronger effect on sustained growth than foreign investment, trade openness, exchange-rate competitiveness, or the strength of political institutions.

Income inequality suppresses economic growth in multiple ways. First, it restricts opportunity for a nation's biggest economic asset—an educated, motivated, and competent workforce. According to a study by the Organisation for Economic Co-operation and Development (OECD), income inequality curtails growth "by hindering human capital accumulation. It undermines education opportunities for disadvantaged individuals, lowering social mobility and hampering skills development." The OECD found that the twenty-one developed countries would have increased their GDP by 8.5 percent over the past twenty-five years if they had not experienced increased income inequality.* If an 8.5 percent loss in GDP does not sound severe, recall that the United States' GDP loss during the Great Recession of 2008–2009 was only 4 percent.

Second, it misallocates the workforce. Too many of the most talented are seduced by the riches of financial manipulation that add little to economic growth, as demonstrated by the Wall Street geniuses who gave us collateralized mortgage-backed securities and credit-default swaps that nearly pushed the economy off a cliff in 2007.

Third, it damages the economy with more crime and incarceration.† The United States incarcerates 2.2 million people—a per-

---

* The Gini index is a widely accepted measure of income inequality. At a Gini index of 0, everyone has the same income. At a Gini index of 1, one person garners all the income. A Gini point equals .01 or 1/100th on the scale between 0 and 1. The OECD study found that "income inequality has a negative and statistically significant impact on medium-term growth. Rising inequality by 3 Gini points, that is the average increase recorded in the OECD over the past two decades, would drag down economic growth by 0.35 percentage point per year for 25 years: a cumulated loss in GDP at the end of the period of 8.5 per cent."

† In theory, increased inequality will lead to more crime, especially property crime. If your alternative is dismal poverty, stealing becomes more attractive and prison is less of a deterrent. This theory is supported by empirical evidence.

centage 5 times higher than the average of developed nations—at an annual cost of more than $80 billion a year. American incarceration and inequality trends since 1980 are highly correlated. Devah Pager, professor of sociology and public policy at Harvard, noted that "the more distant the rich become to the poor, the easier it is to impose policies that are more punitive than others."

Much has also been written on how income inequality imposes higher costs on areas including US health care and public middle-class education. (The United States now ranks twentieth out of twenty-seven advanced nations in the share of young people expected to finish high school.)*

Fourth, high inequality exposes a country to financial crises. As inequality rises, people's household debt increases, making the economy more vulnerable to economic shocks. Earlier IMF research suggested that this might have contributed to the 1929 and

---

Reviewing seventeen relevant studies, Richard H. McAdams, Meltzer Professor of Law at the University of Chicago Law School, concluded, "Many studies found a positive relationship between inequality and crime, many found no significant relationship, and virtually no study found a negative relationship." But the great increase in American income inequality occurred as crime rates were decreasing. Were both the theory and the studies wrong? No, because inequality is not the only factor that influences crime. In "What Accounts for the Decline in Crime," researchers determined that the decline in crime was due to three factors: the increased probability of apprehension, a stronger economy, and the aging of the population (a relative decline in twenty- to twenty-eight-year-old males). They estimated that the crime rate would have dropped dramatically had not inequality increased. "Holding inequality constant at its 1980 level, we could have observed a 55% drop in property crime as opposed to a 17% drop." (Ayse Imrohoroglu, Antonio Merlo, and Peter Rupert, "What Accounts for the Decline in Crime?" *International Economic Review* 45, no. 3 [2004].)

* Joseph Stiglitz, *The Price of Inequality: How Today's Divided Society Endangers Our Future* (New York: W. W. Norton, 2012); David Cay Johnston, *Divided: The Perils of Our Growing Inequality* (New York: New Press, 2014); and Matt Taibbi, *The Divide: American Injustice in the Age of the Wealth* Gap (New York: Spiegel & Grau, 2014).

2008 financial crashes in the United States. Both were preceded by a sharp increase in income inequality and in household debt-to-income ratios. The study found that "long periods of unequal incomes spur borrowing from the rich, increasing the risk of major economic crises."

During the Great Recession, income stagnated for the bottom 95 percent of wage earners. Spending has recovered for the top 5 percent of wage earners, but that was not enough to produce a quick and strong recovery.

Consumer spending is the engine of the American economy, accounting for 70 percent of GDP. With rising inequality, the middle class can become too weak to support consumer spending. The top 1 percent who captured almost all the income growth between 2009 and 2013 tend to save rather than spend; there is a limit to the number of yachts one can own. A 2014 report by former Treasury secretary Lawrence Summers and British Labour Party politician Ed Balls warned that absent government intervention, income inequality will result in "insufficient aggregate demand—too little spending by consumers and businesses to keep GDP at its capacity."

Fifth, rising inequality is often an indication that too much money is flowing to speculators and financiers. Concentration of money and power in the banking sector can damage the functioning of markets and result in massive misallocation of capital. This is what happened in the subprime meltdown. All the money that financed condos in Phoenix and new homes in Riverside, California, between 2003 and 2007 could have and should have been invested in productive assets.

Sixth, inequality leads to political decisions, such as biased tax and regulatory policies, that deter economic growth.

Last and most important, rising inequality erodes trust. Americans recognize the importance of law to a flourishing economy, but trust is even more important. Trust is the lubricant of the capitalist engine. Joseph E. Stiglitz writes:

> Economists often underestimate the role of trust in making our economy work. If every contract had to be enforced by one party taking the other to court, our economy would be in gridlock. Throughout history, the economies that have flourished are those where a handshake is a deal. Without trust, business arrangements based on an understanding that complex details will be worked out later are no longer feasible. Without trust, each participant looks around to see how and when those with whom he is dealing will betray him.

Stiglitz contends, "Increasing inequality means a weaker economy, which means increasing inequality, which means a weaker economy."

WHAT'S IN IT FOR ME?

John Hammergren of McKesson made $145 million in single year. Am I saying that you personally would be better off if Hammergren had made $6 million instead of $145 million? Yes, I am.

If this $139 million difference could be redistributed, each US household would receive a mere $1.21. Add in CEOs Hemsley, Souki, and Zaslav, and you could get about $5.00. Big deal. But add in all the effects of CEO pay and you would get about $12,000. BIG DEAL!

The inflation-adjusted median family income was $53,306 in

1989 and $53,657 in 2014. In twenty-five years, the average house-hold gained virtually nothing. At the same time, per capita real disposable income rose 48 percent. Since the average Joe got none of this additional disposable income, where did it go?

Hammergren and his cronies, the business executives in the top 0.1 percent, seized roughly one-third of it. If we took two-thirds of their haul, still leaving plenty for each executive, and spread it around, the median household income would have risen by $4,784 to $58,441.

Now, assume there is even more to spread around. The OECD study estimated that the increase in income inequality in twenty-one developed countries reduced GDP growth by 8.5 percent over the past twenty-five years. Since the United States suffered a greater increase in inequality than the group, assume increasing inequality reduced US GDP by 10 percent over twenty-five years. Had that additional growth been distributed equally, the median household income today would be $64,928.

Should Hammergren matter to you? Let's review the math:

Median household income in 2014	$53,657
Your share of two-thirds of the per capita income growth that went to top business executives	$4,784
Your share of increased economic growth due to lower inequality	$6,487
Revised median household income 2014	$64,928

Is there a difference between living on $53,657 and $64,928?

If you don't accept my math, ask yourself, "Would I be worse off if CEOs made ten times what they make today and I got no increase?" Most people would answer yes. Well, this is exactly what has happened. After we adjust for inflation, CEO pay increased tenfold since 1980 and the average household got stiffed. To a large extent, since 1980 Hammergren and other CEOs took your share of economic gains.

CEO PAY AND DEMOCRACY

If economics does not move you to want to control CEO pay, maybe preserving democracy will. Democracy and plutocracy are incompatible.

I contend that economic growth under good governance is easy. You do what you do best. I do what I do best. We trade. Through learning, innovation, investment, and technology, we both become more productive each year, and the economy grows. Under proper governance, the market can work miracles.

Unfortunately, good governance is difficult and rare. To enable economic growth, government must ensure stability, the unbiased rule of law, property rights, intellectual property rights, the freedom to contract and exchange, a measure of equality, substantial public investment in education and research and development, acceptable public services, restriction of monopolies, and tax, monetary, regulatory, and fiscal policies that accommodate sound investment, banking, and financing.

But a productive economy tempts interest groups to capture power and exact surpluses and rents. Once empowered, these elites tend to want to maintain the status quo that secures their privileged position. Innovative changes that threaten the controlling groups, be they guilds or kings, are suppressed. (Thus the guilds in Cologne and Aachen blocked the use of textile spinning and weaving machines, while in England, both Elizabeth I and James II stifled the mechanization of textile production. The guilds wanted to maintain their monopolies and the monarchs feared the destabilizing political effects of economic change caused by "creative destruction.")

Empowered elites smothering change and innovation was pretty much the history of imperial and national economies from ancient Rome until the Industrial Revolution in England in the 1800s. But economies where the powerful few claimed all the benefits inevitably floundered. Persistent growth, which has happened only in the last two centuries, demanded inclusive economies that benefit the broad populace rather than the controlling elite.

Where are we in America today? The 1 percent has captured a massive part of all the economic gains since 1980, and they lean slightly to the right: 57 percent Republican, 36 percent Democratic, and 8 percent independent. That those in the 1 percent are not more politically unified may be the only impediment to plutocracy. Over time, could the 1 percent become a unified, cohesive political party or coalition and gain political control? It would not be the first time this has happened in a republic. To preserve its position, would this group dampen creative destruction, thereby halting economic growth? Again, it would not be the first time.

America is already moving toward government of the 1 percent, by the 1 percent, and for the 1 percent. Most of the members of Congress are millionaires with campaigns financed by billionaires. When they leave office, they will get even richer lobbying for billionaires. Astoundingly, America continues to give tax breaks to billionaire hedge fund managers and private equity partners that cost the government $11 billion a year. In 2014, the top twenty-five hedge fund managers made an average of $464 million. In total, these twenty-five made more money than the nation's 158,000 kindergarten teachers. Why? They are job creators. Listen to their apologists:

Q: Why do hedge fund managers and private equity billionaires pay lower tax rates than everybody else?

A: Because lower tax rates for private equity and hedge fund partners benefit all Americans.

Q: Says who?

A: Says Henry Kravis, the billionaire founder of a private equity firm.

Q: Just how do tax breaks for private equity partners benefit all of us?

A: Kravis says the tax breaks create jobs.

Q: So when a private equity firm buys a company, they hire more people?

A: No. The first thing they do is fire a bunch of people.

Q: So how do they create jobs?

A: Stephen Schwarzman, another billionaire private equity partner, spent $15 million on his sixtieth birthday party. Think of all the jobs this created for event planners, caterers, and celebrity chefs.

Q: That makes up for all the people they fire?

A: You don't understand. We must compensate private equity and hedge fund partners for taking risk.

Q: Do private equity and hedge fund partners risk their own money?

A: Are you joking? These are smart people. They risk other people's money.

Q: Why do they need additional tax incentives to risk other people's money?

A: It's a matter of incentives. These guys are already very rich. If we didn't give them tax breaks, they might start showing up at ten a.m., have coffee with each of their partners, and then, coffee being purgative, spend the rest of the morning on the john reading *Forbes*. Then what would happen to the economy?

And what would happen to politics? A recent paper by Martin Gilens of Princeton and Benjamin Page of Northwestern analyzed the relative influence of political actors on policymaking and gauges the impact of elites and interest groups on public policies.

They concluded that the average voter does not matter. Nor do interest groups that claim to benefit the little guys. Politicians respond to the rich people and groups organized to advance their own narrow interests. Compared to economic elites, average voters have a low-to-nonexistent influence on public policies. "Not only do ordinary citizens not have uniquely substantial power over policy decisions, they have little or no independent influence on policy at all."

They summarize their findings in three points:

- Economic elites and organized groups representing business interests have substantial independent impacts on US government policy, while mass-based interest groups and average citizens have little or no independent influence.
- The majority does not rule—at least not in the causal sense of actually determining policy outcomes. When a majority

of citizens disagrees with economic elites and/or with organized interests, they generally lose. Moreover, because of
the strong status quo bias built into the US political system, even when fairly large majorities of Americans favor
policy change, they generally do not get it.

• If powerful business organizations and a small number of
affluent Americans dominate policymaking, then America's claims to being a democratic society are seriously
threatened.

According to Nicholas O. Stephanopoulos, an assistant law
professor at the University of Chicago, "There is near consensus
in the empirical literature that politicians' positions more accurately reflect the views of their donors than those of their constit-
uents."

Political equality is a fundamental American value that may
not survive in an economy dominated by the 0.1 percent, most of
whom are business executives whose pay is driven by that for
CEOs. Democracy cannot flourish without common values. Historically, America's values were middle-class values. Belief in education, family, hard work, individualism, merit, stability, abiding
by the laws, and personal accountability are necessary not only
for the economy to succeed, but for democracy to succeed. But as
President Obama said, "Over the last few decades, the rungs on the
ladder of opportunity have grown farther and farther apart, and
the middle class has shrunk."

The middle class wants to make government more effective,
but rising inequality reduces government's basic effectiveness.
Voting and political participation decreases, since rising inequality reduces voting. Corruption increases, bureaucracies are less

able to deliver services, basic research is curtailed, private goods increase at the cost of public goods. Meanwhile, we see more gated communities and private schools while infrastructure crumbles, and public schools eliminate art classes while hedge fund partners pay millions for contemporary art.

Americans may be tiring of supply-side economics (i.e., trickle-down) since forty years of being trickled on have not helped the common man. In France, the Bourbons tried trickle-down for two hundred years, from the coronation of Henry IV in 1589 through the reign of Louis XVI in 1789. It might have worked if it had been tried longer. Unfortunately, the French Revolution interrupted this experiment.

Bernie Sanders made income inequality the keynote—nearly the only note—of his surprisingly robust campaign for the 2016 Democratic presidential nomination.

"Today, we live in the richest country in the history of the world, but that reality means little because much of that wealth is controlled by a tiny handful of individuals," Sanders wrote. "The issue of wealth and income inequality is the great moral issue of our time, it is the great economic issue of our time, and it is the great political issue of our time.

"America now has more wealth and income inequality than any major developed country on earth, and the gap between the very rich and everyone else is wider than at any time since the 1920s . . . That is unacceptable and that has got to change."

Sanders found it "profoundly wrong" that the top 0.1 percent have as much wealth as the bottom 90 percent, and the real median income for male workers is less than it was forty-two years ago. And he rarely passed up the opportunity to decry CEO pay. He offered a series of tax increases and new government programs including:

- Raising the marginal income tax rates to 52 percent for the highest bracket.
- Decreasing the estate tax exemption from $5.4 million to $3.5 million for individuals and raising marginal estate tax rates to 55 percent.
- Ending tax breaks on capital gains.
- Ending the current $118,500 cap on income subject to social security tax.
- Increasing the federal minimum wage from $7.25 to $15 an hour by 2020.
- Investing $1 trillion in infrastructure to create 13 million jobs.
- Making tuition free at public colleges and universities.
- Enacting a single-payer health care system, Medicare for all.
- Enacting a universal child-care and prekindergarten program.

After the 2016 election, it seems unlikely that any of Sanders's programs will be enacted. Nonetheless, the success of his campaign shows that income inequality will be a major political issue for the next decade.

Capitalism is difficult to defend on the basis of morality or equity. Its economic benefits are its paramount justification. An economic system that serves only 0.1 percent or the 1 percent cannot coexist with true democracy. Either the 1 percent will establish a thinly veiled plutocracy or a populist rebellion will force changes in the economic system. White males with no higher education beyond high school, who formed the backbone of Trump's populist, protectionist campaign, have realized no economic gains since 1980. Millennials propelled the Sanders campaign. Over half of young adults between ages eighteen and twenty-nine do not support capitalism while only 42 percent favor it.

Anyone who believes, as I do, that capitalism and free trade with moderate regulation comprise the least bad economic system should be worried as inequality tears at the economic, political, and social fabric of the nation. Since the Mega Rich are a major cause of income inequality, and since CEO pay drives the incomes of the Mega Rich, inequality is almost certain to increase unless we scrap the CEO Pay Machine and replace it with a reasonable system. But before addressing this issue, we need to understand why the Pay Machine emerged and how it operates. You can't fix what you don't understand.

CHAPTER FIVE

The CEO Pay Machine Emerges

After income is adjusted for inflation, the average American CEO in the 1970s earned only about 4 percent more than his counterpart had in the 1930s.[1] Over that forty-year period, companies gave CEOs annual performance and compensation reviews, just as they gave everyone else. Companies generally didn't use compensation consultants, peer groups, or external equity, nor did they pay large bonuses. Pay for CEOs grew modestly every year, just as did pay for most other workers.

How did CEO pay rise from 26 times that of an average employee in 1978 to between 300 and 700 times today? It emerged from a series of unconnected events, people, and beliefs. There was no plan. No one was in charge.

The emergence of the Pay Machine begins with three totally unrelated actors: Michael Jensen, Milton Rock, and Bill Clinton. Jensen is a professor at the Harvard Business School, Rock was a business consultant, and Clinton, of course, was the forty-second president of the United States. Conspiracy theorists should note these men were neither captains of industry nor CEOs; they weren't corporate directors or partners at Goldman Sachs. They never colluded or met together. I doubt that they even knew each other well. They were not attempting to overpay CEOs and might be stunned and insulted to be grouped together as causal agents.

MICHAEL JENSEN AND SHAREHOLDER VALUE

After World War II, American industry became a global colossus with little foreign competition. Concomitantly, major industries—automotive, steel, communications, broadcasting, business machines, and others—evolved into oligopolies. In this beneficial environment, CEOs, few of whom held material amounts of company stock, valued growth and stability. These goals served the nation and the corporations quite well while they provided CEOs with prestige, good salaries, and security. To ensure growth and stability, American industry tolerated government regulation, high income tax rates, and allowing labor a seat at the table.

When I was in business school from 1966 to 1968, we studied cases that illustrated that good citizenship was usually good business. This was the era when George Romney, Mitt's father, was CEO of American Motors Corporation. In 1960, Romney Sr. turned down a $100,000 bonus after he'd told the AMC board that "no executive needed to make more than $225,000 a year" (about $1.4 million in today's dollars). It's estimated that he turned down $268,000 over five years, about 20 percent of his pay.

Good corporate stewardship protected oligopolies from outraged citizens and government regulators. Aside from shareholders, the other stakeholders—employees, customers, suppliers, financiers, communities, governmental agencies, political groups, and unions—were also to be treated well. It was the right and proper thing to do, and it helped to ensure that the enjoyable and profitable environment would not be disrupted by irate stakeholders. (Later as a television broadcaster, I happily lost money on news and public affairs programming as the price of admission to a government-protected three-network oligopoly.)

In 1981, sixteen major company CEOs drafted a Business Roundtable Statement acknowledging the need to balance the interests of the different stakeholders. "A corporation's responsibilities include how the whole business is conducted every day. It must be a thoughtful institution which rises above the bottom line to consider the impact of its action on all, from shareholders to the society at large. Its business activities must make social sense just as its social activities must make business sense." The roundtable at that time included seventy of the Fortune 100. Their statement also said that "the long-term viability of the corporation depends upon its responsibility to the society of which it is a part. And the well-being of society depends upon profitable and responsible business enterprises."

Prominent CEOs took on statesman-like roles, serving on the board of the Council on Foreign Relations, dining with diplomats, and advising political leaders. GE's Reginald Jones, DuPont's Irving Shapiro, Chase Manhattan's David Rockefeller, and GM's Thomas Murphy "became almost as familiar around [Washington] as the Marine Band," noted *Fortune* magazine. When Jones, Shapiro, Rockefeller, and Murphy all retired, almost simultaneously in 1981, it marked the end of an era. Five years earlier, Michael Jensen and William H. Meckling had lit the fuse that would eventually explode the comfortable world of stake-holders that these CEOs had known.

Jensen, then thirty-six, was a professor of finance at the University of Rochester's business school, and Meckling was the dean. Both had studied at the University of Chicago's business school, ground zero for the efficient market theory and Milton Friedman's free market worship.

In 1970, Friedman wrote an article in *The New York Times Magazine* contending that social responsibility could be justified only in the pursuit of profit. The "social responsibility of business is to increase its profits," he declared. CEOs were "agents" who were supposed to work for their "principals," the shareholders. CEOs with goals other than profits were "unwitting puppets of the intellectual forces that have been undermining the basis of a free society these past decades," and had become "unelected government officials" who were illegally taxing employers and customers.

In 1976, Jensen and Meckling published the seminal work on shareholder value titled "Theory of the Firm: Managerial Behavior, Agency Costs and Ownership Structure," which built on Friedman's opinions with rigorous economics filled with complex formulae such as "$\partial B(X^*)/\partial X^* = \partial P(X^*)/\partial X^* - \partial C(X^*)/\partial X^* = 0$" and graphs like the one on the next page.

Jensen and Meckling realized Friedman's dictum to maximize profits was insufficient instruction. Which profits? Today's or tomorrow's? And how should CEOs accomplish this? What rules should they use? Moreover, why should they do this? What control system can make them maximize share price?

Answering these questions in "Theory of the Firm" and subsequent papers, Jensen was guided by the efficient market theory he

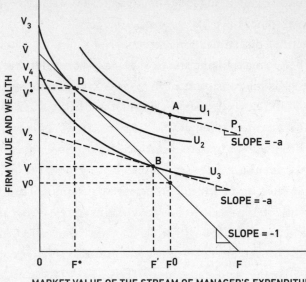

FIRM VALUE AND WEALTH

MARKET VALUE OF THE STREAM OF MANAGER'S EXPENDITURES
ON NON-PECUNIARY BENEFITS

had absorbed at the University of Chicago. Loosely stated, it holds that you can't beat the stock market unless you cheat. (My experience and that of most retail investors and professional investors confirm this. The rare few who beat the market can be explained by random chance. If a thousand investors flip coins, statistics say that one of them will likely flip ten straight heads.)

The theory also holds that the stock market is always right. "The price is right" is the mantra of the Chicago school. How the stock market could have been right on Friday, October 16, 1987, and right again the following Monday, when it dropped 22 percent, is somehow assumed away. But this mantra provided Jensen with his answers. The price of your stock will tell you whether to maximize today's or tomorrow's profits. Weighing the value of today's profits against those in the future is exactly what the stock market does, since the price of a stock, in theory, is the value of all future returns, discounted for time.

Even better, maximizing stock price—i.e., shareholder value—could serve as the consistent and universal criterion for all business decisions. Having multiple goals causes confusion and poor performance, so forget about balancing the needs of customers and suppliers against those of communities and employees. This rule would give CEOs a clear method of setting priorities. Should you spend more on advertising to increase sales or raise prices to increase margins? Choose the option that will raise the stock price the most.

Shareholder value provided control as well as guidance. CEO performance could be monitored and measured daily by the collective wisdom of the stock market. CEOs who enhanced value would be rewarded, and those who dissipated value would be punished. Financial markets would provide the discipline without which CEOs would pursue what benefited them rather than what benefited the shareholders. Jensen believed that the latter course would also best improve the nation's economy.

Jensen then focused on how to compel CEOs to concentrate on shareholder value. His timing was impeccable. The 1970s didn't treat American corporations well. The combination of inflation and economic stagnation, termed "stagflation," damaged business confidence. Stocks went nowhere: The Dow in 1982 was below 1965 levels. The Japanese were eating our lunch. Toyota and Honda were killing the Big Three US automakers. Sony and Toshiba owned the market for electronics. U.S. Steel, Union Carbide, and other industrial giants that once seemed invulnerable were now in trouble. Something had to change. And CEO pay became something that had to change.

Historically, CEO compensation had been tied to the size of the company rather than to share price or company earnings. Jensen and other critics charged that with little ownership in a company, CEOs were motivated to work at empire building. They would focus on increasing the company's assets, revenues, and personnel while ignoring earnings and share price, because the larger the empire grew, the greater the CEO's prestige, compensation, and perks.

Jensen piloted a campaign to change CEO compensation. He called for performance pay to align CEOs more closely with shareholders. In 1985, he joined the faculty of the Harvard Business School, where he is now the Jesse Isidor Straus Professor of Business Administration, Emeritus. In a 1990 article in the *Harvard Business Review*, Jensen dismissed carping about excessive CEO pay: "There are serious problems with CEO compensation, but 'excessive' pay is not the biggest issue. The relentless focus on *how much* CEOs are paid diverts public attention from the real problem—*how* CEOs are paid." Jensen argued, "CEOs act like bureaucrats rather than value-maximizing entrepreneurs." The way to change this was to give them more of the action—a greater part of the value they create for shareholders. His two principles for CEO pay were that "CEOs should own substantial amounts of company stock," and that their "cash compensation should be structured to provide big rewards for outstanding performance and meaningful penalties for poor performance."

Jensen found the right CEO compensation plans in the leveraged buyouts led by private equity firms. Loaded with stock options, these CEOs' compensation was twenty times more sensitive to performance than public company CEOs'. Jensen also blessed hostile takeovers, arguing that they improve economic efficiency while creating shareholder wealth.

Jensen triggered a pronounced shift from stakeholder to shareholder. By 1997, the Business Roundtable had abandoned stakeholders and embraced shareholder value, proclaiming that the principal objective of a business enterprise "is to generate economic returns to its owners" and that if "the CEO and the directors are not focused on shareholder value, it may be less likely the corporation will realize that value."

The move from stakeholders to shareholder value deserves a book of its own, but the shift is relevant here because it launched sky-high CEO compensation. The cultural and economic changes in the era of Reagan and Thatcher, such as deregulation, tax cuts, and celebration of individual riches, reinforced this path. It is debatable that the theory of shareholder value accomplished anything other than further enriching already Mega Rich, financial fiddlers, and CEOs.

Jensen can be accused of overlooking the effect of shareholder value on employees. If you are a sole proprietor of a business, would proclaiming that your paramount objective is to maximize your share price motivate your employees? Shareholder value alone was no more a silver bullet than any other all-encompassing theory.

Regarding CEO pay, Jensen got many things right. He saw the link between the structure of compensation and the behavior of CEOs. His first principle, that CEOs should own a substantial amount of company stock, is spot-on. Absent this, CEOs will be tempted to place their own interests ahead of the companies'.

Jensen's second principle that cash compensation should be structured to provide big rewards for outstanding performance erroneously assumes that corporate boards can and will accurately measure and reward performance.

Jensen's reform might have worked had it been tried, but corporate America heard what they wanted to hear from Jensen and disregarded the rest. They enthusiastically welcomed his message that CEOs should be paid more. Boards also embraced his call for performance pay but implemented it in a distorted, ineffective, and economically harmful fashion.

For Jensen, long-term economic returns to shareholders were the sole measure of performance. Few corporations adopted this definition of performance. Instead, they tied bonuses to annual financial results, such as earnings per share and cash flow. In addition to being shortsighted, these measures introduced the subtle issue of trust. If a company has a good CEO, it should allow him to become a significant shareholder and then rely on him to act in the shareholders' interests. It shouldn't give him a bonus for, say, increasing EPS. In doing so, the board says, "We believe increasing earnings per share is critically important, but even though you are a significant shareholder, we don't trust you to do this unless we pay you extra for doing it."

American statesman Henry L. Stimson famously said, "The chief lesson I have learned in a long life is that the only way you can make a man trustworthy is to trust him; and the surest way to make him untrustworthy is to distrust him." By not trusting the CEO to act in the interests of the shareholders, the board encouraged him to serve himself first and negotiate performance measures that allow him to snatch money from shareholders. This may explain why public confidence in big business is lower than its confidence in any other American institution with the sole exception of Congress.

STOCK OPTIONS VS. STOCK OWNERSHIP

Boards also misapplied Jensen's counsel that the CEO should own a significant amount of company stock. Instead, due in part to Bill Clinton, boards granted CEOs massive stock options, a practice that Jensen never championed.

Stock options and stock ownership are different animals. Stock ownership has an upside and a downside. Having invested their own money, shareholders face an outcome of "Heads we win, tails we lose." With options, the CEO is offered the bet "Heads I win, tails I break even." His options may become worthless, but he paid nothing for them, so he breaks even. How much should a rational person bet on this proposition? The correct answer is "everything he has plus everything he can borrow." A CEO with stock options faces something like this bet. Consequently, he has an economic interest in taking more risk than the shareholders would probably want him to take.

Corporate apologists might argue that possession of stock options would not push CEOs to act against the interests of their shareholders. But the same apologists advocate that CEOs must have economic incentives for everything else that they do. A CEO does have a reason not to bet everything: he could lose his job and reputation if the coin comes up tails. Still, he receives greater rewards and suffers fewer penalties for taking risks than do the shareholders. Moreover, armed with superior knowledge of the company, the CEO should be able to time the execution of options and the sale of stock to maximize his gains.

Should we be surprised that bankers loaded with options took extreme risks, leveraged themselves to the hilt, and financed themselves with overnight money in 2007? Did their stock options align their interests with those of the shareholders?

PAY FOR LUCK

A compensation system loaded with massive stock option awards necessarily incorporates pay for luck. Stock options give the CEO enormous windfalls when the stock goes up, whether or not his performance, or the company's performance, has been superior.

The stock market—not the CEO's performance—determines most of the price movements of his company's shares. General market conditions account for 70 percent of any individual stock's movements. Market upswings—not the CEO's good performance—determine most of his short-term gains from options.

When the stock market rallies, the CEO can make money even if his company performs poorly. If the market is up 15 percent and his company is up only 5 percent, his options are still in the money. Similarly, he will benefit when the Fed lowers interest rates or Wall Street falls in love with his industry.

Given the degree to which business success is due to random, unpredictable events, equity pay for performance is largely pay for luck. In October 2007, the *New York Times* columnist Joe Nocera spoke to Ira Kay, head of the executive compensation practice at Watson Wyatt, one of the major compensation consulting firms. "It is not a coincidence that the Dow Jones industrial average, which stood at 5,000 in 1996, is now well above 13,000," Kay said.

"While U.S. executive pay practices do not entirely explain this rise, there is little doubt that it would not have occurred without them." Nocera argued in his column that Kay had "cause and effect exactly backward. It was the rising market that made the lucky fellas running America's corporations look like geniuses—and made them richer than they'd ever imagined, thanks to the shift to stock options as the primary way to reward executives." I wonder what Mr. Kay had to say thirteen months later when the Dow crashed below 7,500.

Marissa Mayer was a beneficiary of pay for luck to the tune of $214 million in her first fifteen months as CEO of Yahoo. Yahoo's revenues and income have declined during her tenure, but its stock rose because of its 24 percent stake in Alibaba, the Chinese Internet giant. "Simply put, without Alibaba, Ms. Mayer's options would probably be worthless and her pay package would be worth $10 million," *The New York Times* reported. Thanks to Alibaba, which is not managed by Yahoo, she stood to collect $214 million as of 2014.

In the pay-for-performance model, corporate boards, but not Jensen, saw stock options as the panacea that would align the interests of the CEO and the shareholders and reward the CEO for increasing earnings and stock price.

Depending on the company and the plan, stock options may vest either over time or upon achieving some performance measure.

Options were not only magic, they were free! Until 2005, a company could award stock options without including them as part of the CEO's compensation or recognizing them as an expense. Throughout the nineties, neither the SEC nor the Financial Accounting Standards Board (the association that then regulated the accounting industry) had the backbone to compel companies to account for stock option awards as an expense.

Because stock option awards didn't affect the bottom line and because performance pay was infinitely tax deductible, their use exploded in the 1990s. By 2000, options constituted the largest part of CEO compensation. More than three-quarters of Hammergren's $145 million and nine-tenths of Hemsley's $102 million came from exercising stock options they had been awarded in previous years.

Recognizing the problems caused by stock options, some companies have cut back on them and increased restricted stock and performance awards. At their peak in 1999, stock options accounted for about 78 percent of the average executive's long-term incentive package. By 2012, they represented just 31 percent.

MILTON ROCK AND COMPENSATION CONSULTANTS

After serving in the Air Force and getting a PhD in psychology, Milton Rock joined the Hay Group, a human resources consulting firm. Rock helped them become the most influential firm in America regarding executive compensation. By the time he left the Hay Group in 1986, it had a hundred offices in twenty-seven countries. Rock then became a prolific author and editor, producing some of the most influential publications in the field of management consulting.

As CEO pay began to rise and become more complex, corporate boards turned to compensation consultants for both their expertise and their supposed objectivity. In the 1950s, Rock and Edward Hay developed the Hay point system, which assigned numeric values to job requirements, duties, and responsibilities, and the total points were then pegged to a compensation range. Using confidential information from his clients on the compensation of their senior executives, including the CEO, Rock then provided the clients with comparisons to guide their compensation decisions.

This precipitated a profound change in CEO compensation. In the old stakeholder world, pay was guided by the principle of internal equity—how it compared with that of other managers and employees within the company. By providing comparative data from other firms, Rock introduced the principle of external equity, which pegged pay to what other CEOs, presumably with comparable responsibilities, were paid. This promised the benefit of objectivity.

Consulting for a client, Rock would survey CEO pay at similar companies, and the board could then decide where their CEO should be placed within this "peer group."

At first glance, this appeared both fair and prudent. As they recognized the positive effect compensation consultants and peer groups had on their own pay, CEOs began to find them indispensable. If challenged about any compensation decision, the board could justify it with mountains of "objective data" compiled and analyzed by independent third-party experts. This also explains why pay consultants are now a foundational component of the CEO Pay Machine.

This adoption of peer groups as a guideline for CEO pay wasn't driven by a coherent theory or a compelling philosophy or any evidence of effectiveness. It was blessed neither by academic studies nor by industry conferences. Instead of reducing costs, it increased them. Then why did the use of peer groups quickly become ubiquitous? Because both CEOs and boards saw it was in their self-interest. CEOs got more money and boards found a justification to keep CEOs happy.

In 2006, the SEC required companies to disclose the companies in their peer groups. This had scant effect because once established, peer groups changed little from year to year. But comp committees should study the matter more carefully. They might notice that their peer group never includes foreign companies, even when those companies are their fiercest competitors. A few foreign firms would radically depress CEO pay.

The comp committee might be shocked—shocked—to learn that firms select highly paid peers to justify their CEO compensation. Writing in the *Journal of Financial Economics*, Michael Faulkender and Jun Yang found that "compensation committees seem to be endorsing compensation peer groups that include companies with higher CEO compensation, everything else equal, possibly because such peer companies enable justification of the high level of their CEO pay." Another study noted "significant structural bias in the selection of compensation peers." When the CEO is also chairman of the board, as is the case with McKesson and Cheniere, even more highly paid peers are selected.

Peer groups have come under attack periodically, especially when they insanely inflate pay. In 2003, a firestorm erupted when the peer group chosen by the board of the New York Stock Exchange produced a $140 million payday for then-chairman Richard A. Grasso. Even though the Big Board was then a nonprofit organization, the peer group included highly profitable investment banks and huge financial institutions.

Tellingly, when companies compare *performance* against others, they almost always ignore their peer group, and instead use a

broad market index such as the S&P 500 or some internally prepared bogey that they almost always exceed.

The use of different peer groups—one to calibrate executive
pay, another to measure company performance—is near universal in corporate America. Not a bad deal for the CEO. He gets
paid according to his peer group, but his performance is never
measured against it. We will so frequently encounter the practice
of using a peer group to establish pay targets and then ignoring it
when evaluating performance that I've created the acronym
PUPNUP for "peer groups used for pay, never used for performance." The Fortune 500 loves PUPNUP.

BENCHMARKING

A peer group alone cannot determine CEO pay, so Rock and other
compensation consultants introduced the practice of benchmarking. The board or comp committee should decide where to rank
their CEO within the group. Should he be paid as much as the
average CEO in the group or should he be paid above or below the
average? Once the board decided that the CEO should be paid at
the 50th or 75th percentile, they could apply this to Rock's peer
group data and calculate a precise target for CEO pay.

Benchmarking, like peer groups, displays a cursory logic: you
get what you pay for. If you want to perform better than your
peers, you should pay better than your peers. When Rock introduced peer groups and benchmarking to a few clients, he may not
have considered the consequences of everybody using these two
practices. Yet with universal use, they guaranteed constant escalation of CEO pay. They form the core of the CEO Pay Machine.

Every board on which I've served set its benchmark at either the 50th, 75th, or 90th percentile. Benchmarks below the 50th percentile almost never occur. The net result is a corporate Lake Woebegone where all CEOs are above average.

How can everyone be above average? Easy. No board wants to benchmark pay at, say, the 25th percentile, because that says, "We're a lousy company, and we don't even aspire to be better."

At any company, directors can easily justify paying above the 50th percentile. At a high-performing company, the CEO deserves it. At a mediocre one, the board can defend high pay on the theory that they need to attract better people, who will improve things. Directors at a hopelessly lousy company can conclude that performance was poor because they weren't paying enough.

So all companies benchmark pay at the 50th or 75th percentile, except for those that benchmark at the 90th. The above-average benchmarking of pay within peer groups creates a relentless upward spiral in pay—a game of CEO leapfrog. Every time a CEO leaps, he establishes a higher compensation base for the next CEO in the group to leap over. CEOs don't have to wait long to jump over the peers who have just jumped over them. Almost all of them have their compensation reviewed annually.

To illustrate how peer groups and benchmarking interact to magnify CEO pay, assume a board, like most boards, benchmarks its CEO at the 75th percentile. The peer group is loaded with highly paid CEOs, a quarter of whom make above $10 million a year, which becomes the 75th percentile of this group, and therefore the CEO's target pay. As in the fairy tale, he can double or triple this target.

After calculating all his bonuses, he may be paid $25 million. Next year his $25 million is fed back into the group survey that the boards of his peer CEOs will use. Most of them, also benchmarked at the 75th percentile, will have their targets raised and will generally exceed them. Next year, his survey will reflect those big pay increases, and he will get a bigger increase and begin the cycle again.

A CEO need not achieve anything to be benchmarked at the 75th percentile. Hemsley, Hammergren, Souki, and Zaslav did not have to perform better than 75 percent of their peer group; they deserved to be pegged at least at the 75th percentile based on the divine right of CEOs for PUPNUP.

In economic theory, this should not happen. Companies are supposed to minimize costs by striking the best deal they can. But in the real world, the cost of the CEO is treated differently from all other costs.

ROCK'S CHILDREN

Arthur Rock spawned a major industry. Today, virtually all large companies retain compensation consultants. In 2003, a blue-ribbon panel of the Conference Board, an international association of large companies, recommended hiring compensation consultants as a "best practice" of governance. Pay consultants were part of the team that made that recommendation. Lack of chutzpah is seldom a problem with these guys.

Here is Warren Buffett's opinion of compensation consultants: "You don't suggest [compensation] consultants who are Dobermans. You get cocker spaniels and make sure their tails are wagging." Buffett's partner, Charles Munger, is more blunt. "I would rather throw a viper down my shirtfront than hire a compensation consultant," he said.

Not surprisingly, CEO pay is higher at companies that use

compensation consultants. Studies indicate that "compensation consultants are hired to justify higher CEO pay to the board, shareholders, and other stakeholders." In fact, when a company first retains a consultant, the CEO receives 7.5 percent more than he would have otherwise. And the higher the increase in CEO pay, the more likely the consultants will be rehired.

Six major consulting firms—Towers Perrin, Mercer Human Resource Consulting, Hewitt Associates, Frederic W. Cook & Co., Watson Wyatt Worldwide, and Pearl Meyer & Partners—once dominated this business with a collective market share of more than 75 percent, but they lost share to boutiques beginning in 2009 when the SEC decided to aim its all-purpose weapon— disclosure—at pay consultants. Fees would have to be disclosed if the consulting firm provided other services along with compensation consulting. This rule produced unintended consequences. Andrew Ross Sorkin reported in *The New York Times*:

> A cottage industry of boutique compensation consultants sprang up in the wake of the new rule, in part because then the companies do not have to disclose consulting fees if the firm does not provide other services. Some Mercer partners left to start Compensation Advisory Partners, and Towers Watson announced that it would partner with a newly created spinoff, Pay Governance L.L.C.

Companies that switched to these boutiques paid their CEOs 9.7 percent more than a matched sample of companies that did not switch.

For the big consulting firms, services such as designing pension and health plans are a larger and more lucrative part of their business than executive compensation work. Prior to 2009, nearly half of large companies used a compensation consultant that did other work for the company. The fees for the other services were 11 times greater than those for executive compensation.

Can a consulting firm dependent on the CEO for major fees give unbiased advice about what he should be paid? With no intention of disparaging the integrity of the industry, I note that when consultants provided other services to a company, the CEO's pay was substantially higher.

Compensation consultants would deny that they are among those professions—appraisers, PR flacks, lobbyists—that are paid to lie. Their defense would be that they don't make decisions—they simply provide objective data and technical advice. In other words, they are not paid to lie; they are paid to aid and abet.

Boards do not retain compensation consultants to help control CEO pay. Directors would have to be brain dead not to know that the consultants—and the Pay Machine they helped construct—generate excessive CEO compensation. Boards hire pay consultants to provide cover for directors, and because everyone else does. In fact, the entire $200 billion management consulting industry is driven in part by the fact that directors and executives want to avoid responsibility for some decisions and need a ready scapegoat for bad ones.

A recent SEC rule encouraged the comp committee to hire its own independent compensation consultant who does no other work for the company. To implement this rule, the New York Stock Exchange and Nasdaq required listed companies to consider and disclose whether their compensation consultants had conflicts of interest, but did not require independence. As long as both companies and consultants embrace the Pay Machine, "independent" consultants advising a board on CEO pay will have little reforming effect. Independent consultants can slightly restrain CEO pay only if the comp committee has backbone. Otherwise, the consultant provides the board with further justification for higher CEO pay.

BILL CLINTON

Rather than understanding and overhauling the Pay Machine, misguided reformers aggravated the problem.

Aiming to restrain CEO pay, the government screwed up bigtime. The graph on the next page plots the ratio of CEO pay to average worker pay since 1980. Note the sharp increase between 1995 and 2000.*

CEO pay was 20 times higher than worker pay in 1965 and 87 times higher in 1994—an average annual increase in the pay ratio of 5 percent. Between 1994 and 2000 the ratio more than quadrupled to 376, posting an average annual increase of 27 percent.

You—and CEOs—can thank Bill Clinton and congressional Democrats for that expansion. It took an act of Congress to open the floodgates. CEO pay became a prominent political issue when President George H. W. Bush visited Japan in January 1992 accompanied by highly paid American CEOs. Bush played up jobs and trade, but media attention was focused on the huge CEO pay disparities between Japan and the United States. At that time, Japanese CEOs reportedly made only 10 times as much as the average employee.

During the presidential campaigns that fall, Bill Clinton

---

* This is the same graph that was superimposed on the share of income garnered by the Mega Rich on page 41. Recall that they are revealingly similar.

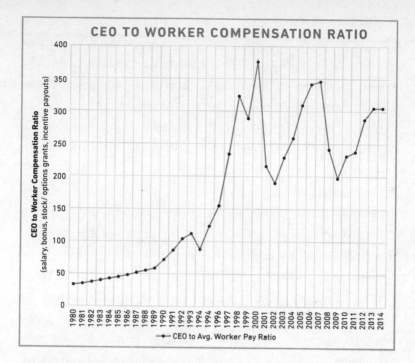

CEO TO WORKER COMPENSATION RATIO

CEO to Worker Compensation Ratio
(salary, bonus, stock/ options grants, incentive payouts)

— CEO to Avg. Worker Pay Ratio

promised to clamp down on excessive executive compensation. Under existing law, there was no ceiling on how much compensation companies could deduct as a business expense. Clinton proposed eliminating tax deductions for executive pay in excess of $1 million per year. When business leaders strongly objected to this idea, Clinton modified his stance after the election, asking only that "excessive" pay not be deductible, which he defined as "unrelated to the productivity of the enterprise."

Business was still unhappy. Finally, Clinton and congressional Democrats agreed to exempt stock options from this cap, signaling that options were an acceptable form of compensation, even in large amounts. This provision was appended to Clinton's budget bill, the Omnibus Budget Reconciliation Act (OBRA) of 1993. In the fierce battle over new tax rates, this provision was hardly noticed. Clinton's bill raised top income tax rates from 31 percent to 39.6 percent for income above $250,000; raised corporate tax rates from 34 percent to 35 percent for income from $10 million to $15 million, 38 percent for income from $15 million to $18.33 million, and 35 percent for income above $18.33 million; applied the 2.9 percent Medicare tax to all income, removing the previous cap of $135,000; increased the portion of Social Security benefits subject to income taxes from 50 percent to 85 percent; and raised the alternative minimum tax rate from 24 percent to tiered rates of 26 percent and 28 percent.

Republicans united against the new taxes, and the bill faced two cliffhanger votes. On August 5, 1993, the bill passed the House 218 to 216, with 217 Democrats and 1 independent (Bernie Sanders) voting in favor and 41 Democrats and all 175 Republicans voting against. If only one more Democrat had voted with the opposition, the bill would have failed on a tie vote.

The next day, the Senate outcome remained in doubt until 8:30 p.m., when Senator Bob Kerrey of Nebraska, the last senator to vote, came out in favor of the bill; Vice President Al Gore cast the tie-breaking vote. Clinton and congressional Democrats celebrated their legislative victory and may have thought they had taken a small step toward controlling CEO pay. Pay consultants correctly predicted companies would simply shift from cash compensation to stock options.

Ironically, the unlimited tax deductibility for "performance pay" became law without a single Republican vote. The OBRA law is emblematic of failed reform. It attempted to control CEO pay by mandating lawyerly procedures. For compensation to qualify as "performance pay," it had to meet several requirements: it must be solely for attaining performance goals; the goals had to be established by an independent committee consisting of two or more outside directors; the goals and the terms of the compensation had to be disclosed to and approved by shareholders; and before payment, the committee had to certify that the goals and other terms were met.

Boards could now pay unlimited amounts as long as they could pass it off as "performance based" and could grant unlimited stock options with no performance requirements. Checking all the boxes provided UnitedHealth Group, McKesson, Cheniere, Discovery, and everyone else with safe harbors, even when their CEO pay was in the nine figures.

I doubt Clinton and the congressional Democrats realized that they were opening the floodgates. More likely, they viewed the legislation as a partial victory and a step toward controlling CEO pay. Legislation often backfires because the majority of congressmen are lawyers who try to fix most things through imposing procedures and regulations rather than altering incentives. These lawyer-legislators prefer to force the sinner to repent rather than making virtue more attractive. Perhaps they ignore incentives, since in their careers, they have experienced only two: bill more hours and get reelected. In this instance, corporate America and their lobbyists stood a proposed reform on its head. They objected, exerted pressure, were heard, and were mollified.

The immediate consequence of this legislation was that many companies that had paid their CEOs a salary of less than $1 million raised it to $1 million, and bonuses that had been issued at the discretion of the board—subjective bonuses—were replaced with ones determined by quantitative formulas. Under IRS regulations issued pursuant to this legislation, plugging data into a formula will qualify as "performance pay" no matter how absurd the result, but a discretionary bonus based on the board's after-the-fact subjective judgment will not. The mandate of blind objectivity proved far more remunerative than discretionary bonuses had been.

Between 1995 and 2000, huge option awards and a booming stock market fueled the exponential growth in CEO pay. And by restricting salary and allowing unlimited options and defining "performance pay," the government inaugurated the megabonus era. Kevin Murphy, professor of finance and business economics at USC, wrote, "The explosion in stock options that led to the escalation in pay was in large part the (arguably unintended) consequence from government policy."

Jensen wanted to pay good CEOs more and bad CEOs less.* Rock wanted to bring systematic logic and objectivity to CEO pay. Clinton wanted to limit excessive CEO pay. However well-intentioned, they did not understand how their interconnected actions would provide the foundation for the CEO Pay Machine. In complex systems, few can foresee the emergent consequences of their actions.

SUNLIGHT GROWS WEEDS AT THE SEC

Jensen, Rock, and Clinton were not the only ones whose ill-informed reforms made things worse. In 1991, the SEC ruled that

---

* Jensen later changed his views on CEO compensation. In 2007, he coauthored *CEO Pay and What to Do About It*, in which he admitted that compensation can be both excessive and not subject to sufficient risk. Such pay systems might incent CEOs to act in ways that destroy value. The authors argued that boards should negotiate tougher with CEOs and make them accountable for the "Strategic Value" of the company. The book explains how to design and implement such a plan.

CEOs and others could sell stock immediately after exercising options instead of having to wait at least six months, reasoning that this would allow market forces to work more efficiently. When CEO pay became a big political issue in 1992, Richard C. Breeden, then-chairman of the SEC, stated that market forces, not the SEC, should control CEO pay. Earth to SEC: Market forces have nothing to do with CEO pay. There is no market for CEOs. Peer groups and the rest of the CEO Pay Machine do not simulate a market. They simulate a racket.

You wouldn't expect public disclosure of CEO compensation to be part of the problem, but it is. Once any information is out there, other CEOs can use it to improve their bargaining positions. Warren Buffett once remarked that envy might be a greater motivation than greed for CEOs. They can't stand someone who isn't as great as they are making more money than they do.

The SEC believes that "sunlight is the best disinfectant"—disclosure is the cure for everything from insider trading to cancer. Had they hired a few gardeners to complement their staff of brilliant lawyers, they might have learned that sunshine also makes weeds grow. As the SEC required more disclosure about CEO pay, pay increased relentlessly because more disclosure made it easier for everyone to know what everyone else was making—and to leapfrog to the next higher level.

CONGRESS MOTIVATES THE CEOS

Despite the Clinton tax increases, Congress lowered marginal tax rates from 1980 to 2005. The top marginal rate averaged more than 90 percent from 1945 to 1963 and remained at 70 percent through 1981. The Reagan and Bush tax cuts reduced it to 35 percent with dividends and capital gains taxed at 15 percent. Thomas Piketty thinks these rate decreases explain much of the CEO pay explosion:

> In the 1950s and the 1960s, executives in British and American firms had little reason to fight for such raises, and other interested parties were less inclined to accept them, because 80–90% of the increase would in any case go directly to the government. After 1980, the game was utterly transformed, however, and the evidence suggests that executives went to considerable lengths to persuade other interested parties to grant them substantial raises.

Piketty makes a good point. But if he hung out with more CEOs, he might observe them fighting for every pretax dollar, regardless of marginal tax rates, because that is their competitive yardstick. Perhaps CEOs are less rational than economists.

When CEO compensation was escalating steadily in the 1990s, scholars, commentators, institutional investors, regulatory agencies, and the Delaware judiciary blamed toothless corporate boards and demanded reforms. They called for changes in board composition, independent directors, open elections, and the alignment of the compensation consultants with the boards that retained them. Many of these changes have become standard practice in publicly traded companies. Independent directors now must control a majority of board votes, and the compensation and audit committees must be entirely made up of independent directors. At most large companies, the board comp committee, not management, now usually hires the compensation consultants.

Disclosure requirements regarding management compensation are more stringent and shareholders have received new tools— such as "say on pay"—to keep management in check. Despite all of this, CEO pay continues to explode.

Why have all these reforms failed to make a difference?

First, they haven't changed anybody's motivation or behavior. Having only independent directors on the comp committees does nothing to change the dynamic between the CEO and the board. Directors are now no less sympathetic toward the CEO. Consultants hired by the comp committee rather than management are no less eager to please a CEO for whom they may do other work. Additional mandatory disclosures of compensation data provided evidence for other CEOs to ask for more.

Second, none of these reforms recognized the real problem. CEOs are overpaid not because the comp committees lack independence or because disclosure is insufficient. CEOs are overpaid thanks to the Pay Machine. Even if CEOs were not acquisitive, even if the board bargained with them at arm's length, and even if CEOs exercised no influence on the compensation process, compensation would have risen exponentially due to the procedures and practices built into the Pay Machine. That most CEOs are mercenary and influence their own pay while boards collaborate simply compounds the problem.

CHAPTER SIX

The CEO Pay Machine Constructed

Pay consultants dictated the architecture of the Pay Machine. The three components of CEO compensation should be as follows:

1. Salary that is paid in cash and not related to performance. Because executive salaries in excess of $1 million a year are not tax deductible, many large companies limit salary to $1 million.

2. A cash bonus that is related to performance and is tax deductible. This is typically awarded for annual performance and labeled a "short-term" bonus. Bonuses were awarded as early as the 1940s, but they were not common enough to have a noticeable impact on median compensation until the late 1950s.

3. Equity awards of stock options and/or restricted stock.

Today this composition is accepted as axiomatic, though few directors could explain why. They might argue, "The equity bonus aligns the CEO with the shareholders, while the annual cash bonus focuses him on annual objectives," but why have both? Don't they interfere with each other? And why salary? "Well, most of his pay is performance related, but we have to pay some salary to be competitive" might be the lame explanation. Most directors would answer that there are three parts to executive compensation because everyone knows that this is how executive compensation is done.

The proportions of these basic pay elements have changed over time. Between 1950 and 1970, total CEO bonuses ranged between 15 percent and 20 percent of compensation. Today, those proportions are reversed. Salary is typically a small portion of CEO compensation, normally 3 to 10 percent at larger companies. So-called performance bonuses account for more than 80 percent. Cash bonus plans vary widely, but on average account for 37 percent of total compensation, while equity bonuses, often termed "long-term incentive" bonuses, comprise 54 percent of compensation.

The dictionary definition of "bonus" is "something in addition to what is expected or strictly due: as money or an equivalent given in addition to an employee's usual compensation." But bonuses now constitute four-fifths of CEO pay.

TARGETS AND ACTUAL COMPENSATION

While peer groups and benchmarks are the foundation of the Pay Machine, they produce only a *target* for CEO compensation. Somehow this target needs to be transformed into actual compensation. Once again, no one planned the process of how to proceed from target compensation to actual compensation. It simply evolved as boards and consultants suggested and boards adopted "best practices" that were built into the Pay Machine.

But evolution is not random. It is propelled by survival within a specific environment. To survive and become part of the Pay Machine, each and every pay practice had to pass two tests: First, when each one is considered in isolation, the board had to find it logical and justifiable. Second, the practice must work to increase CEO pay. As a class, CEOs were able to veto any practice that diminished their compensation, so by this Darwinian selection, the Pay Machine evolved to relentlessly push the numbers into the stratosphere.

Having used peer groups and benchmarks to set targets for CEO pay, the comp committee decides how to allocate that target among the three compensation components. Given a $10 million compensation target, the comp committee may decide to allocate $1 million to salary, $4 million to a short-term cash bonus, and $5 million to an equity bonus. Then each bonus has its own target, and the comp committee establishes performance measures, bonus bogeys, and bonus ranges to determine whether the actual bonus paid is higher or lower than the target. In combination, these "best practices" ensure that the CEO will exceed his target bonuses 80 percent of the time.

In order for CEO pay to be "performance based," the board must decide how to measure performance. The CEO controls certain resources, and the board wants to measure what he achieved with them.* To do this, the board often looks at a ratio—a simple

---

* Since more than 95 percent of Fortune 500 CEOs are men, I will use the male pronoun when referring generically to CEOs. Women may be more willing to tolerate this practice because many of my references to CEOs are less than charitable.

fraction—where the denominator represents resources the CEO controls: for example, assets (the gross value of everything the CEO controls), equity (the shareholders' money he controls), invested capital (the total money, including debt, the company has invested), or shares of stock outstanding. The numerator represents what the CEO has accomplished with these resources (in terms of profit after tax or cash generated from operations, usually defined as earnings before interest, tax, depreciation, and amortization—EBITDA—or some other measure). You don't need to understand the differences between EBITDA and profit after tax, or between return on assets and return on invested capital. You just need to know that the board looks at a ratio of returns to resources, which is a measure of what the CEO achieved with the resources at his disposal. How much he got out of the resources he had is a measure of his performance.

In our fairy tale, your annual performance was measured by the ratio of loans made this year to loans made last year. Your CEO's bonus, like UnitedHealth Group's and McKesson's, was based on the increase in earnings per share (EPS).

While this is one of many useful measures of company performance, EPS is problematic as the primary performance measure for the CEO's bonus. First, it's easily manipulated. Using a few accounting tricks, I could always make EPS jump up and dance the Macarena. Second, an EPS increase may be due to nothing more than a good economy, increased industry demand, or even a mild winter. The stock may be down, the competition eating our lunch, but the CEO still gets his bonus if he hits the EPS bogey. PUPNUP. I know of no board that requires the CEO to beat his peer group in EPS growth or any other measure to get a bonus.

When they use an EPS measure, the directors are essentially setting a profit bogey. EPS is profit divided by the number of shares of stock outstanding. Absent a stock repurchase program, the number of shares outstanding is predictable; the only unknown is profit. The directors must base their profit estimate on a budget or forecast prepared by management, or pluck a number out of the air. The former approach is far more likely.

Though a common practice, this tying of bonuses to budgets or some forecast prepared by management is a bad idea. Here again, the CEO possesses a lot of information about next year's earnings, but the board hasn't a clue. Tying a bonus to a budget encourages a CEO to "sandbag," i.e., to submit an easy budget. It pays the CEO for dishonesty and penalizes him for honesty. It also corrupts the financial information system that is critical for controlling and monitoring the organization. Nevertheless, the CEO can often get a budget approved that is highly likely to generate a whopping bonus.

Tying bonuses to improvements over the prior year is another bad idea. In a bad year with no annual bonus in sight, CEOs can write off everything and "take a bath," making this a terrible financial year that will be easy to beat next year. In a good year with a full bonus certain, CEOs have incentives to push unneeded earnings into the following year, which will lower next year's denominator and increase next year's numerator—and his bonus.

One CEO's bonus was based on return on equity (ROE). The board set a 15 percent ceiling, and the executive believed his firm could easily surpass this number. He told an interviewer, "I'd have to be the stupidest CEO in the world to report an ROE of 18 percent. First, I wouldn't get any bonus for any results above the cap. Second, I could have saved some of our earnings for next year. And third, [the board of directors] would increase my target performance for next year."

The use of any ratio at all in an annual bonus is troublesome. You can improve the ratio either by increasing the numerator—profits—or decreasing the denominator—assets, equity, or invested capital. The board may want the CEO to accomplish the difficult task of increasing profits, but he may find it easier and more rewarding to decrease the denominator even if this harms the company in the long run. A share repurchase program, selling a growth division, or limiting new investments to those with initial high expected returns could help the CEO achieve annual bogeys for, respectively, return on equity, return on assets, or return on invested capital, even if any of these actions would be detrimental to the company in the long term.

BONUS BOGEYS

The bogey is the number that the CEO must hit to receive a bonus. For example, if he will get his bonus only if EPS are up 9 percent over last year, then 9 percent is the bogey. If the board sets a bogey of $15.25 EPS, then the CEO receives no bonus if EPS are $15.24 or less.

Cash bonuses can be considerable and bogeys can be outright gifts. When Leslie Moonves, CEO of CBS, took home a $25 million cash bonus in 2014, David Gelles wrote in *The New York Times*, "Some cash bonuses seemed to reward simply doing one's job. In the case of Mr. Moonves, $12 million of that bonus was tied to the performance of the company, while the remaining $13 million was doled out by the compensation committee partly in special recognition of his 'leadership and direction in the creation of premium content.' In other words, the television studio C.E.O. got a big bonus for being a television studio C.E.O."

The CEO can engineer a bonus simply for doing his job because he holds better cards than the board. Most boards and comp committees meet four to six times a year; the CEO is there every day and he knows what measures are and are not within his power to achieve, honestly or through manipulation. He knows everything the board knows, but the board knows only a bit of what the CEO knows. The directors get most of their company-specific information through him; he controls a large organization with staff, information systems, and institutional memory. The board has none of these, making it difficult for them to assess what is and what is not achievable within one year.

Skills one can expect in every CEO are expertise at internal politics and the ability to manipulate the board. How do you think they got their jobs? I was much better at board-level politics than I was at running a company, which is one reason I was never fired. (Woody Allen once said, "Eighty percent of success is showing up." He might have said, "Eighty percent of success is sucking up.")

The CEO's advantages in compensation negotiations are most evident when it comes to bonus bogeys. A compensation consultant reporting to the comp committee can advise on the size of the bonus but has no basis for assessing whether an 8 percent increase in earnings or a 12 percent return of equity is a high or low hurdle for the coming year. The CEO has all the information. Asked by the comp committee if an 8 percent earnings increase is low, he can present reams of data showing that last year was unusually sunny and a great deal of rain is forecast for the coming year. Therefore, 8 percent is aggressive.

BONUS RANGE

Like most parts of the Pay Machine, a bonus range makes sense at first glance. If you accomplish more, you get paid more. It seems almost like piecework, in which, for example, a seamstress gets a fixed payment for each shirt she sews. But there are two big differences. The seamstress produces a standard finished product that is easily counted, while the CEO's output is so difficult to measure that it is usually mismeasured. Moreover, the CEO also gets a big salary and an equity bonus, and the seamstress does not.

As in the fairy tale, the CEO's bonus usually exceeds the targets. The bonus range sets an upper limit, with the lower limit usually being the bogey, though sometimes the CEO is awarded a bonus for coming close to the bogey, as Discovery's David Zaslav was in 2014.

For his annual bonus, a rational CEO wants easy goals, flexible measures, and the best chance of reaching 200 percent or 300 percent of his target. In negotiations, he will run rings around the board, comp committee, and consultants, most of whom may be on his side to begin with.

I can find no hard data on how often CEOs exceed their negotiated bonus targets. My experience is that they achieve this more than 80 percent of the time. All of us, CEOs included, would like to receive a bonus for fogging a mirror. Heads I win, tails I win. CEOs can often negotiate this happy result.

Consider Angelo Mozilo. When he was CEO of mortgage lender Countrywide Financial, his cash bonus was based on growth in EPS. In 2004, Countrywide's EPS declined by 13.2 percent, yet Mozilo received a $17.3 million cash bonus.

How did he accomplish this miracle? Read the fine print. His bonus was set by a formula that multiplied his previous year's bonus by a ratio. The numerator was the EPS for the current year and the denominator the EPS for the previous year. Dividing the 2004 EPS of $3.63 by the 2003 EPS of $4.18 produces a ratio of 0.8684. Mozilo's 2003 bonus of $19.89 million was multiplied by 86.84 percent to produce a 2004 bonus of $17.3 million.

One reporter noted: "If you follow the math, you quickly discover that killing Mozilo's bonus is as difficult as killing Count Dracula. It would take a 100 percent decline in EPS to achieve that amazing feat."

EQUITY BONUS

Business is a constant struggle to balance the long term against the short term. Rather than leave this to the continuing, on-the-spot wisdom and judgment of the CEO and board, corporate America has a bonus system that gives the CEO cash for the short term and equity awards for the long term. Though both are severely flawed, boards tacitly assume that two bad practices can achieve the proper balance between short- and long-term concerns.

Public companies are required to obtain shareholder approval for equity compensation plans that set aside a number of stock options or restricted shares that the board may award to management. When these have been distributed, the board must ask for approval of a new plan. On occasion, these plans are challenged, but they are rarely rejected. When some disgruntled Pfizer shareholders pushed for a resolution to terminate executive stock options, only 4 percent of shareholders voted for it.

Depending on the plan, stock options may vest either over time or upon achieving some performance measure. Three of the four companies we will examine—UnitedHealth Group, McKesson, and Discovery—did not require the CEO to accomplish anything to receive an equity bonus. He received this "performance" award by not getting fired.

ADJUST THE NUMBER (UPWARD)

If the annual bonus game is not sufficiently rigged, the CEO can always count on the sympathy of the board. At UnitedHealth Group, McKesson, and Discovery, the board played with the books, after the fact, to increase the CEOs' bonuses. When it rains, directors are sympathetic and quick to make upward adjustments that increase earnings because the rain wasn't the CEO's fault. But when the sun shines, the board almost never makes downward adjustments. Why penalize the CEO when the company had a good year? Anyway, with the CEO reporting the weather, the directors may not be aware of the true amounts of rain and sunshine.

Kevin Crutchfield, CEO of Alpha Natural Resources, did not qualify for an annual bonus in 2011 because the company experienced its biggest loss in history. Nonetheless, the directors awarded him a $528,000 bonus for total pay of $6.7 million, citing his "tremendous efforts" toward improving worker safety. The language is telling. When did "effort" become "performance"?

In 2011, Mylan's board decided that CEO Robert Coury deserved an extra $900,000 because the European debt crisis and the Japanese tsunami that hammered the company's financial results were beyond his control. The same year, Nationwide Mutual Insurance doubled its CEO's bonus by arguing that claims from

US tornadoes shouldn't count against his performance measures. And here I thought weighing the risks of unusual occurrences was what insurance was all about.

William S. Simon, president and CEO of Walmart's US unit, was due a bonus for 2013 if sales grew more than 2 percent. When sales grew only 1.8 percent, the board decided to adjust for un-expected events, including the federal government's cutting food stamp benefits. I am not making this up. It is disclosed in the Walmart proxy. Walmart also adjusted for the costs of terminat-ing a joint venture in India, store closures in Brazil and China, a change in historical lease accounting practices in China, con-tingent liabilities related to non-income taxes in Brazil, settle-ments of employment claims in Brazil, the restructuring of Sam's Club, the pending sale of its Vips restaurant operations in Mexico, the sale of Walmart's interest in 1-800-Contacts, and decisions not to open previously planned stores and unexpected delays in store openings in certain international markets. Based on these adjustments, sales rose 2.03 percent, and Simon enjoyed total compensation of $13 million.

The above examples are not unusual. A study of executive com-pensation noted the "Compensation Committee's willingness to deviate from the benchmarks its own processes had established."

IF THE PERFORMANCE MEASURES are objective and the actual results easily obtainable, awarding a bonus should be a simple mathematical calculation. However, boards leave themselves am-ple wiggle room. At McKesson, Hammergren's bonuses were nearly doubled when the board conjured up an "individual performance multiplier." The largest part of CEO compensation, stock options, are often awarded with the curt explanation that it is in line with the CEO's peer group.

To review, the Pay Machine begins with highly paid peer groups and benchmarking usually at the 75th percentile of the group to produce a generous compensation target for the CEO. The Pay Machine then transfigures this target to actual compensation by establishing bonus targets, performance measures, and bonus bogeys ranges that push compensation well above target 80 percent of the time. If this is not enough, the board can always fiddle with the numbers or apply an "individual performance multiplier."

Theft is an unpleasant word, so I will say that the CEO Pay Machine allows CEOs to liberate funds that would otherwise belong to their shareholders. By law, the CEO is a fiduciary with duties to the shareholders. The Pay Machine enables him not only to "liberate" monies from his shareholders but also to come back and liberate more next year to keep pace with his peers, who have been engaged in the same activity.

OTHER COMPENSATION

"Other compensation," which excludes salary, cash bonus, and equity bonus, makes up about 9 percent of total CEO compensation and comes mostly from perks and retirement benefits. While these are reported as compensation, comp committees usually treat them as add-ons. They are like a corner office, nice to have but not a component of the Pay Machine. Since peer practices vary widely, perks and retirement benefits are not derived from peer groups and benchmarking. Instead, they are driven by company practices and negotiations with the CEO.

The comp committee reviews the list and costs of CEO perks, adding and revising but rarely subtracting. CEO perks may include a company car and driver, free use of corporate aircraft, expanded health plans (Live Nation Entertainment spent $121,318 in a year on health insurance premiums for chairman Irving Azoff in 2011), home security, enhanced retirement plans, deferred income plans, and financial counseling (Tom Ward of SandRidge Energy received $783,533 worth of "accounting support" from company employees in 2011).

For the hundred highest-paid CEOs of American companies with revenues of more than $5 billion, the average 2012 perks package was worth $320,635.

Some of my favorites:

- Sheldon Adelson, the gambling billionaire who financed Newt Gingrich's 2012 primary campaign, received $2.6 million from a company he controls to pay for security protection for himself and his family. Anyone who financed Newt Gingrich's primary campaign needs psychiatric care more than security protection, but few companies provide this benefit as a CEO perk. It's possible to get security for less than that. Oracle paid a paltry $1.4 million for CEO Larry Ellison's home security system. Goldman Sachs spent a miserly $258,701 on security for CEO Lloyd Blankfein. How does that make him feel?

- Steve Wynn, another humble and frugal casino owner, racked up more than $1 million in personal travel in 2012 on his company's private jet. Wynn Resorts purchased the first G650 jet to roll off Gulfstream's assembly line, and the $65 million plane flies Mr. Wynn back and forth between

Las Vegas, where he lives in a villa that the company purchased for $451,574 in 2012, and New York, where he
owns a $70 million penthouse overlooking Central Park.

- Wynn's travel budget was austere compared to that of
Barry Diller, the chairman of Expedia and IAC/Inter-
ActiveCorp, who in 2010 got $1.28 million worth of per-
sonal use of a jet jointly owned by the two companies.

- Abercrombie & Fitch's stock dropped 61 percent in 2011,
but CEO Michael Jeffries still received $719,182 in perks
as part of his $48 million package; he made 1,640 times the
average salary of an Abercrombie employee and ranked as
number two on the CEO pay ratio scale. Only Ron Johnson, whom we will meet in chapter 12, bettered him. Johnson's ratio at JCPenney was 1,795 to 1 before he was fired.

- When Edward Mueller became CEO of Denver-based
Qwest, the company provided him and his wife and daughter free use of the company jet to commute to and from
California, where the daughter was in school. The cost
to Qwest for the Muellers' use of the jet in 2007 was
$281,162. Qwest also purchased a California home from
Mueller for $1.8 million above its market value. As a mem-
ber of the 2011 McKesson comp committee, Mueller may
have found it hard to be miserly to his fellow CEO John
Hammergren.

- My all-time favorite perk: Tyco CEO Dennis Kozlowski
threw his wife a party in Sardinia. Tyco picked up the $2
million tab.

Kozlowski served time for fraud, which proves there is some
justice in the world. Meanwhile, Adelson, Ellison, Wynn, Jeffries,

and Mueller are all still at large, indicating that the amount of justice has not become excessive.

Since there are no standards for CEO perks, the comp committee finds itself in the position of a parent negotiating with a teenager over allowance: It is never enough, and all the other kids get more. If the CEO can make the case that comparable CEOs get jets, cars, drivers, massages, and mandatory concession of four-foot putts, the comp committee will often oblige him with similar toys and treats.

In 2006, the SEC did try to curtail perks by ruling that when the value of a CEO's perks exceeds $10,000, the company must disclose the cost of all of them, including company-provided aircraft, club memberships, personal travel using company vehicles, use of other company-owned property, and clerical or secretarial services devoted to personal matters. No one seemed to care except for an occasional journalist—and, of course, the other CEOs. The disclosures provided CEOs proof that the other kids did indeed get higher allowances.

While perks have obvious value, consultants and boards tend not to include them when comparing, establishing, and allocating overall compensation. When the board reviews CEO perks, the best it can hope for is not to increase the existing package. Once given, perks are difficult to reclaim. Who wants a CEO as surly as a teenager whose allowance has been cut?

Sometimes companies buy back perks previously awarded. In 2009, the Abercrombie board terminated Mr. Jeffries's unlimited use of the company jet and capped his personal travel reimbursements at $200,000 a year and gave him a $4 million lump-sum payment in return. This was a bizarre arrangement; shareholders would have been better off had Abercrombie continued Jeffries's unlimited use of the jet and kept the $4 million. Heads, Jeffries wins; tails, the shareholders lose.

RETIREMENT AND GOLDEN PARACHUTES

Like perks, pension and retirement benefits are established outside of the peer group benchmarking process. Typically, these are negotiated as part of the CEO's employment contract and not subject to annual review. However, as we will see in the case of Mc-Kesson and Hammergren, the board can interpret the contractual language in ways that greatly benefits the CEO. At less generous firms, a single retirement and pension plan may apply to all employees. Even here, the CEO will get a larger pension, since most pension plans are based upon the individual's earnings.

The bounteous severance packages known as "golden parachutes" are classified as neither compensation nor perks, because the CEO doesn't receive anything when they're awarded. But the packages may include retirement bonuses, extended stock options, and pensions that can have a total worth of $100 million or more.

Parachutes triggered by a change of control are supposed to relieve the CEO of financial worries when selling his company. Suppose ABC Corporation wants to acquire XYZ Company. If the CEO of XYZ is not financially secure, he might negotiate a sweetheart deal with ABC in the hope that he can retain his—or an equivalent—job once ABC takes charge. In theory, a parachute that gives him future financial security will position him to negotiate aggressively to get the best possible price from the buyer.

As a CEO motivator, a golden parachute is double-edged. If it becomes too attractive, the CEO may want to sell the company.

Harvard professor Lucian Bebchuk found that companies that gave generous golden parachutes were more likely to be acquired, presumably because their CEOs were more amenable to this course. These companies also tended to sell for lower acquisition premiums—in other words, less money for the shareholders—perhaps because their CEOs were happy to be bought out.

Did these CEOs sell out their companies to cash out their parachutes? Who knows? I pocketed parachute money when King Broadcasting was sold. I was grateful, but I would have preferred to keep my job. I think most CEOs want to keep their jobs. Nonetheless, $100 million seems a high price for a company to pay to ensure that a CEO remains honest during a sale.

Even those publicly shamed by their contributions to the subprime meltdown received colossal severance pay. Fired from Citigroup in November 2007, Charles Prince walked away with $40 million. One month earlier, after reporting a $2.24 billion loss, Merrill fired CEO Stanley O'Neal. He left with $161.5 million in stock awards and retirement benefits. John Thain lasted a little over one year as CEO of Merrill Lynch, for which he received $83.8 million. During his brief tenure, Merrill paid out $230,000 to his driver and $1.22 million to redecorate his office. Washington Mutual's Kerry Killinger took home a $25.1 million paycheck in 2008, received a $15.3 million severance payment in September 2008, and also got a $445,200 lump-sum payment for vacation benefits and a $300,669 "special payment." This is not pay for performance. It's "parachutes for failure."

CHAPTER SEVEN

The Players

Before examining just how Stephen Hemsley made $102 million, John Hammergren $145 million, Charif Souki $142 million, and David Zaslav $224 million in a single year, we need to understand how the players who operate the Pay Machine interact: the board of directors, the comp committee, and the CEO. The shareholders, who actually own the company, don't have a seat at this table.

THE BOARD OF DIRECTORS

When I was nearing retirement, I lined up seats on corporate boards, joking that they were what I'd been looking for all my life: authority without responsibility, stimulation without anxiety, prestige without striving, and pay without bosses. A good corporate board is like a club where you work on interesting problems with intelligent, congenial companions. Travel, good restaurants, and other amenities are provided free of charge. Best of all, instead of paying club dues, the club pays you.

Over the last thirty years, I've served on over a dozen boards and chaired the comp committee at both private and public companies.

In theory, the shareholders elect the board to represent them, but in practice, corporate boards are self-perpetuating. The board nominates itself. Absent a rare takeover battle, shareholders routinely elect whoever the board nominates. Approval ratings for corporate directors rival those of Kim Jong-un. In 2012, of the 17,081 corporate directors nominated for board positions, only sixty-one, about one-third of 1 percent, were not approved by a majority of shareholder votes.

Even if directors lose, they can win. In 2012, directors at forty-one publicly traded companies received less than 50 percent shareholder approval but remained on the board because no one else was on the ballot. Be thankful that board seats are not yet inheritable.

Corporate boards typically consist of seven to twelve directors, with an average being 9.2. They oversee management and, working with the CEO, help to develop corporate strategy, policies, and objectives; approve and review performance against budgets and financial plans; and monitor everything from product planning, executive compensation, risk management, internal controls, shareholder relations, financial reporting, and disclosure to quality of products and services and executive succession and development.

Despite these responsibilities, the board does not and cannot manage the company. That is the job of the CEO and his subordinates. The board's most important job is to hire and oversee the CEO, and replace him if necessary. On paper at least, the board is the CEO's boss, but when the CEO also chairs the board, he is captain of the team and often a dominating presence.

If the company is reasonably successful, the board usually selects a new CEO from within the company. The board will have watched top management and will have a good understanding of each internal candidate's strengths and weaknesses.

If the company is in trouble or lacks a strong internal candidate, a board committee will usually hire an executive search firm. The committee and the firm will compile a list of the capabilities and experiences they want in a new CEO. The firm will then approach executives who meet the criteria. They may describe the position and ask a potential candidate if he knows of anyone who might be interested in the job in the hope that the candidate will suggest himself. After the firm compiles a list, the board committee will narrow the selection and interview the finalists. Then they will begin negotiations with their first choice.

The board provides advice and is often the sounding board for the CEO. Directors may be the CEO's best source of independent and unbiased advice. Employees who work directly or indirectly for the CEO are reluctant to challenge him no matter how much he says he wants them to.

Dealing as they do with high-level issues and strategies, corporate boards prefer generalists to specialists. Sitting CEOs are the most desirable board members, since they generally face the same challenges as the company's CEO. There aren't enough sitting CEOs to go around because their own boards usually limit them to serving on one or two outside boards, so retired CEOs become the second choice. They've had the CEO experience and now have time to do the committee work that boards require. In 2014,

Fortune 500 companies filled 339 new board seats with independent directors, and 47 percent were current or former CEOs and 20 percent current or former CFOs. In five of the past six years, CEOs and CFOs together comprised more than two-thirds of the new appointments.

Large-company boards today resemble an old men's club (the average age is sixty-three) that has been recently pressured to admit women and minorities. In 2014, white males chaired the boards at 93 percent of the S&P 500 companies. Women accounted for only 19 percent of total directors, unchanged from 2013, and minorities about 13 percent.

As I can attest, corporate boards are a good gig, so plenty of qualified people are eager to join. I can recall only two instances when someone turned down an invitation to join a board. This does not mean boards can get anyone they want. Bill Clinton will not join your board unless you offer an astronomical board fee. Warren Buffett will not join your board unless he buys a large part of the company. However, within the range of the achievable, boards enjoy a high acceptance rate.

Turnover on boards is low. Few directors resign for any reason other than reaching a mandatory age, typically seventy-two for public companies. In 2012, the reappointment rate for directors was 94 percent. My guess is that the remaining 6 percent either turned seventy-two or died, or both.

How do you get invited?

In theory, the board identifies the needs of the company and the gaps in director capabilities. You get invited if you best fill these needs and gaps. In practice, it's who you know and who those people know. Approaching retirement, I told everyone I knew that I was seeking board positions. One invitation came from the private equity partner who had financed my buyout of a corporate division. He was investing in a company and looking for board members. A second invitation arrived when some people back east bought a Seattle-based company and wanted someone local on the board. Two of them were on a board whose CEO knew me and suggested my name. A third offer came from a good friend who owned a company. Then the family company I mentioned was searching for a non-family director and I knew some people who knew some company directors.

Most directors serve on boards because, like me, they enjoy it. In corporate America, it's often said that no one joins a board for the money. I would modify this. Few businesspeople do it only for the money. If you have been successful enough in business to be invited on boards, you can probably live without the money. However, if you are from the world of government, the military, nonprofits, or academia, a board fee of $100,000 or more can be very meaningful. And no one turns down the money. I have noted that few directors, though well off, are so indifferent to money that they fail to bill the company for all expenses, including car mileage at the maximum rate allowed by the IRS.

Annual director compensation for public companies ranges from $35,000 at small companies to a median of $258,000 at the two hundred largest US public companies, about double what they were in 2000. The highest-paid directors do even better. Oracle paid its directors an average of $780,000 in FY 2015. Perhaps in gratitude, they paid CEO Larry Ellison more than $300 million since FY 2012. *The Boston Globe* reported that in 2014, among Boston-area directors, Michael Heffernan earned $1 million from

Ocata Therapeutics, including stock and stock options. William D. Young received $1.7 million in compensation from Vertex Pharmaceuticals. Phillip A. Sharp hauled in $1.9 million from Alnylam Pharmaceuticals.

Serving on a corporate board entails roughly 150 hours of work a year—preparing for and attending committee and board meetings, teleconferences, and staying up-to-date on technical matters—so directors at the higher end of the scale make around $3,000 an hour.

Boards are collegial and consensual. In my twenty-five years, over tens of thousands of board votes, less than ten were not unanimous. This degree of unanimity is not as startling as it appears. Group consensus is quite common; juries composed of twelve strangers who will never again work together make unanimous decisions 95 percent of the time. Directors know each other, know that they will meet many times again, and are often led by a strong individual. Additionally, a dissenting vote on a critical issue such as the sale of the company could expose a director to endless litigation.* Consequently, if one or two board members voice concerns, an issue is tabled until an accommodation can be forged, usually outside of a board meeting.

---

* I was a director of a public company that was acquired. Within ten minutes of the announcement, five law firms filed suits claiming the directors of the selling company ate babies for breakfast. None of these firms had done any research. In fact, one of them substituted our name at the head of a prior complaint but left in the name of the prior defendant. These sleazebags hoped that the case got sent to a naive state judge who would find the allegation of eating babies serious and enjoin the sale pending a hearing. In this case, the buyer was eager to close the sale, so it "settled" by paying hundreds of thousands in legal fees. Our shareholder got nothing other than our agreement to make innocuous and vacuous additional disclosures, such as September 21 fell on a Wednesday. Had a director voted against this sale, the extortion demand would have increased while the director would spend weeks being deposed.

The relationship of the board to the CEO is not a superior-subordinate relationship. While in principle they oversee the CEO, directors are also colleagues and often friends. In fact, the CEO may have recruited them or could have vetoed them. Unless there's a proxy fight, directors are rarely added to a board over the objections of the CEO. Especially if he's also chairman, the CEO's relationship to the board is often that of first among peers. At over half of large companies, the CEO is also chairman of the board. This is one reason he can negotiate his compensation while other employees cannot.

When hiring a new CEO, the board, with the help of consultants, may establish a compensation plan that is not negotiable. This is often the case with internal promotions, where the incoming CEO has little bargaining leverage. The longer the CEO remains in the job, the more the board becomes his board and the annual compensation review becomes more of a negotiation.

Board members naturally want to help, as well as oversee, the CEO, but mixing help with oversight is tricky. I've tried to ask tough questions on strategy, finances, and new initiatives, while telling the CEO that these are in his self-interest and noting that while I was a CEO I encountered troubles on occasion because my own board was insufficiently diligent.

While the board approves annual operating and capital budgets, executive compensation is the only significant costs it directly controls,* and it almost always defers to the comp committee.

Were the costs of insurance or shipping escalating for a few years, some board member would ask management for an explanation. Part of a director's job is to ask the questions that don't get

---

* The board, through its audit committee, also directly controls audit fees.

asked internally. The board might then ask the CEO to present a plan to contain insurance or shipping costs. But despite all the bad publicity surrounding CEO pay, directors are reluctant to criticize or even question the compensation proposed by their peers on the comp committee. The committee has studied the issues and the data, met with the consultants, and usually negotiated, directly or indirectly, with the CEO. Warren Buffett, who served for fifty-five years on nineteen boards, stated, "I never heard of a vote against a compensation plan voted by the compensation committee." Though a vocal critic of CEO pay levels, he admitted that he has voted for compensation plans with which he disagreed.

THE COMP COMMITTEE

The comp committee comprises three or four board members who recommend compensation levels, plans, and practices to the full board. We might expect the members, especially those who are current and former CEOs, to sympathize with the CEO and be guided by Jesus's advice to "Do unto others as you would have them do unto you."

The committee conducts an annual CEO compensation review, typically receiving a report prepared by the company's human resources (HR) department, usually accompanied by comments from the pay consultants. Compensation negotiations are idiosyncratic and depend on the personalities involved. Negotiations between a relatively new CEO and an established board with its own chairman are very different from those between a veteran CEO who is also the chairman on a board filled with people he helped recruit.

Unless they retain independent pay consultants, the comp committee has few defenses. Management has all the information and can claim to have been guided by "unbiased" pay consultants to produce a fair compensation package. Any effort by the committee to make significant changes in the management/consultant recommendations might now look like a rebuke to the CEO. Comp committees are unlikely to seek board approval of a package that hasn't been accepted by the CEO.

The comp committee can receive less biased and more useful information by retaining its own independent pay consultant. However, all this information is of little use if the committee, especially the chair, is not willing to stand up to the CEO.

The board is always at a disadvantage when negotiating with the CEO. Even under the best of circumstances, it's difficult for such negotiations to be at arm's length. It's impractical, if not impossible, for board members committed to being supportive players on the team to transform themselves into hard-nosed negotiators. The comp committee is in no position to be proactive, having neither staff nor institutional memory. Even if the board has its own pay consultant, the CEO retains the initiative—he makes the first moves and sets the parameters of negotiations.

Friends from outside the world of business ask incredulously, "Why doesn't the board just set a salary for the CEO and tell him to take it or leave it? Nobody ever negotiated compensation with me. Why does the board negotiate with him?"

The simple answer is that directors find it in their self-interest to negotiate generously with the CEO. For a multitude of reasons, they choose to err on the side of paying more, especially since they know that "independent" consultants will bless any amount of compensation.

The board wants to keep the CEO happy. He is the captain of the team, often their friend. If he is resentful about his compensation, he may do a bad job. The company will be in trouble, and the board that chose the CEO will look bad.

The CEO always holds the implicit threat of moving to another company for better pay. While the board may know that it's highly unlikely he would do so, the possibility can make the comp committee anxious. Were this to happen, the committee would look like incompetents, and the company would face the risky and expensive procedure of finding a new CEO.

The CEO negotiates for himself, while the directors negotiate for the shareholders. The CEO pockets what he gets, but the directors pay with the shareholders' money, not their own, a recipe for a one-sided negotiation. Directors cannot gain status or prestige or augment their reputations by being tough on CEO pay because they cannot go public about it. No board can announce, "We saved the shareholders $25 million by not agreeing to excessive CEO pay demands," and no director can claim credit for paying the CEO at the 25th percentile.

Most directors got where they are by looking out for number one. They are practical and pragmatic rather than idealistic and ethically pure. They have scant incentive to rock the boat and disturb board congeniality by getting tough on CEO pay, especially when they can hide behind supposedly impartial third-party consultants.

The board and comp committee know they cannot be personally liable no matter how much they pay the CEO. The "business judgment rule" gives the board broad discretion. Derived from case law, the rule accepts that business is inherently uncertain, volatile, and risky and allows directors to exercise their best judgment without liability for unprofitable decisions, or even incompetence and stupidity. Unless the directors have blatantly violated their fiduciary duty, courts will not question their decisions. In 2006, Disney's board of directors was ruled not to have breached its fiduciary duties or committed waste when it allowed a $130 million severance payment to its former president Michael Ovitz after his disastrous fourteen-month tenure.

Then there is safety in numbers. Directors can reassure themselves that they are acting precisely as all other Fortune 500 boards act, and even rationalize that the profligacy of those other boards created this problem. Those boards acted irresponsibly, established ridiculous CEO pay levels, and left us with no choice but to match them.

A friend of mine became the chair of the comp committee for a company roughly the size of UnitedHealth Group and McKesson. After his first year, he decided that while he disliked wrestling with a CEO about compensation, he disliked rolling over even more. The internal HR staff, whose director reported to the CEO, prepared all executive compensation data, analyses, and recommendations, and the CEO's own lawyer represented him in compensation negotiations.

My friend hired a pay consultant to report directly to the comp committee and he questioned everything on executive compensation generated by the company's HR department. My friend ceased negotiating with lawyers and initiated sessions where the CEO faced a unified compensation committee that often reduced the CEO's recommended package. He said that with these changes, the CEO's winning percentage dropped from 98 percent to between 60 percent and 65 percent. He thought this was about as good as he could do. Given the CEO's advantages, he concluded that compensation negotiations could never be a fair match.

Even with able, energetic, and independent leadership, a comp committee may dispute some numbers, but it never challenges the basic structure of the CEO Pay Machine. Without giving it much thought, boards accept that the proper process for setting CEO compensation is the Pay Machine, incorporating pay consultants, peer groups, benchmarking, performance bonuses, bonus bogeys, overall pay targets, and other practices we examine in detail. If directors were asked why they used this structure, most would reply that it's the standard structure, a best practice, a time-tested technique. In other words, everybody else does it. So long as this structure remains in place, the best the comp committee can do is avoid obscene overpayment.

THE CEO

Fortune 500 CEOs are overwhelmingly male (95 percent) and white; minorities—African-Americans, Latinos, and Asians—account for only 4 percent. Their average age is fifty-seven, and 93 percent graduated from college. A third majored in engineering and another third in liberal arts. Collectively, these 500 executives earned about 200 MBAs (Harvard, Penn, and Stanford counting for 40, 13, and 10, respectively) and about 140 other graduate degrees. Half said they were Republican, while only 2 percent admitted to being a Democrat. Only 5 percent served in the military.

How do you get to be CEO? To start, you learn how to get promoted. This is one skill that all CEOs possess. Then you *look* like a

CEO—a tall, fit, good-looking white male. The typical Fortune 500 CEO is three inches taller than average and better looking than average. They work out and are trim. Overweight CEOs are as rare as Trotskyist CEOs. It is possible that such physical attributes make them better leaders by inspiring confidence. It is much more likely the white male directors, the majority of the board, pick someone who looks much like themselves. Of Fortune 500 CEOs, 30 percent began their careers in finance. The second-largest starting point was 20 percent in sales and marketing. Half were promoted from chief operating officer (COO), the number two position in the company, and 5 percent were promoted directly from CFO. In sum, these CEOs are a lot like me, only taller and richer.

What does a CEO do?

He helps devise the company's strategy. He selects and coaches people to implement this strategy. He sets company goals and measures progress against them. He coordinates finance, production, sales, research and development, marketing, and personnel. He leads through suasion and example. He uses carrots and sticks. And he sells—to his customers, to his employees, to his shareholders, and to his board. I have learned, painfully, that no matter what business you think you're in, you're in sales.

Harold Geneen, the legendary head of ITT, gave an excellent description of a CEO's job:

The best way to run a business with the best hope of eventual success is to do it as you would cook on a wood-burning stove. . . .

Because you know that you cannot control all the elements of fire, wood, air flow, etc., you keep your eye on everything at all times. You follow the recipe to an extent, but you also add something extra of your own. You do not measure out every spice and condiment. You sprinkle here, you pour there. And then you watch it cook.

You keep your eye on the pot. You look at it and check it from time to time. You sniff it. You dip your finger in and taste it. Perhaps you add a little something extra to suit your own taste. You let it brew a while and then taste it again. And again. If something is wrong, you correct it.

Whatever you do, the most important thing is to keep your eye on it. You don't want it to be ruined when you are off doing something else.

When it is done to your satisfaction, you're right there to take it off the stove. In the end, you will have a pot roast or a lamb stew that is the very best you could possibly make, a joy to your palate and a tribute to your ability as a cook. It will taste far better than any slab of meat you cook automatically by pushing buttons on a microwave oven.

That is how you would cook on a wood-burning stove when nothing is preset. And that is the frame of mind to take into the art of conducting and building a successful business.

Ultimately, the CEO has a simple job description: *run the company the best you can.* You're on your own; the job is pretty much what you decide it is. Your board meets four to six times a year. It can help you with goals and strategy and serve as a sounding board. But it cannot tell you what to do today or how to do it. Some CEOs focus intensely on numbers, others on customers, and others on recruiting and developing talent within the organization. Some are control freaks; others delegate everything. The average Fortune 500 CEO spends only about 15 percent of his time working on his own. Sixty percent of his time is taken up in meetings and another 25 percent is occupied with phone calls and public events.

Being a CEO is a tough job. It can be emotionally exhausting, because when there are mistakes, you have nobody to blame but yourself. On becoming a CEO, I quickly learned that no one was paid enough, and no one's assistant was paid enough. Now in retirement, I wake up every morning and think, "A whole day lies before me in which no one is going to complain to me about pay. Life is wonderful."

Calvin Trillin once said of CEOs, "The very fact that they devote their lives to making more money than anybody could possibly use indicates that they behave that way not because they want more money but because they don't know any better." After you meet the highest-paid CEO in 2011, 2012, 2013, and 2014, you may decide that Trillin was right.

CHAPTER EIGHT

The Highest Paid

I started writing this book in 2013. When I learned that Stephen J. Hemsley of UnitedHealth Group, who made $102 million, and John Hammergren of McKesson, who made $145 million, were named the highest-paid American CEOs in 2011 and 2012, I wondered what they had done that could have justified that pay.

The SEC requires companies to disclose information in two annual statements: a proxy statement issued before the shareholders vote at an annual meeting, and a 10-K statement to disclose all relevant information to potential buyers and sellers of the stock. The proxy sent to the shareholders is apparently authored by PR flacks and filled with boasts about how the company is dynamic, profitable, and responsible, especially in regard to executive compensation. Mandated disclosures about CEO pay often fail to confirm these claims. Lawyers, not PR flacks, write the 10-K statement that provides a comprehensive description of each company's business, performance, and risks. Whenever a stock takes a tumble, plaintiffs' lawyers sue, alleging the company failed to disclose detrimental information. Therefore, as protection, company lawyers disclose that this company is more risky than investing in tulip bulbs. They state:

- XYZ, Inc. ("the company"), is engaged in the business of manufacturing widgets.
- Manufacturing widgets is inherently risky and volatile.
- The widget business is economic lunacy. There is no demand for widgets. We don't even know what widgets do.
- Major risks faced by the company include plague, famine, pestilence, nuclear war, and a rain of tailless amphibians from the order Anura, including, but not limited to, frogs and tadpoles.
- Whoa! What if the Chinese start manufacturing widgets? Holy shit, we would be toast!
- Management may be guilty of fraud, misfeasance, and malfeasance. Did we mention that they are not the sharpest arrows in the quiver?

Aside from the comic relief, proxies and 10-Ks, if you know how to read them, are very revealing. I was stunned by what I found in UnitedHealth Group's and McKesson's proxies and 10-Ks. The directors of these two major American corporations were at best asleep at the switch, and at worst, aiding and abetting the CEOs as they pocketed funds belonging to shareholders. The directors had set easy bonus targets, chosen highly paid peers to target compensation, ignored these peers when evaluating performance (PUPNUP), fiddled with the numbers after the fact to increase the CEOs' bonuses, misled their shareholders, and awarded eye-popping bonuses for mediocre results.

These examples were so alarming that I later investigated the highest-paid CEOs of 2013 and 2014: Charif Souki of Cheniere Energy, who made $142 million, and David Zaslav of Discovery Communications, who made $156 million or $224 million, depending on how you count. Each of these four CEOs demonstrated a different way to be preposterously overpaid—Hemsley and Hammergren by cashing in options previously awarded, Souki through multiple awards of restricted stock, and Zaslav with a large signing bonus plus option gains. However, the small details, such as how the board set easy bogeys, cavalierly granted equity, and changed the numbers after the fact, are more revealing than the astounding pay amounts. Incredibly, none of these four companies produced exceptional financial results in the year in question. In fact, three of the four had bad years financially. What is remarkable is not how much these four CEOs achieved, but how little they achieved relative to their compensation.

You would think that you might have heard of at least one of the highest-paid CEOs, but this group includes no visionary technology entrepreneurs like Mark Zuckerberg of Facebook, Sergey Brin of Google, or Steve Jobs of Apple. No industry pioneers such as Starbucks' Howard Schultz, Amazon's Jeff Bezos, or Tesla's Elon Musk. No famous businessmen such as Warren Buffett or Rupert Murdoch, and no iconic companies such as IBM, General Electric, or AT&T. So let me introduce them to you.

STEPHEN HEMSLEY OF UNITEDHEALTH GROUP

UnitedHealth Group, the largest health insurer in the United States, ranked number six in revenue in the Fortune 500 in 2015.

It provides health care access to 29 million Americans through networks that include more than 850,000 physicians and health care professionals and approximately 6,100 hospitals and health facilities. It is either the largest or second-largest insurer in twelve states: Maryland, North Carolina, Missouri, Louisiana, Georgia, Nebraska, Arizona, Colorado, Iowa, Arkansas, Wyoming, and Rhode Island. In 2015, insurance produced about two-thirds of UnitedHealth Group's $157 billion in revenues.

UnitedHealth also owns Optum, a platform offering health services such as care delivery, care management, consumer engagement, financial services, operational services, health information technology services, and pharmacy services. Optum accounts for roughly one-third of UnitedHealth Group revenues, but it is growing faster than the insurance side.

Stephen J. Hemsley was named CEO in 2006. He had served as COO since 1998 and has been a board member since 2000. Prior to joining the company in 1997, he was managing partner and CFO for the accounting firm Arthur Andersen.

He made news in 2008 when the SEC charged that between 1994 and 2005 UnitedHealth Group had backdated stock option grants to hide more than $1.5 billion in executive compensation. Backdating is stealing from shareholders; there is no other way to characterize it. Suppose a company granted its CEO 400,000 options when the stock was trading at $100. Subsequently, these are backdated to the stock's low point during the year when the stock was trading at $85. The backdating allowed the CEO to steal $6 million ($15 x 400,000) from the shareholders.

Backdating enabled Hemsley and other UnitedHealth Group executives to receive stock option grants priced on the single lowest trading day of the year four years in a row. *The Wall Street Journal* estimated that the odds of this honestly happening were 1 in 200 million.

When the scandal broke, Hemsley voluntarily returned $190 million of stock option value to the company. The SEC investigations forced the then-CEO, Dr. William McGuire, to resign, pay a $7 million civil penalty, and forfeit $461 million in stock options. Despite the scandal, McGuire's "golden parachute" was reported to be around $1.1 billion, the largest in corporate American history.

An internal investigation largely cleared Hemsley, claiming he played a "more limited role in the option-granting process." Despite the fact that the backdated grants had been prepared by the HR department, which ultimately reported to Hemsley, he told investigators that he "was unaware of how the grant dates were selected" or other precise terms.

Later, the California Public Employees' Retirement System was the lead plaintiff in a shareholder suit against the company, alleging that "Hemsley personally offered backdated options to new hires, was required to approve all grants in excess of 5,000 shares, [and] approved backdated mass grants." UnitedHealth Group denied the allegation.

Whatever Hemsley's direct participation in backdating, it is hard to believe that he was unaware of the practice. When he joined UnitedHealth Group in June 1997, he received a grant of 400,000 stock options. The options were dated five months earlier, when he was still working for Arthur Andersen. This backdating produced a built-in gain of $2.9 million for Hemsley. Hemsley said that he "didn't recall focusing at the time" on the fact that that his options carried a discounted price. Remember, he is a numbers guy. He had been CFO for Arthur Andersen, then one of the biggest accounting firms in the nation. He negotiated his contract with UnitedHealth, specifying, among other things, 400,000 options, and we are asked to believe that he never noticed that he made $2.9 million when he received options dated months before he joined the company or the additional $187 million he made from backdating in subsequent years.

Incidentally, Arthur Andersen advised UnitedHealth Group's comp committee as they negotiated Hemsley's contract. In 2001, Hemsley hired William Spears, then the chair of the comp committee, to manage his personal money. Spears resigned in 2006 when the scandal revealed that he managed $55 million for the then-CEO, Dr. McGuire. Very cozy.

JOHN HAMMERGREN OF MCKESSON

McKesson is a middleman, the largest pharmaceutical distributor in North America. With revenues of $181 billion in 2015, they ranked number five on the Fortune 500. Headquartered in San Francisco, they buy drugs, equipment, and health care and beauty products from manufacturers and distribute them to doctors, hospitals, pharmacies, retail chains, mail order and mass merchandisers, and institutional health care providers. They also deliver products to physician offices, surgery centers, long-term care facilities, and home care businesses, and directly to consumers. McKesson's technology solutions arm provides software, information technology, electronic health records systems, health plan payment management, and other consulting services to hospitals, physicians, and other health care providers. This business is growing, but it accounted for only 2 percent of their revenues in 2015.

John Hammergren grew up in the business. His father was a

medical supply salesman, and Hammergren often accompanied him on sales trips during school vacations. An Eagle Scout and outstanding student, Hammergren received a scholarship to the University of Minnesota. After graduating in 1981, he took a sales job with American Hospital Supply. As he climbed the corporate ladder, he earned an MBA from Xavier University.

He joined McKesson in 1996 as president of a new unit that sold pharmaceuticals to hospitals. Hammergren quickly built the unit up, and four years later, it accounted for a third of the company's US drug-distribution revenue.

Three years after Hammergren arrived at the company, McKesson was rocked by an accounting scandal when the board discovered that between 1997 and 1999, its chief executives had inflated revenues and backdated contracts. The board removed five executives, including the CEO, Charles W. McCall, who was later indicted for securities fraud and sentenced to ten years in prison. The company was forced to restate earnings downward for three prior years, and its stock price plummeted from a high of $96 to a low of $15.

Hammergren, described as "squeaky clean" and "the last man standing," became president and co-CEO in 1999 and sole CEO in 2001, and was credited for stabilizing, even rescuing, the company. Gary Rivlin wrote in *The Daily Beast*, "By all accounts, Hammergren has done a topnotch job managing the company's core business: the delivery of prescription drugs and other medicines to hospitals, nursing homes, and large retail chains like Walmart and Rite Aid. Less impressive, though, have been his efforts to broaden the company's offerings, starting with the lucrative health-technology business."

In 2005, McKesson settled a shareholders' class action suit related to the accounting scandal for $960 million, which cleared the way for a series of acquisitions: two health care information services companies in 2006; US Oncology, a distributor of medications and services in 2010; and PSS World Medical, a distributor of medical and surgical products in 2012.

By the end of fiscal year 2011, McKesson stock had recovered, reaching $85, but it was not all smooth sailing. Between 2005 and 2012 McKesson faced a series of lawsuits when the federal government, twenty-nine states, pension plans, and other health care payers sued, alleging that the company colluded with publishers of listed drug prices to inflate prices. McKesson denied any wrongdoing, but eventually settled for $151 million.

CHARIF SOUKI OF CHENIERE ENERGY

Cheniere Energy is in the liquid natural gas (LNG) business. It is one of those companies that never makes money, so its stock is always on a roller-coaster ride perhaps because its price-to-earnings ratio is meaningless, since there never are earnings. The stock was at $21 in April 1994, down to 47 cents in June 2002, up to $43 in April 2006, down again to $2 in December 2009, and way up to $80 in August 2014. The collapse of oil prices drove the stock down to $43 by the end of December 2016.

Charif Souki became CEO in 2002, having previously served as chairman of the board from June 1999 to December 2002, while he was also working as an investment banker specializing in oil and gas. His track record is one of a gambler who, having made a good bet, almost loses it all, then doubles down and wins big, but never quits when he is ahead. He has made a lot of money for himself while losing billions for the Cheniere shareholders.

He was born in Cairo in 1953, and his family moved to Beirut when he was four. His father, a journalist and author, became a well-connected adviser to the region's business and political elite. Souki went to college in the United States and graduated from Columbia Business School.

As a native Arabic speaker with an MBA and good Middle Eastern contacts, he was recruited by Blyth, Eastman Dillon, where he steered large investments from Middle East moguls to the firm.

Souki then decided to go out on his own, and after a few follies, he opened two restaurants in Aspen and Los Angeles. The latter, Mezzaluna, was patronized by Nicole Brown Simpson, the ex-wife of O.J., and employed a young waiter named Ron Goldman. After the Simpson and Goldman murders, he left the restaurant business and lost a lot of other people's money in oil and gas wildcatting. Then through the newly founded Cheniere Energy, he made a huge bet on importing natural gas into the United States. He could not have picked a worse time. Fracking was about to erupt, and by 2009 America was swimming in domestic natural gas.

At that time Cheniere was burning through $50 million a year and its stock was trading below $2. Souki decided to turn his lemons into lemonade. Instead of importing natural gas, Cheniere would export it. It would retrofit its import terminals to make them export terminals at a cost of $12 billion—a lot of money, but raising money was Souki's forte.

The Cheniere board, having no better option, went along. "The board's attitude was that it was a Hail Mary pass, fourth and 25 on our own five-yard line. . . . They were fatigued," a former board member explained.

By 2014, Souki believed that Cheniere was about to become one of the world's major exporters of LNG, capturing 10 percent of that market by the end of the decade. Its stock hit a high of $80.

The roller-coaster ride continued. The collapse in oil prices in 2015 may have eliminated the price advantage of domestic LNG relative to oil. "We're all going to have to adapt," Souki said. "I think it's pretty unsettling, as it is now. I really can't imagine anything that gets worse, and I speak from experience."

"We're stuck in an industry where we make investments for forty years, and things change every five years," he said. "It's not a very comfortable situation. But if you do it right and you look at all the options, you can determine where the opportunities are and try to take advantage of them."

In September 2015, activist investor Carl Icahn bought another 5 percent of Cheniere, increasing his stake to 13 percent. Three months later, the board fired Souki, who had never turned a profit and had run up cumulative losses of over $3 billion under his leadership.

Other members of the Souki clan benefited from Cheniere's largess. In 2014, his brother Karim was paid about $40,000 a month for consulting services and received a $600,000 bonus for his work in 2013. Charif's son Tarek was a vice president at Cheniere's London-based subsidiary, with a salary of about $300,000.

DAVID ZASLAV OF DISCOVERY COMMUNICATIONS

Discovery Communications is a global media company that provides programming in forty languages and 220 countries. Its networks include the Discovery Channel, TLC, Animal Planet, Investigation Discovery, Science, and Velocity. The flagship Discovery Channel is available to approximately 409 million households worldwide and 96 million households in the United States.

In 2008, Discovery was spun off from Liberty Media, a company controlled by John Malone. The author Ken Auletta once described Malone, the master of complex media deals, as "a man who plays chess against opponents who merely play checkers." According to *Forbes*, Malone's deal making and operational skills have generated a net worth of $8.6 billion.

Malone hired Zaslav, who had previously overseen NBC Universal's cable services, in January 2007. A teenage tennis prodigy and recovering lawyer, Zaslav began his career at the ill-fated firm LeBoeuf, Lamb, which went bankrupt after merging with Dewey Ballantine.

At Discovery, Zaslav immediately cleaned house by cashiering 25 percent of Discovery's personnel, including most of its executive staff. He then injected showbiz pizzazz by moving the Discovery Channel from documentaries to reality TV programming (*Dirty Jobs* and *Deadliest Catch*) and speculative investigations (*MythBusters, Unsolved History,* and *Best Evidence*). Animal Planet added flamboyance with shows such as *My Cat from Hell* and *River Monsters*. "The original theory was that all the programming should be rated G," Zaslav said. "But the animal kingdom isn't rated G. A lot of those stories about nature and animals involve mysteries and danger. So we relaunched Animal Planet as a more aggressive and compelling brand. And we're finding some meaningful success."

At first glance, 2014 was not a good year for Discovery. Its stock was down 25 percent while the S&P 500 was up 11 percent. For the five-year period ending 2014, its stock performed 30 percent worse than its board-selected peer group. Nonetheless, their proxy proclaimed, "We had a strong year in 2014, reporting increases in revenue and adjusted operating income before depreciation and amortization (OIBDA): Revenues increased 13 percent to $6.265 billion; and adjusted OIBDA increased 4 percent to $2.491 billion. Our free cash flow also increased 2 percent to $1.198 billion."

The above increases were largely due to acquisitions that provided $576 million in revenue and $87 million in OIBDA. Excluding them, OIBDA would have been flat and growth in revenues an anemic 4 percent. So not a great year for Discovery, but a great year for CEO David Zaslav, who pocketed $224 million.

THE FOUR HIGHEST-PAID opera singers today are Anna Netrebko, Karita Mattila, Roberto Alagna, and Renée Fleming, who make between $15,000 and $20,000 per performance. People can argue over whether they are the four best opera singers working today, but they are certainly in the top ten. Can the same be said of Hemsley, Hammergren, Souki, and Zaslav? If not, isn't something askew in corporate America? These four CEOs made an average of $153 million for one year's work, a figure they could not have received without considerable assistance from compensation consultants and sympathetic boards.

UnitedHealth Group retained Towers Perrin to act as its independent compensation consultant and paid them $363,150 for executive compensation consulting alone and approximately $3.5

million for other services. The comp committee determined that paying them almost ten times as much on other services would not jeopardize the independence of their consulting, since the $3.5 million did not exceed 2 percent of Towers Perrin's gross revenue. Apparently, the committee believes that Towers Perrin won't sell out for chump change, only for big bucks.

McKesson hired Compensation Strategies Group, a very small firm whose prior work for them had been advising management on its own pay proposal that was submitted to the board. In 2012, the firm switched sides and advised the compensation committee on how to react to management's pay proposal.

If Compensation Strategies helped put together management's package of peer groups, benchmarks, bonuses, bonus bogeys, long-term incentives, and other factors, how could it then provide an unbiased review of those proposals for the compensation committee and the board? Indeed, how could the firm challenge anything in management proposals that was rooted in their prior work?

The McKesson board also retained Compensation Strategies to advise them on what board members should be paid. Using the same firm to advise on both board and management compensation is problematic. By recommending higher board fees, the consultants can purchase directors' collaboration, connivance, or at least lack of vigilance regarding CEO compensation. Though directors seldom do it for the money, they might find it hard to be tightfisted with the CEO if the company has just treated them well. The fact that Alton Irby, the chair of McKesson's comp committee, had cashed out $2 million of McKesson stock in the prior year may have restrained his parsimonious side.

In October 2013, Cheniere's compensation committee hired

Pearl Meyer & Partners as its independent consultant. Their previous consultant, Deloitte, had performed other consulting services for Cheniere. Perhaps Cheniere no longer wanted to disclose how much they paid for compensation consulting.

Discovery's comp committee retained the Croner Company, which had worked for Discovery management through 2010. As at McKesson, the committee hired a consultant to review the procedures and practices that the consultant helped design.

The consultants at three of our four companies either had conflicts due to prior compensation work for management, were concurrently advising the board on its own compensation, and/or were accepting large fees for other consulting work. None of them allowed their compromised position to interfere with endorsing preposterous CEO compensation.

Consultants routinely blessed ridiculous peer groups selected by management. Hemsley had worked for only two companies in his entire career: the accounting firm Arthur Andersen and United-Health Group. Nonetheless, his "peer group" was loaded with large, complex corporations that have nothing to do with health insurance: Amazon, American Express, Apple, Bank of America, Cisco, Citigroup, Coca-Cola, Costco, Dow Chemical, General Electric, Goldman Sachs, Google, Hewlett-Packard, McDonald's, Microsoft, Morgan Stanley, Oracle, Procter & Gamble, Walmart, and Wells Fargo.

Hemsley appears to be a highly competent executive, but it is laughable to think that any of these companies would attempt to hire him away. When it came to setting compensation for him, whatever Amazon, American Express, Apple, Bank of America, etc., paid their CEOs was irrelevant. They would never hire a CEO with no industry experience. Nonetheless, the comp committee benchmarked his pay between the 50th and 75th percentile of this distinguished peer group. For the trailing five-year period, this group's stock performance was up 6 percent, while UnitedHealth Group's was down 30 percent. PUPNUP.

McKesson's peer group for FY 2011 included General Electric, IBM, and Oracle. Oracle's CEO had averaged $179 million in compensation for the prior six years, so that figure inflated Hammergren's payday. The comp committee had approved the same peer group the year before, so they probably didn't give it the attention it deserved. That neither General Electric nor IBM nor Oracle would ever have hired Hammergren as their CEO underscores the risibility of this peer group.

The consultants provided data on executive compensation from thirty-three companies in McKesson's peer group. The majority were other health care companies that were smaller than McKesson. Therefore, McKesson's HR staff correlated CEO compensation with company size and upwardly adjusted peer group CEO pay to what it might have been, in their judgment, had the company been as large as McKesson. No doubt that made very good sense to the directors; they were quite familiar with upward adjustments.

When McKesson compared its performance against others in its annual report and proxy statement, it ignored this peer group. It compared its shareholder returns against the S&P 500 and the Value Line Healthcare Index that replicates the average of all heath care stocks. PUPNUP.

McKesson said it benchmarked cash compensation at the 50th percentile of the peer group and equity bonus at the 75th percentile, but it reserved the right to depart from these guidelines for any number of reasons. The McKesson proxy disclosed: "Ultimately due to a number of variables including share price, individual performance and company performance, total direct compensation delivered to our executive officers may be higher or lower than the 50th and 75th percentiles of our Compensation Peer Group." I offer 100 to 1 odds to anyone who will bet on lower.

Cheniere selected fifteen energy companies as their peer group. As Cheniere had no earnings, the comparisons presented in their proxy featured stock price performance. The comparisons showed that they beat the S&P 500 and the peer group median.

Cheniere said it did not benchmark, explaining, "While we spend considerable time benchmarking levels of pay against similarly situated executives in the marketplace, we do not have a set formula for targeting pay at any particular level of the marketplace. Rather, we use such information as a market point of reference, from which the Compensation Committee applies discretion in setting compensation."

Discovery's peer group—AMC Networks, Cablevision Systems Corporation, CBS Corporation, Charter Communications, DIRECTV, Netflix, Scripps Networks Interactive, Viacom, and Yahoo—seems quite reasonable. They are all closely related businesses.

Discovery benchmarked Zaslav "significantly above the 75th percentile," but none of his performance measures required him to perform "significantly above the 75th percentile" to get a bonus. Truly, all CEOs are above average.

The comp committee lamely explained that "based on an overall review of the Comparative Financial Measures, the Company was performing well as compared to its peers." They made this statement in 2014 after Discovery's share price had dropped 24 percent, while the S&P and Discovery's peer groups were up 11 percent. In its comparative review, Discovery gave itself high marks in meaningless measures such as revenue growth and absurd ones such as the growth rate in enterprise value. The latter is the total market value of stock plus debt and cash. This can be increased simply by going further into debt.

COMPENSATION TARGETS

UnitedHealth Group and McKesson used the strict Pay Machine practice of setting a target by selecting a percentile ranking of their peer group. This produced a $9.1 million target compensation for Hemsley, and I estimate Hammergren's target to be roughly $20 million. Cheniere did not explicitly benchmark, perhaps because they could not find enough companies losing $500 million a year. Perhaps Souki's target was simply the highest number any director could think of. Discovery set no overall target for Zaslav, as his contract fixed 96 percent of his total compensation. The only variable was his cash bonus, targeted at $6.6 million. What his peers were paid no doubt influenced his contract negotiation, but not in a formal way.

SALARY, CASH BONUS, AND LONG-TERM BONUS

Let's now analyze how the four companies dealt with three types of compensation, beginning with salary.

UnitedHealth Group kept Hemsley's salary at $1,300,000, the same as the prior year. Hammergren nobly eschewed a salary increase and his salary remained at $1,664,615. Souki's salary was $800,000. The proxy states that the compensation committee decided not to increase Mr. Souki's base salary but rather "rely on the performance-based elements of his pay to ensure that he is fairly compensated." They relied on performance-based elements to the tune of $133 million. Zaslav negotiated a new six-year employment agreement with Discovery on January 2, 2014, specifying key provisions for his compensation, including that his base salary would remain flat at $3 million for the seven years beginning 2014.

In all cases, salary was a relatively insignificant portion of compensation, ranging from 0.6 to 1.3 percent. Therefore, I wonder why these companies did not limit salary to $1 million, thus making it all tax deductible.

How these four companies calculated and awarded cash bonuses further illustrates the strength of the Pay Machine and the fecklessness of the boards.

UnitedHealth Group set a target cash bonus for Hemsley at 125 percent of his salary, or $1,625,000. Hemsley could, and did, receive more than his target.

UnitedHealth Group selected three performance measures, each weighted one-third, for this bonus:

- Revenue
- Operating income and cash flow
- Stewardship (customer and physician satisfaction, employee engagement and employee teamwork)

Selecting revenue as a bonus measure is inexplicable. A CEO can increase revenues by reducing prices or increasing promotion spending. Both might diminish profits, but he still gets a bonus. Operating income and cash flow are easily manipulated, since the first excludes interest charges and the second excludes depreciation. Heavy capital spending and acquisitions coupled with debt financing will increase both operating income and cash flow even if the returns on these investments are poor. The third criterion, stewardship, is meaningless jargon. How can a company honestly measure results for employee engagement and employee teamwork?

As I read the UnitedHealth Group proxy, I asked myself, and not for the first time, "What were these people thinking?" For the largest health insurer in America, why are revenue growth and employee engagement two of the critical objectives? How about the health of their 29 million customers?

For each of these three performance measures, UnitedHealth Group set a bonus bogey and a bonus range. The bonus bogeys were charitably undemanding: a 6 percent increase in revenue, a 4 percent increase in cash flow, and a 4 percent decrease in operating income. The S&P 500 EPS more than tripled in 2009, but Hemsley got a bonus bogey of minus 4 percent in operating income. Falling off a log would have been tougher.

It turned out not to be a great year for UnitedHealth Group. Their stock was up 15 percent, but the S&P 500 was up 23 percent. Nonetheless, Hemsley was awarded a $1,950,000 cash bonus, or 120 percent of his target short-term cash bonus of $1,625,000. The comp committee explained in its "rationale for individual compensation decisions" that Hemsley had done a lot of good work that year, including "achievement of overall performance for the 2009 annual cash incentive award that was between the target and maximum goals."

The proxy then adds another reason to shower Hemsley with riches: he met the three-year EPS bogey. This EPS bogey was a cumulative $10.09 for the three-year period. The actual three-year

EPS was $9.06, 10 percent below the bogey. To hit the bogey, the directors had to make adjustments, so they added $1.2 billion in earnings. Before the adjustment, the earnings total for that year was $3.8 billion. They had to goose the number by at least 32 percent to hit the bogey.

The company's plan, approved by the shareholders, allows adjustments for extraordinary items and nonrecurring items. Where did they find $1.2 billion? What was their rationale? For legal, audit, and tax purposes, UnitedHealth Group's board had to document the rationale for and the effect of these adjustments, but they chose not to disclose this information to shareholders.

McKESSON

McKesson specified a target short-term cash bonus of $2,750,000 if Hammergren hit a $4.82 EPS bogey. If he surpassed it, he could receive up to three times his target bonus. Here, Hammergren was able to negotiate very easy bonus bogeys: $4.82 EPS for FY 2011 was a modest 5 percent increase over the comparable 2010 figure of $4.58.

How was 5 percent chosen? We are not told. Maybe the board and/or Hammergren thought 2011 would be a tough year. Maybe they had previously agreed on a budget that was up 5 percent. Regardless, they decided to award Hammergren a bonus for a 5 percent increase in EPS.

As it turned out, the S&P 500 EPS increased 26 percent over the same period. When they set the 5 percent bogey, McKesson directors obviously did not know S&P earnings would be up 26 percent. However, if the board had set Hammergren's bonus bogey at beating 50 percent or 75 percent of the McKesson peer group's increase in EPS, he would have received no bonus. PUPNUP.

Hammergren did beat his bogey, but only after the directors fudged the numbers. McKesson reported $4.65 in EPS in both its annual report and its 10-K. Strangely, this number never appears in the proxy statement that discloses executive pay. The proxy states that the EPS number was $4.82. The explanation—in small print—is that the proxy number excludes litigation charges. Hey, it's not Hammergren's fault that some bastards are suing us.

The directors then decided that some additional adjustments to EPS were "appropriate to reflect certain unusual events that were not included in the Company's FY 2011 operating plan." The directors added back $37 million of acquisition expenses to arrive at $5.00 EPS and then used this number to calculate Hammergren's bonus. At the director-adjusted $5.00 EPS, Hammergren beat his bogey by 5 percent. According to the board, he was then due 123 percent of his initial target bonus award.

After modifying earnings to benefit Hammergren, the McKesson comp committee proceeded to increase this 123 percent bonus to 185 percent. Their reason for doing that? The committee applied an "individual performance modifier . . . to recognize the executive officer's performance against non-financial objectives and initiatives." Based on achieving 185 percent of his $2,520,000 target, Hammergren received $4,649,400 for his short-term cash bonus.

Hammergren's long-term cash bonus was based on a cumulative three-year EPS bogey of $12.89 per share. The actual three-year result for FY 2009 through FY 2011, after board-directed adjustments, was $13.35 per share, which was 3.6 percent higher than the bogey. For this achievement, the compensation committee determined that Hammergren deserved 193 percent of his target bonus. The target was $2,700,000, so his long-term cash bonus was $5,211,000. For exceeding a bogey by 3.6 percent, Hammergren gets 193 percent. Nice work if you can get it.

CHENIERE

Cheniere's comp committee determined that aggregate short-term cash bonuses should be approximately 10 percent greater than last year's, largely because its stock was up. Since Cheniere was losing money, the committee could not use financial bonus measures, so it looked toward accomplishments, such as:

- Managing the capital budget and operating expenditures within 10 percent of the approved 2013 expenditure budget.
- Completing the financing for and commenced construction of Trains 3 and 4 at the Sabine Pass LNG terminal in May 2013.
- Initiating FERC prefiling for Trains 5 and 6 at the Sabine Pass LNG in February 2013.
- Corpus Christi Liquefaction entering into its first LNG SPA with Pertamina in December 2013.
- And a score of other achievements I could not understand.

The board increased Souki's target bonus by 15 percent, from $3,200,000 to $3,680,000. They stated no reason for this, but it could have been a reward for holding shareholder losses to only $507 million in 2013 following a $332 million loss in 2012.

Souki also received a $4,200,000 long-term cash bonus. This was his second installment, 20 percent of the long-term bonus granted in 2012 for the issuance of Notice to Proceed to commence. Cheniere gave no further explanation.

DISCOVERY

Under his contract with Discovery, Zaslav's cash bonus target was $6.6 million for 2014, with further increases in the subsequent years. This bonus was based 50 percent on financial achievement and 50 percent on nonfinancial individual accomplishments.

The financial measures were increases in (1) revenues, (2) OIBDA, essentially cash generated before tax and interest on debt, and (3) free cash flow, i.e., the cash available for redeployment defined as after-tax cash generated by operations, less capital expenditures. All are problematic as performance measures. Revenue increases are irrelevant unless they produce more earnings. OIBDA, since it ignores depreciation and amortization, can be increased by capital spending and acquisitions, as it did here. Zaslav was credited with the OIBDA generated by acquisitions, but not charged for the economic cost of these acquisitions, the interest on debt, and the dilution on equity to finance the acquisition and the depreciation and amortization of assets acquired. The third measure—free cash flow—can be easily manipulated by deferring capital investment.

In any case, the board set specific bonus bogeys for each:

- Net revenue $6.534 billion
- Adjusted free cash flow $1.340 billion
- Further adjusted OIBDA $2.649 billion

Zaslav missed all his numbers. On page thirty of their proxy, Discovery showed net revenue of $6.265 billion (4 percent lower than the bogey), adjusted free cash flow of $1.198 billion (11 percent lower), and adjusted OIBDA of $2.491 billion (6 percent lower). So did Zaslav get no bonus? Don't be silly.

On page forty-nine, the company presented new numbers: net revenue of $6.449 billion (1 percent lower than the bogey), adjusted free cash flow of $1.389 billion (4 percent above the bogey), and adjusted OIBDA of $2.616 billion (1 percent lower). On average, these numbers had risen by 3 percent, 16 percent, and 5 percent in a mere nineteen pages. What happened? Surprise! The board had adjusted them upward to account not only for unplanned initiatives but also for shortfalls caused by items such as "Russia/Ukraine geopolitical issues" and impairment of programming "as a result of the 2014 Mount Everest avalanche." An avalanche in, of all places, Mount Everest. Surely Zaslav didn't cause the avalanche, so let's not penalize him. The board ignored downward adjustments for continued peace between the United States and Canada and the absence of avalanches on Kilimanjaro, K2, and Mount Fuji.

Even after these changes, the committee determined that Zaslav missed his quantitative financial bogeys by 4 percent.

His qualitative short-term bonus goals were:

- Manage growth across networks through continued content investment, including brand-defining content, and strategic allocation of assets for long-term growth (20 percent).
- Drive revenue through affiliate sales growth and securing advertisers for cable, free-to-air, and digital platforms to outperform peers in domestic and international markets (20 percent).

- Drive international growth through potential new acquisi-tions, integrate completed acquisitions, and build a strong content presence in local markets (20 percent).
- Further develop management succession plans for key op-erational roles (15 percent).
- Further develop strategies on content and distribution that protect and move our business forward with emerging technologies (15 percent).
- Continue to attract, retain, differentiate, and reward ex-ceptional talent in cable, new media, free-to-air, and edu-cation at all levels on a global basis (10 percent).

This sounds more like Zaslav's job description than achieve-ments that merit a bonus. Moreover, the committee determined that he'd missed his qualitative goals by 6 percent. Combining quantitative with qualitative, it calculated that he'd missed his ag-gregate goals by 8 percent. So Zaslav gets no bonus? I told you, don't be silly.

Missing by 8 percent meant that he made 92 percent, and we all know that 92 percent is an A minus. So the committee then deter-mined that he was due a cash bonus of $6,082,359.

COMMON THREADS

The companies used performance measures for cash bonuses that were foolish (revenue growth, employee teamwork, managing the capital budget, developing strategies) or easily manipulated (oper-ating income, cash flow, and EPS).

The companies set undemanding bogeys such as a decrease of

4 percent in operating income at UnitedHealth Group and a 5 percent increase in EPS at McKesson, filing forms at Cheniere, and developing a succession plan at Discovery. In Souki's case, the board gave him a cash bonus because he had done a bunch of swell things.

Three of the four—UnitedHealth Group, McKesson, and Discovery—changed the numbers after the fact to pay cash bonuses. UnitedHealth Group miraculously found $1.2 billion of earnings. McKesson adjusted $4.65 in EPS to $5.00. Discovery adjusted for avalanches. Only Cheniere did not fiddle with the numbers, but they didn't need to, since Souki's bonus was not based on numbers.

The "target" for a bonus served largely as a floor, as bonus ranges and payout formulas were generous. Hemsley got 120 percent of his target bonus. McKesson applied payout formulas that defied reason. For beating the EPS target by 5 percent, they paid Hammergren 185 percent of his target short-term bonus. He did better on his long-term cash bonus, getting 193 percent of targets for beating his bogey by 3.6 percent. Zaslav missed his bogeys by 8 percent, but got 92 percent of his bonus. He was protected on the downside, but unlimited on the upside.

All four CEOs received multimillion-dollar cash bonuses for little more than doing their job. It is difficult to point to a single objective achievement among them that warranted a large cash bonus. The S&P 500 beat UnitedHealth Group by 8 percent. Zaslav's stock was down 24 percent while his peer group was up 11 percent. PUPNUP. Even after adjustment, Hammergren's EPS were up 5 percent compared to the S&P's increase of 26 percent. PUPNUP. Souki lost over half a billion dollars. PUPNUP.

EQUITY AWARDS

For an equity award, the UnitedHealth Group comp committee, one month into the year, awarded Mr. Hemsley 115,385 "performance shares" worth $2.74 million at the time of the grant, 57,692 restricted stock units (RSUs) valued at $1.37 million, and 169,683 stock appreciation rights (SARs) worth $1.44 million.* SARs are the functional equivalent of stock options that entitle the executive to the appreciation in the company's stock, but the company never has to issues new shares.

UnitedHealth Group explained that these awards "were determined by the Compensation Committee after considering competitive market data; the desirability of utilizing a balanced system to mitigate risk, encourage superior performance, and build ownership; and the need to retain and motivate the executives to deliver sustained performance." I think this means that Hemsley had to have a pulse. Don't ask the shareholders. They were left in the dark as to how and why Hemsley got his equity bonus.

Stock options and SARs need not be performance based to be tax deductible. Since they gain value only if the stock goes up, the

---

* Not to complicate an already difficult subject, I have not distinguished between restricted stock and restricted stock units (RSUs). Many companies now utilize RSUs instead of restricted stock. An RSU is the economic equivalent of a share of company stock. However, similar to phantom stock, with an RSU, no stock is issued until the restrictions lapse. RSUs differ from restricted stock in accounting and tax treatment. Their benefits are (1) RSUs do not count as outstanding shares until shares are actually issued after vesting, while restricted stock counts immediately; (2) in general, RSUs are easier to administer; (3) the company can avoid paying cash dividends until vested; and (4) it is easier to enforce clawbacks with RSUs. I prefer RSUs to restricted stock and used them in the private company plan in chapter 1.

higher stock price is considered de facto performance. But if restricted stock or RSUs are awarded without being based on performance, the company gets no tax deduction. Stunningly, UnitedHealth Group did not base their RSU award on performance, and therefore, it was not tax deductible.* They awarded $15.5 million in RSUs grants to their five top executives without any performance test, thus forgoing $5.4 million in tax savings. They used stock in a cookie jar from their 2002 plan that did not require performance. They even took steps to preserve this cookie jar by issuing SARs, because these "have a similar accounting treatment to stock options and result in a smaller number of shares being issued from our 2002 Stock Incentive Plan."

Since the directors stated that their first principle of executive compensation is "pay for performance," I wondered how they could justify paying Uncle Sam $5.4 million by ignoring performance. UnitedHealth Group limply explained, "The Compensation Committee seeks to structure most elements of our executive compensation program to meet this [performance] exception. However, to maintain flexibility to promote varying corporate goals, we have not adopted a policy requiring all compensation to be deductible."

McKesson awarded bonuses in the form of both stock options and restricted stock. The McKesson proxy is opaque about how the directors determined the number of stock option grants. Option awards were "consistent with the [compensation committee's] review of stock option awards granted to similarly situated

---

* The UnitedHealth Group proxy states, "The most recent equity-based compensation plan, the 2002 Stock Incentive Plan, is the source of current awards. RSUs granted under the Company's 2002 Stock Incentive Plan do not qualify as performance-based compensation."

executives by companies in the Compensation Peer Group." This criterion is not quite "whatever strikes our fancy," but it's not far from that. In May 2011, Hammergren was awarded 402,000 options. McKesson estimated that they were worth $7,370,750, and Hammergren did not have to beat any bogey to get them. They were simply the comp committee's reward for all his diligence and the way he parts his hair. Justifying the option awards, the directors stated in the proxy: "Since stock option awards provide value to the holder only if the company's stock price appreciates, the use of such incentives directly aligns the interests of our executives and stockholders." As the Duke of Wellington once said, "If you believe that, you'll believe anything."

At the start of each fiscal year, the McKesson board established target bonuses and corresponding bonus bogeys for restricted stock. In May of 2010, they set a target bonus of 127,000 shares of restricted stock for Hammergren. The proxy reveals little about how and why they settled on this number. With McKesson shares then trading around $68, this target bonus would have a market value of $8.6 million. The restricted shares vested over four years.

As with the cash bonuses, Hammergren could get more, up to 225 percent of target, if he beat his bogey. McKesson used the same bogey for Hammergren's restricted stock bonus as they had for his cash bonus, achieving a 5 percent increase in the same EPS. Because of board-directed upward adjustments, McKesson beat its EPS bogey of $4.82, and Hammergren was eligible to receive 116 percent of his initial restricted stock targets under the comp committee's formula. But wait, that's not all!

The board also applied Hammergren's "individual performance

modifier," which increased his initial target of 127,000 shares to 220,980 shares—74 percent above target.

The proxy does not explain how an "individual performance modifier" is calculated, except that "modification of payouts based upon individual performance, inclusive of assessment against our 'ICARE' principles (i.e., integrity, customer first, accountability, respect and excellence)." I will have more to say on ICARE later.

With the stock then trading around $84, the award had a total market value of $18.6 million. This was tax-deductible "performance pay" awarded for performance that according to the company's own chosen metric was far below average. PUPNUP. As in the case of the short-term cash bonus, Hammergren missed his target and beat it only by 4 percent after the board fudged the numbers. For this he deserves 174 percent of his target equity bonus.

Cheniere provides a murky exposition in its proxy of how it determined Charif Souki's equity bonus. Since the company has never made money, the comp committee decided to base long-term incentive awards on meeting a series of milestones. Souki received $132.9 million of stock in the following increments:

- $27.2 million for Milestone 1: The first installment of 30 percent of the Milestone Awards vested upon the closing of financing and issuance of notice to proceed ("NTP") to begin construction of Trains 3 and 4 at the Sabine Pass LNG terminal
- $18.1 million for Milestone 2: Payment of 60 percent of original contract price of EPC contract

- $18.1 million for Milestone 3: Substantial completion of Train 4
- $27.2 million for Milestone 4: First anniversary of substantial completion of Train 4
- $21.7 million for Cheniere's stock price averaging over $25 for 120 days
- $20.6 million for Cheniere's stock price averaging over $35 for 120 days

My cynical opinion is that meeting milestones established by a friendly board is a lot easier than actually making money. It certainly was for Souki. He never met a milestone he didn't like. As the company continued to lose money, one might expect the CEO to meet some milestones for the $9.1 million he was paid in cash. Did Cheniere need to pay him an extra $133 million to motivate him to do his job?

They also seemed to pay him three times for everything he did:

- In cash—$9.1 million is significant compensation, even for a CEO
- Bonuses for accomplishments and meeting milestones
- Bonuses for the increase in stock price

Since the company continued to lose money, the stock price should reflect anticipated future earnings. If "Completion of Train 4" or "Payment of 60 percent of original contract price of EPC Contract" increased anticipated future earnings, the stock price should also rise. Paying for one meant paying for both.

Though immense, Discovery equity awards were structured

more sensibly than those of the other three corporations, a very low bar. All of Zaslav's equity awards were part of his new six-year employment agreement. His largest equity award was an up-front bonus of RSUs valued at $94.6 million. Probably half of the SARs valued at $50.5 million could also be considered a signing bonus. In real economic terms, about $120 million of Zaslav's 2014 equity awards should have been spread over the six-year life of his contract, but the accounting profession does not allow this. One could argue that Zaslav's reported compensation of $156 million is overstated by $100 million (five-sixths of $120 million). However, I will later contend that his reported compensation was also understated by $68 million, so making both adjustments puts him at $124 million.

OTHER COMPENSATION

The Pay Machine does not deal with other compensation, which includes perks and retirement benefits. Not surprisingly, the four companies differed sharply in the way they handled these.

UnitedHealth Group stated, "We do not believe that providing generous executive perquisites is either necessary to attract and retain executive talent or consistent with our pay-for-performance philosophy." Stunningly, they appear to be telling the truth. No executive officer received more than $10,000 in perks, so the company did not have to disclose the amounts of individual perks.

Toward the other end of the spectrum, John Hammergren received $267,040 in perks. He was reimbursed $122,177 for home security costs. He also got a chauffeur to drive his company car, free use of the McKesson corporate jet for personal travel worth $100,560, and an extra $17,000 a year to pay for a financial planner, because handling all those millions himself would have left him little time to devote to running the company.

Like UnitedHealth Group, Cheniere boasted of their frugality regarding perks. "We generally do not provide benefits to our executives that are not offered to all of our employees." Reading a little further, however, reveals that "Mr. Souki occasionally uses Company-chartered aircraft to commute to the Company's headquarters." His personal guests were permitted to join him on all flights, and his personal use of company aircraft totaled $334,159 for the year. In line with their stated policy of not providing benefits to executives that were not offered to all employees, many other Cheniere employees must have used the company aircraft at a cost of more than $300,000, but the proxy doesn't elaborate.

David Zaslav surpassed Hammergren, with perks totaling $384,287, including $296,930 for personal use of aircraft including family travel, $50,324 for tax gross-ups for business associate/spouse travel, $16,800 for a car allowance, $3,614 for home office expenses, and $16,619 for personal security services.

With perks, we see how payments not generated by the Pay Machine vary widely even for the highest-paid executives. Zaslav gets $384,287 in perks and Hemsley gets less than $10,000.

RETIREMENT AND GOLDEN PARACHUTES

Upon retirement (or termination for any reason), Hemsley will receive a lump sum of $10.7 million. This supplemental benefit was frozen in 2006. Therefore, there was no increase and no expense for Hemsley in the year in question. Hemsley did receive $8,575 for his 401(k) and $75,583 for an executive savings plan match. Through his own contributions, company matching, and earnings, Hemsley had accumulated $6,601,529 in the executive savings plan that he can receive upon retirement.

McKesson contributed $729,119 to Hammergren's retirement plan. In 2011, the present value of his pension benefits—which are not tied in any way to performance—increased by $13.5 million. When he retires, Hammergren will receive lifetime benefits, including a personal assistant, an office, and the services of a financial counselor. It's estimated these will cost $350,000 annually. Even Hammergren's death will not derail the gravy train. If his wife survives him, she will continue receiving his base salary for six months and will get $2 million in after-tax income, with McKesson paying the tax.

In June 2013, McKesson disclosed that if Hammergren had left voluntarily on March 31, he would have received a lump sum of $159 million. *The Wall Street Journal* reported that "McKesson is giving Mr. Hammergren credit for extra years of service and for pay that he didn't receive. It's also waiving a penalty for early retirement. And the company has long used a favorable formula to calculate the current value of a pension that will be paid over many years."

"Without those advantages, Mr. Hammergren's pension would have been valued at about $36 million as of March 31." According to the *Journal*'s analysis, this is less than one-quarter of the sum he would actually have collected.

Cheniere offers only a 401(k) matching plan as a retirement benefit to all employees including the CEO. Souki did not participate in this plan in 2013.

Discovery offered a 401(k) defined contribution plan to all employees and a supplemental deferred compensation plan (SRP) to senior management including Zaslav and contributed $1,533,300 to Zaslav's SRP in 2014. This brought the value of his plan to $52.3 million at the end of 2014.

Pension benefits vary widely depending on the company. Hammergren could leave with a $159 million lump sum to cushion retirement; Souki gets only what is in his 401(k), to which he and Cheniere made no contribution in 2012.

While technically not part of CEO compensation, generous golden parachutes helped spark shareholder backlash. If Hammergren were to lose his job because McKesson was sold or merged or otherwise underwent a change of control, he would receive an immediate $469 million payout. At Cheniere, Souki must get by with a $96.4 million parachute. Zaslav's parachute is good for only $230 million, about what he made in 2014. And I thought Malone paid well.

Hemsley is due only an $8 million parachute if there is a change of control. Though a large number to anyone except a CEO, it is less than 2 percent of what Hammergren would get, further evidence that payments not driven by the Pay Machine, such as pensions and golden parachutes, differ greatly between companies.

COMMON THREADS

CEOs got stock options for being CEOs. They did not have to accomplish anything else. Hemsley was awarded 169,863 SARs, Hammergren 301,000 options, and Zaslav 3,702,660 SARs, with no performance hurdle. UnitedHealth Group awarded options "after considering competitive market data; the desirability of utilizing a balanced system to mitigate risk, encourage superior performance, and build ownership; and the need to retain and motivate the executives to deliver sustained performance." McKesson stated that this award was "consistent with its review of stock option awards granted to similarly situated executives by companies in the Compensation Peer Group." Discovery explained that the options were part of Zaslav's contract. The rationale at these three companies seems to be that everyone else gets a whopping number of options. Why not our guy?

The enormity of the equity awards at our companies is breathtaking. Souki received restricted stock worth $133 million. Zaslav got stock and options worth $145 million. Hemsley, Hammergren, and Zaslav cashed in options and stock for gains of $96 million, $112 million, and $68 million, respectively.

All four CEOs played a significant role in setting their own compensation.

- At UnitedHealth Group, "Management recommends appropriate enterprise-wide financial and non-financial performance goals. Management works with the Compensation Committee to establish the agenda and prepare meeting information for each Compensation Committee meeting."
- McKesson's executive vice president of HR, who reported directly to CEO Hammergren, oversaw the initial work of identifying peer companies, assembling salary surveys, assessing McKesson's financial performance, and making the first recommendations to the compensation committee.
- At Cheniere, management participated in the review of external market data to determine the competitiveness of the executive compensation packages.

- At Discovery, the CEO "provides the Committee with proposed goals for himself."

You don't need a fairy godmother if you have your hand on the controls of the Pay Machine.

CHAPTER NINE

How Much Did He Make?

Thanks to an accounting anomaly, the simple act of reporting CEO pay, as required by the SEC, allows companies to ignore the largest component of CEO compensation—the appreciation on stock options. According to UnitedHealth Group and McKesson, their CEOs were only moderately overpaid. UnitedHealth Group reported that Hemsley made less than $9 million. According to McKesson, Hammergren made $46 million. But these amounts are far less than the $102 million for Hemsley and $145 million for Hammergren reported by *Forbes* and other monitors. This is because, in a good stock market year, appreciation on options can amount to more than 80 percent of total realized compensation. It accounted for 41 percent of CEO realized compensation in 2012, the most recent year for which this number is available.

Corporate boards do not report appreciation on stock options as compensation. They hold that the only thing that counts is the value of the options at the time they were granted. When the CEO later cashes them in, the board treats him as a lucky shareholder who benefited from a higher stock price, even though he had paid nothing for them.

How can this be? Excuse me while I delve into the obscure art of accounting.

There are two kinds of executive compensation: realized and earned.

Realized compensation is the compensation received by the CEO. It's the total value of what he took home this year. It's what he can spend.

You may ask, "How can there be an alternative definition?" The answer is among the mysteries that can be fathomed only by the priestly class of accountants, who speak an incomprehensible language of their own.

I have chaired the audit committee at five different companies. (As I mentioned earlier, the second dumbest director chairs the audit committee.) I've often wondered if auditing firms are in the business of extortion: "Nice company you have here. It would be a shame if it didn't get a clean audit opinion." Without a clean opinion from the external auditor, few companies can survive.

When they have abetted fraud, as with Enron, accounting firms have a solution—more auditing. In response to Enron, Congress, in one of its more cockamamie acts (a very high standard), approved Section 404 of the Sarbanes-Oxley Act, which requires a company's external auditor to opine on the company's system of internal controls on financial reporting. Enron did not go bust because its accounts payable system lacked proper internal controls. Enron went bust because it committed fraud while its external auditors connived with the fraudsters. But why should such facts interfere with legislation that shifts hundreds of millions of dollars from shareholders to accounting firms?

Aside from doubling audit fees, Section 404 accomplished nothing. Until Lehman went bankrupt in 2008, its external auditors were signing off on scams such as "repo 105" and SIVs (structured investment vehicles) that magically moved debt off its balance sheet.* The fact that Lehman's accounts payable system had adequate internal controls was not sufficient to save the company.

So, now that we're clear on all that . . .

Realized compensation is what the CEO can spend. It includes the value received when he exercises his stock options. If the CEO holds options with a strike price of $20 and exercises them when the stock is selling for $50 a share, he makes $30 a share.

Earned compensation is an accounting concept. It relies on estimates and does not disclose all the benefits an executive received. Earned compensation is the value of compensation an executive "earns the right to keep." This construct is what corporations report as compensation, then show as an expense on their books.

The major difference between the two categories is that earned compensation leaves out the price appreciation the CEO receives when he exercises his stock options. Instead, the value of the options is estimated when the options are awarded. To calculate this value, most companies use a complex mathematical model known as Black-Scholes, which was formulated by Nobel Prize winners.

Suppose a CEO is awarded stock options to purchase 1,000,000 shares at a price of $20 each. Using a complex mathematical

---

* Repo 105 is an accounting maneuver where a short-term loan is classified as a sale. The cash obtained through this "sale" is then used to pay down debt, allowing the company to appear to reduce its leverage by temporarily paying down liabilities—just long enough to reflect on the company's published balance sheet. After the company's financial reports are published, the company borrows cash and repurchases its original assets. SIVs are investment pools that usually aim to profit from credit spreads. For reasons I cannot understand, SIVs do not appear on banks' balance sheets, and this allows the banks to have much greater leverage than they reveal.

model, the company might calculate that at the time of the award, each option is worth $3. Therefore, the CEO's earned compensation is $3 million when the options are awarded, while his realized compensation is zero. Suppose the stock increases by 150 percent—to $50 in eight years solely because the broad stock market was up the same amount. Now the CEO exercises his options for a gain of $30 a share (today's price of $50 less the $20 option price). The CEO pockets $30 million. "Realized compensation" says the CEO was paid $30 million when he exercised the options; under the earned definition, he earned nothing.

UnitedHealth Group reported that Hemsley's total compensation was $9 million. He actually made $102 million largely by exercising stock options that produced a gain of $98.6 million. Where did this $98.6 million come from? According to the company, it came from the tooth fairy. The rest of the shareholders lost money because their shares were diluted when the company printed more shares to give to the CEO.* The CEO pocketed $98.6 million, but UnitedHealth Group and the earned method of accounting say nothing happened.

UnitedHealth Group's income was reported as if Hemsley was an outside investor. If you owned their stock and sold it for a gain, they would not report anything. The fact that you bought your stock on the open market while Hemsley was given his for nothing is a distinction that they do not find germane. They had to disclose in their proxies the $98.6 million gain their CEO

---

* Technically, the company would exchange "treasury stock" for the options. Treasury stock may have come from a repurchase or buyback from shareholders, or it may have been authorized but never issued to the public in the first place. To the layman, this is a distinction without a difference.

realized; but instead of including it in the discussions of CEO compensation, they put in elsewhere.*

When McKesson reported Hammergren's compensation for 2011, the company employed the earned method, which ignored the value received on the exercise of options. In FY 2011, Hammergren exercised options on 3.3 million shares of stock for $112.1 million. These were options he had been awarded in prior years. Don't worry; he got more options in 2012 to make sure he stayed motivated.

In FY 2011, Hammergren's stock with a market value of $6.6 million became vested, meaning he could sell it immediately if he wanted. So, in total, he received $118.7 million from the exercise of options and the vesting of restricted stock.

As with UnitedHealth Group, McKesson neither reported this as compensation nor recorded it as an expense. Instead, they estimated the value of Hammergren's stock options plus the restricted stock he had earned the right to keep at $19.6 million. The difference between what Hammergren realized and what McKesson reported as earned was $99.1 million.

---

* Hemsley's realized and earned compensation for the year were:

	Realized Compensation	Earned Compensation
Salary	$1,300,000	$1,300,000
Cash bonuses	1,950,000	1,950,000
Restricted stock	0	4,122,694
Value of options (SARs)	0	1,442,306
Options exercised	98,578,350	0
Vesting restricted stock	44,600	0
All other	86,916	86,916
Total	$101,959,866	$8,901,916

When *Forbes* and other media reported Hammergren's compensation, they cited his higher, realized compensation rather than the lower, earned compensation.* Is it possible that the board members, all sophisticated businesspeople, didn't know there were two ways of reporting CEO pay? Some certainly knew Hammergren had exercised options worth $98.6 million because this was disclosed in the proxy even though it was not reported as compensation. However, the directors may have thought they were approving $46 million (Hammergren's earned compensation), not $145 million (his realized compensation).†

At $46 million, the board had no reason to expect an angry explosion. The previous year, they had reported Hammergren's compensation as $54.6 million and gotten away with it. That year,

---

* It is easier to report earned compensation numbers since they are clearly presented in the proxy. To obtain realized compensation, one has to locate and then add and subtract numbers from different parts of the proxy. *Forbes*, traditionally and in Hemsley's and Hammergren's case, calculated realized compensation. More recently, the media, including *The New York Times,* have reported CEO compensation numbers compiled by Equilar, a privately held company that provides information on executive compensation. Using the earned compensation method, Equilar and *The New York Times* and other media named Souki and Zaslav as the highest-paid CEO in 2013 and 2014, respectively.

† Hammergren's realized and earned compensation were:

	Realized Compensation	Earned Compensation
Salary	$1,664,615	$1,664,615
Cash bonuses	9,860,400	9,860,400
Pension & misc.	14,072,640	14,072,640
Restricted stock	0	12,185,796
Value of options (SARs)	0	7,370,750
Options exercised	112,121,910	0
Vesting restricted stock	6,552,247	0
All other	511,951	511,951
Total	$144,783,763	$45,666,152

Hammergren had ranked number 22 on the *Forbes* list of highest-paid CEOs, but since McKesson also ranked number 14 in revenues in the Fortune 500, the directors suffered little adverse publicity. For FY 2011, their figure of $46 million appeared to have been a reduction of over $8 million in Hammergren's total comp, down 16 percent from the previous year. The directors even stated in the proxy that "these changes are having the effect of moderating the compensation provided to our CEO." They probably thought they were in good shape—except for that extra $99 million that Hammergren got.

I wonder what Hammergren did with his $145 million. I read that he likes golf and has a 12 handicap, slightly better than average, but far short of exceptional. Money can't help him here. He can't walk into his pro shop and purchase a 3 handicap, even for $145 million. In addition, memberships in exclusive golf clubs such as Augusta, Cypress, Pine Valley, and Fishers Island are not for sale for any amount of money. Maybe Hammergren will soon taste the joys of collecting contemporary art. With $145 million, he could purchase two and a half *Balloon Dogs* by Jeff Koons.

As I tried to understand exactly how Hammergren made $145 million, I remembered "ICARE." According to the proxy, the CEO's individual performance modifier was based in part on the McKesson board's assessment of his performance against the company's "ICARE" values:

Integrity
Customer first
Accountability
Respect
Excellence

Reading these words, I had a revelation. Hammergren beat his EPS bogey after the board fiddled with the numbers. Then I guess that he knocked it out of the park on ICARE. Accountability? He accounted. Respect? He respected. Integrity? He integrated. Excellence? He excelled. And he put the customer first—or at least ahead of the shareholders. Impressively, he did all this in the face of ruthless competition. Look at his competitors:

Microsoft's values included Integrity, Passion for Customers, Respect, Excellence, and Accountability. JPMorgan Chase's values were Customer Focus, Respect for Each Other, Teamwork, Initiative, Professionalism, and Quality. Aetna's values were Integrity, Quality Service and Value, Excellence and Accountability, and Employee Engagement. The Bank of New York's values were Integrity, Respect, Personal Responsibility, Teamwork, and Excellence.

You might think that Aetna is in insurance, JPMorgan Chase in banking, Microsoft in software, and McKesson in drug distribution. But in fact these guys are in the same business, the Integrity and Excellence business, and—let's face it—the competition is intense, especially in the Respect and Teamwork sectors. Consider Washington Mutual, whose values were Ethics, Respect, Teamwork, Innovation, and Excellence. Perhaps because money was not one of their values, they went bankrupt. The same thing had happened to Enron, whose values were Respect, Integrity, Communication, and Excellence. They didn't care about money either.

Perhaps Hammergren deserves every penny of his $145 million for his ICARE achievements.

At least McKesson and UnitedHealth Group reported how much their CEOs gained from exercising stock options even if they did not include them in their compensation totals. Discovery did not even report the gains. They simply reported that Zaslav had realized $107.2 million by exercising option and stock awards received in prior years. They didn't disclose his gains on stock options or include them as part of his compensation. I calculated his gains at $68 million. He must pay federal income tax on this amount, but it is not reported as compensation. Add in gains on stock options and Zaslav's compensation comes to $224 million, not the $156 million Discovery reported.

Is he worth it? Media CEOs have traditionally been paid well. For the thirteen media companies among the largest two hundred companies in 2014, the median CEO salary was more than $40 million. "It's good to be in media and technology," said Robert Jackson Jr., a professor of corporate governance at Columbia Law School. "The financial crisis has focused the government's attention on banks and financial services, where you used to go to get paid . . . At John Malone's companies, there's still a great deal of inside baseball in setting executive pay," and after looking at the compensation of Malone CEOs, Jackson noted, "It's hard to see how that's what they need to be paid competitively."

"Media executives have perpetuated the myth that there is something so unique about success in this industry that C.E.O.s cannot be judged or paid by conventional standards," said Michael Pryce-Jones, director of corporate governance at the CtW Investment Group, which pushes for shareholder rights. "Malone is an exponent of this fantasy, so it isn't surprising to see it perpetuated at the companies he influences."

Even if John Malone is right, and his track record is quite good, there is still a tax issue. The bulk of Zaslav's compensation was essentially a $145 million signing bonus. But a signing bonus is not performance related and therefore not tax deductible. Discovery weakly camouflaged this bonus as performance related, explaining that it would be earned if "Mr. Zaslav meets the performance metrics for 2014, as determined by the Compensation Committee." In February 2015, the committee determined that the performance metrics had been achieved in full and the signing bonus vested. Discovery did not reveal just what these performance metrics were. They may have had a lot to do with showing up.

It would be hypocritical to castigate Discovery for gaming the tax man. Over my corporate career I developed a simple guideline for dealing with the IRS: Give them documents or give them money. If you give them a lot of documents, you won't have to give them much money. I'm sure Discovery has a lot of documents, but I wonder why the IRS did not challenge this deduction. I would happily take the IRS's position, on contingency, in a lawsuit. With the penalties and interest, I could finally make big-time CEO money.

Cheniere had to report everything. On top of a salary of $800,000 and cash bonuses totaling $7,880,000 and other compensation of $339,280, they gave Souki $133,000,000 in direct stock awards, all performance pay for passing milestones while losing half a billion.

CHAPTER TEN

Four Boards

Gigantic CEO pay sparked shareholder protests at all four companies. At UnitedHealth Group's annual meeting following Hemsley's $102 million year, shareholders considered a proposal for annual advisory votes on executive compensation ("say on pay"). It came very close to passing, with 46 percent of the vote, but had little effect; Mr. Hemsley made $48.8 million the subsequent year.

At McKesson's annual meeting in 2012, negative publicity about Hammergren's exorbitant payday provoked shareholders to offer two resolutions, both of which were opposed by management: The first would have split the roles of CEO and chairman of the board, and the second would have allowed shareholders to act by written consent in lieu of a meeting. While they failed to pass, 38 percent of shares voted against the company's pay plan. In 2013, McKesson shareholders said they had had enough of excessive CEO pay packages, and the proxy advisory firm ISS urged them to vote against all four members of the compensation committee for failing to fully address persistent compensation issues.

Shareholders overwhelmingly rejected the board's pay plan, with 78 percent voting against it in a nonbinding vote. They also approved an advisory measure to recapture executive compensation in cases of subsequent poor performance, the first time a clawback policy had won majority support. Attempting to mollify shareholders, Hammergren later agreed to reduce his record-setting $159 million pension benefit by $45 million. Even then, he was due a lump-sum pension of $114 million, still among the richest pensions in corporate history. In the face of this shareholder outcry, McKesson's Pay Machine produced a $131 million compensation package for Hammergren in 2014.

Despite Cheniere's high stock price at the end of 2013, shareholders were not happy with Souki's compensation. They sued, arguing that shareholder votes authorizing the stock award plan had been inaccurately counted and would have failed had abstentions counted as negative votes. The suit demanded that $1.6 billion in compensation be returned to the company and forced Cheniere to delay its 2014 annual meeting from June to September.

In a "say on pay" vote at the September meeting, 88 million shares voted against the executive compensation plan; only 76 million shares supported the plan. Moreover, 53 million shares opposed the reelection of David Kilpatrick, chairman of the compensation committee, to the board. As a peace offering, Souki reduced his yearly salary from $800,000 to $1.

At Discovery's 2014 annual meeting, shortly after Zaslav's compensation was publicized, 41 percent of the voted shares rejected Discovery's pay practices.

John Malone set up Discovery with two classes of stock. He owns 93 percent of the class that has ten votes per share and

0.4 percent of the class that has one vote per share. Two classes of stock and undemocratic voting are quite common in the media industry. Over four-fifths of the eighty-six largest publicly traded media companies are controlled by a single shareholder or family, including Rupert Murdoch's News Corp. and Sumner Redstone's Viacom.

Corporate governance experts criticize two classes of stock because they divorce economic ownership from voting control. Assuming that Malone voted in favor of his own decisions, then 69 percent of the economic ownership repudiated the board's decisions on pay. The company and board refused to comment on the vote when queried by a *New York Times* reporter. The shareholders won't have another opportunity to vote on the pay of the CEO until 2017 because Discovery schedules "say on pay" votes every three years, the longest period allowed under Dodd-Frank.

All four companies paid their CEOs hundreds of millions for a single year's work and were tone-deaf to shareholder complaints. Who were their directors and what were they thinking?

UNITEDHEALTH GROUP

Excluding Hemsley, UnitedHealth Group's directors averaged sixty-six years in age and $369,000 in board fees. The board can be divided into two groups: the old guard who joined the board between 1973 and 1993, and the new kids who were added between 2007 and 2009.

The old guard:

- Richard Burke, retired CEO of UnitedHealth Group
- Douglas Leatherdale, retired CEO of Travelers Insurance

- Dr. Gail Wilensky, a health care economist with extensive federal government experience
- William Ballard Jr., retired CFO of Humana

The new kids:

- Robert Darretta Jr., retired CFO of Johnson & Johnson
- Michele Hooper, a consultant working with corporate boards to increase their independence, effectiveness, and diversity
- Glenn Renwick, CEO of the Progressive Corporation, an auto insurance holding company
- Dr. Kenneth Shine, executive vice chancellor for health affairs of the University of Texas System

This is not a group likely to shake things up: four directors are retired, four have served for decades, and the four employed directors come from the worlds of government, consulting, auto insurance, and academia. Few would expect them to wrangle with a CEO who had served since 2000.

They didn't. They sanctioned a conflicted compensation consultant, absurd peer groups, PUPNUP, mindless performance measures, and billion-dollar upward adjustments, and even agreed to paying extra taxes to avoid subjecting Hemsley to any performance test before granting massive equity awards.

But they did not lack chutzpah. Their proxy stated, "Although Mr. Hemsley's total compensation is below the median as compared to other CEOs in the Company's peer groups, the Compensation Committee and Mr. Hemsley agree that it is sufficient to motivate and retain him." It was noble of Hemsley to stay on for a mere $102 million that year and $49 million the following year.

MCKESSON

McKesson paid its directors an average of $289,000. Their average age was sixty-seven, and five of the eight were retired. The board had three women and one African-American and included:

- Andy Bryant, executive vice president and chief administrative officer of Intel
- Wayne Budd, retired and former general counsel of John Hancock Financial Services
- Alton Irby, an investment banker and founding partner of a private investment firm
- M. Christine Jacobs, CEO of Theragenics Corporation, a manufacturer of prostate cancer treatment devices and surgical products
- Marie Knowles, retired CFO of ARCO
- Dr. David Lawrence, retired CEO of Kaiser Foundation Health Plan and Kaiser Foundation Hospitals
- Edward Mueller, retired CEO of Qwest Communications
- Dr. Jane Shaw, retired CEO of Aerogen, which specialized in the development of products for improving respiratory therapy

McKesson's proxy proudly declared that they had decreased CEO compensation for the year, an astounding statement when their CEO made $145 million. They also trumpeted their "legacy of continuous refinement to our executive compensation system," such as "embracing shareholder feedback and 14 recent specific improvements."

McKesson's board of successful, independent, and business-savvy directors produced a $145 million CEO payday that was driven by compromised consultants, a stacked peer group, undemanding bonus bogeys, lavish equity grants that were nearly doubled based on an "individual performance multiplier" that was never explained, embarrassingly indulgent retirement benefits driven by the board that ignored its own rules, and a record-setting parachute.

CHENIERE

On average, Cheniere's directors were sixty-three years old and were paid $180,000 for their service. Excluding Souki, five board members came from private equity and investment banking, three from the oil and gas industry, and three through Washington's revolving door, two of whom are women. On paper, they look great:

DEAL MAKERS
- G. Andrea Botta, an investment banker and president of Glenco LLC, a private investment company
- Keith F. Carney, who is engaged in private investments after working as a securities analyst and an oil and gas exploration geologist
- Nuno Brandolini, a partner of Scorpion Capital Partners, a private equity firm

- David I. Foley, a senior managing director of the Blackstone Group, one of the largest and most successful private equity firms
- Donald Robillard Jr., CFO of a private holding company with interests in oil and gas exploration and production, refining, real estate development, and private equity

OIL AND GAS

- Randy A. Foutch, the founder and CEO of Laredo Petroleum, an oil and gas exploration and production company
- Paul J. Hoenmans, retired executive vice president of Mobil Oil
- David B. Kilpatrick, who has thirty years of industry experience and runs his own consulting firm

REVOLVING DOOR

- Vicky A. Bailey, former assistant secretary of the Department of Energy
- John M. Deutch, former undersecretary of the Department of Energy, undersecretary and deputy secretary of Defense, and director of the CIA
- Heather R. Zichal, former deputy assistant to the president for energy and climate change

Like Hammergren, Souki is both CEO and chairman of the board. For years, activist shareholders, institutional investors, proxy advisory firms, and regulators have demanded that these roles be separated, but when the CEO is also chairman, any initiatives to reform CEO pay practices are unlikely to appear high on the board's agenda.

In its proxy, Cheniere boasted that they had limited perks, used a single peer group, prevented employees from hedging in their stock, employed independent consultants, had limited employment agreements, and maintained strong risk management, etc.

Otherwise, their CEO compensation resembled a *Saturday Night Live* skit. The company loses $508 million, but the CEO gets $142 million because he hit some milestones and promoted the stock. If the milestones had real economic meaning, the board could wait until they paid off and let Souki muddle through with $9.1 million in cash. Had they adopted this practice, Souki would still be waiting; in 2014, Cheniere's loss increased to $548 million.

DISCOVERY

The board of Discovery Communications is a throwback to a bygone clubby era: nine old white guys, average age sixty-six, plus one of their sons, who were paid an average of $223,000.

The Discovery directors could be labeled Malone cronies, but given his success, this can be taken as a compliment. They all came either from cable TV or a money management/investment background.

The cable crowd:

- S. Decker Anstrom, retired; headed cable TV's lobbying efforts before becoming CEO of the Weather Channel from 1999 to 2001 and COO of Landmark Media Enterprises from 2002 to 2008
- Robert R. Bennett, who served as one of Malone's chief lieutenants for decades, and now spends his time managing his own money

- Robert J. Miron, formerly at Advance/Newhouse Communications and Bright House Networks
- Steven A. Miron, the son of Robert Miron, who succeeded his father as CEO of Advance/Newhouse Communications
- M. LaVoy Robison, former partner at the accounting firm Peat, Marwick, Mitchell & Co. (later known as KPMG), where he specialized in cable TV

The moneymen:

- Robert R. Beck, a professional money manager
- Paul A. Gould, a managing director of Allen & Company, an investment bank and deal maker active in media
- J. David Wargo, president of Wargo & Company, a private investment company specializing in the communications industry. Since 2004, he has served on the board of a number of Malone's companies.

Malone was both a cable veteran and a consummate deal maker. As CEO from 1973 to 1996, he made his first fortune by building TCI into the largest cable TV company in America. He then started wheeling and dealing at Liberty Media.

Discovery is one of twenty-three companies in the Fortune 500 that have no women directors. The Discovery board opposed a 2014 shareholder initiative to push for the creation of a more diverse board. The resolution was supported by 23 percent of the shareholder vote.

Malone believes in paying top dollar. Liberty Global and Liberty Media, two other companies he controls, paid their CEOs

$112 million and $74 million in 2014, respectively. Malone is one of the smartest men in business. If he chooses to overpay, at least he knows that he is doing it. Since he's not on the comp committee, I don't know if he focused on the fact that it was done with a conflicted consultant, lame performance measures, and forgiving bonus ranges, PUPNUP, and adjusting the numbers after the fact.

CHAPTER ELEVEN

Collective Delusionality

Given what these four companies paid their CEOs and what they got in return, it's tempting to believe that the directors are either fools or knaves. But they were mostly successful, knowledgeable, and experienced business leaders, attributes seldom found in fools. Their first priority may be to benefit number one, but this applies to almost everyone else in the for-profit sector. If these directors are knaves, so are the other 100 million Americans engaged in business.

If neither fools nor knaves, how could they condone hundred-million-dollar paydays? I have a more plausible explanation for their behavior. The directors of these four boards are collectively delusional.

To deter libel suits, I need to define these terms. "Delusional" is holding false beliefs, beliefs that can be disproved by evidence. "Collectively delusional" is the dynamic that circulates and reinforces false beliefs within a group. In corporate boards, this results from a combination of groupthink and acceptance of corporate dogma. The directors accept a set of beliefs as a matter of faith, and as is true of many religions, these beliefs are not subject to empirical validation and critical examination. The desire for harmony, consensus, and conformity produces a groupthink that refuses to consider the possibility that their decisions are irrational and dysfunctional.

Apart from aliens from the galaxy Zork-El, corporate directors are the only sentient group who think that CEO pay levels today are justified. In one survey, 86 percent of directors said the compensation programs at their firms were effective or very effective. Roughly the same percentage said that the pay difference between a CEO and the other members of their firm's management team is "about right." Only in an isolated echo chamber can an intelligent and informed group maintain such bizarre beliefs. Directors listen to each other, their consultants, free market economists, and business-friendly politicians. Critics are job-killing, antibusiness leftists who can be ignored.

In 2012, JPMorgan Chase lost more than $6 billion when Bruno Iksil, the "London whale," picked the wrong side of huge derivative bets. In response, the board reduced CEO Jamie Dimon's incentive compensation to $10 million, down 53.5 percent from 2011.

The JPMorgan directors, like those of UnitedHealth Group, McKesson, Cheniere, and Discovery, refused to alter or even question the CEO Pay Machine. They merely made a onetime gesture, and revved it up again the next year. I can imagine a board member saying, "I like Jamie. We all like Jamie. But we have to do something or we'll get murdered by the press and end up testifying before some dingbat senator." I cannot imagine a board member saying, "We don't need to pay Jamie $20 million to keep him motivated. He's the most competitive, motivated person I have ever met. Our CEO compensation is insane. We cannot squander shareholder money in this fashion. We need to change our pay system." This statement is unthinkable because it contradicts corporate dogma.

AARON RODGERS

We expect the highest-paid quarterback to be the best quarterback in the NFL. In 2014, Aaron Rodgers of the Green Bay Packers was the highest-paid quarterback in the NFL and the Most Valuable Player. He was paid only ten times the average of the other fifty-eight Green Bay players under contract. His compensation was blessed neither by independent board members nor expert third-party compensation consultants. Rodgers received no performance pay, no cash bonus, and no equity awards.* His pay was not based upon peer groups, benchmarking, and measurable achievements such as percentage of passes completed, average gain, and number of touchdown passes.

Rodgers received no perks. No company car. No use of the corporate jet. No free financial counseling. He was offered no special retirement plan. If he is traded, he does not even get a parachute.

By the standards of corporate boards and compensation consultants, this was a terrible compensation plan. According to the corporate model, the Packers did everything wrong. Yet they got the right results—Rodgers delivered the performance they paid for. UnitedHealth Group, McKesson, Cheniere, and Discovery correctly executed all the procedures prescribed by experts and built into the Pay Machine, yet they all got a grotesque result and

---

* Rodgers's contract included a "workout bonus," payable for coming to voluntary workout camps, and a "roster bonus," for being on the team's roster as of certain dates. These are salary cap items and are not performance related.

wasted immense amounts of money; they could have paid their CEOs 90 percent less and obtained the same performance.

We would expect the highest-paid CEOs to be *the* best or at least among the best CEOs of the year. But their financial results suggest that none of our four CEOs were MVPs.

Thus far, I have argued that directors act rationally in their self-interest to overpay CEOs. But directors, being human, also have irrational sides. The four boards accept five delusions as gospel truth:

1. The importance delusion: The CEO is responsible for the performance of the company. If the company does well, he should get most of the credit and the rewards.
2. The market delusion: There's a competitive market for CEOs that is driven by supply and demand. High prices reflect the low supply of good CEOs and the large number of companies that want to hire them.
3. The motivation delusion: Bonuses are the best way to motivate CEOs to do their job.
4. The performance delusion: Corporate boards can effectively measure and reward CEO performance.
5. The alignment delusion: Stock options and measurable bonus goals align the interests of the CEOs and shareholders.

These delusions work in tandem to reinforce each other. Thus, if directors believe that they can properly measure and reward CEO performance, they don't want to question whether this is the best way to motivate him, and if they believe he is best motivated by money, then they want to believe that they can properly measure and reward him. And believing these two delusions leads to justifying acceptance of the alignment delusion and so on.

These are not revealed truths. At best they are hypotheses, and when tested, the overwhelming weight of evidence shows that all five are erroneous. I find it incongruous that modern business corporations pride themselves on rigorous quantifying, analyzing, and testing and then choose to pay their CEOs hundreds of millions based upon beliefs that are demonstrably false and pay systems that are rigged. But directors hold these five fallacies to be axiomatic. If they were subjected to empirical validation or questioning, the CEO Pay Machine would implode, and directors would have to start from scratch.

THE IMPORTANCE DELUSION

In the 1840s, Thomas Carlyle popularized the Great Man Theory of history. His idea was that men who were brilliant, charismatic, and bold determined the course of history. "The history of the world," Carlyle wrote, "is but the biography of great men." Debunking this theory provided gainful employment for historians for the next 170 years. Today, any self-respecting university would not tolerate a follower of this theory. However, a Carlyle disciple could be invited to join the board of a Fortune 500 company.

The first delusion that leads to outrageous CEO pay is the misconception that the CEO is the company. You pay him $100 million for one year's work because everything depends upon him.

The CEO's unique importance allows the boards of United-Health Group, McKesson, Cheniere, and Discovery to justify their munificence. In 2011, McKesson paid Hammergren more than they paid their shareholders in dividends the year before. Cheniere and Discovery forked over hundreds of millions to their CEOs and paid no dividends at all.

The CEO is so important that you should pay him 300 to 700 times what the average employee makes, or in McKesson's case, 2,000 times the pay of the average of their 38,000 employees, despite the harmful effects on morale.

I was a CEO for fourteen years. I ran a communications company, King Broadcasting, that had TV, radio, cable, and ancillary broadcasting properties. When King was sold, I led a buyout of the division that supplied mobile facilities for sports broadcasting. A private equity firm and I put up one-third of the purchase price and borrowed the rest. Our timing was fortunate. With the proliferation of cable sports channels, sports broadcasting was expanding. We bought the division for $20 million, put up more capital for three acquisitions, and sold it for $55 million. The investors more than doubled their money in five years. In the booming nineties, this was considered a solid single. Today it would be extra bases.

We sold to another private equity firm. They were smarter and more sophisticated than my first private equity partner and me. I was so impressed that I reinvested part of my profits from the sale in their new company, but shortly after their acquisition, the industry began suffering from overcapacity. The new firm lost money and sold to another private equity firm that ran the company into bankruptcy.

Most retired CEOs who write books proclaim, "I was a great CEO. Follow my advice and you too can be great." But the truth is that the top 20 percent of CEOs are very good, the bottom 20 percent are bozos, and the rest are mediocre. Since I was never fired, I place myself above the bottom 20 percent. Since I probably deserved to be fired, I make no claim to be in the top 20 percent.

When I was in the right place at the right time, I was a genius.

When I was in the wrong place at the wrong time, I was a moron. If I was in the right place at the wrong time or the wrong place at the right time and was lucky, I was a leader who could succeed in the face of adversity. If unlucky, I was in over my head and wilted under stress.

When I was with King Broadcasting, we acquired an unprofitable independent TV station in Honolulu. We had a plan. Our plan failed, but we lucked out and made money in spite of ourselves.

The competition to our independent TV station in Honolulu was the three stations affiliated with ABC, NBC, and CBS. They were coining money. Because Hawaii is eight hours behind New York time, all network programs were played on tape delay. When advertising demand was high, the three stations would expand network breaks and fill them with extra ads until the late-night news might start fifteen minutes late.

Our plan was to offer to remove all this extra clutter if the networks would switch their affiliation to us. We thought we couldn't lose. If one network switched, we would make good money as an affiliate. If they didn't switch, we expected them to use our offer to compel their affiliates to stop expanding break time, and the extra ads would move to us. As an independent, we had plenty of time available.

We miscalculated. The networks used us as leverage. But instead of asking their affiliates to stop expanding breaks and run programs on time, they stopped paying their Honolulu affiliates certain forms of compensation. We lost a lot of money in our first year. Then Rupert Murdoch started the Fox network. We never thought a fourth network could be profitable, but with no better option, we became Fox's Honolulu affiliate. A few years later we were making money.

Remember the old joke that goes "The operation was a success but the patient died"? With King's Honolulu TV station, the operation failed, but the patient recovered. Such is the serendipity of business. I have made money when my plans failed and lost money when they succeeded. In business, as in many other pursuits, as Ecclesiastes 9:11 states, "The race is not always to the swift nor the battle to the strong . . . but time and chance happeneth to them all."

My concise management advice to aspiring CEOs:

- Be in the right place at the right time.
- Avoid the wrong place at the wrong time.
- If in the right place at the wrong time or the wrong place at the right time, be lucky.

When asked what type of generals he preferred, Napoleon replied, "Lucky ones." He understood business. In support of the theory of randomness and drift, I point out that Coca-Cola began as a pharmaceutical company, Tiffany as a stationery store, Raytheon as refrigerator manufacturer, Nokia as a paper mill, and DuPont as a manufacturer of explosives.

Most people refuse to accept this degree of randomness because we are hardwired to find patterns. Given a string of random numbers, people will find a pattern. We accept after-the-fact explanations for success. We look for simple narratives to explain complex phenomena. "The stock went up because the CEO had a brilliant strategy" suggests a compelling narrative linking a concrete result to a single human actor. It has explanatory power because it combines a surface logic, an after-the-fact understanding, and a simple cause and effect. It accords with the Great Man

Theory. It's easier to accept this narrative than the true one: "The stock went up. Nobody knows why."

Even with sophisticated computer models, complex nonlinear systems cannot be predicted or even understood. That is why there's no recipe for corporate success. Look at the companies celebrated by the iconic management books *In Search of Excellence* (1982) and *Built to Last* (1994). Both authors set forth timeless business principles that ensured lasting success. But the timeless principles didn't work. Of the excellent companies cited in *In Search of Excellence*, 58 percent performed below the S&P 500 between 1980 and 1989. The companies in *Built to Last* were worse: 62.5 percent of them underperformed the S&P 500 from 1990 to 2000.

There are great CEOs. In my hometown of Seattle, Jeff Bezos of Amazon and Howard Schultz of Starbucks are superb. Steve Jobs was a great one. So was Bill Gates. All four were founding CEOs, a different breed from professional managers like me.* Apple, Amazon, Microsoft, and Starbucks would not exist were it not for founders who transmitted inspiring visions and authentic values to their employees rather than the fatuous pabulum spouted at larger, more established corporations. Founders were seldom formally trained in business, a fact that may explain their success. While by 2010, 42 percent of the CEOs of the Fortune 100 had MBAs, none of these four founders did. Two did not complete college.

The founder often runs the company for a long time, and his vision and methods become part of the company's DNA, reflecting his drive, his personality, and the people he hired and trained.

---

* Technically, Howard Schultz was not a founding CEO. But since he acquired Starbucks when it had only four stores, he might as well have been.

In contrast to founders, the average tenure of a Fortune 500 CEO is only 4.6 years. How much can a CEO accomplish in such a short period? A company's success is built largely on its personnel, but most CEOs rely on personnel recruited, trained, and promoted by their predecessors. We might better judge CEOs by the success of their successors.

Successful founding CEOs seldom pay themselves much. Larry Page, CEO and cofounder of Google, gets $1 a year in compensation, as does Mark Zuckerberg of Facebook. From 1998 through 2015, Jeff Bezos received a salary of $81,840. Bill Gates's annual compensation never exceeded $1 million. Of course, these men have large ownership positions in their companies. Page has a net worth of $34.8 billion, Zuckerberg $35.7 billion, Bezos $43.5 billion, and Gates $79.3 billion. In my opinion, they deserve their riches. They didn't steal anything from their shareholders. Their shareholders got a bargain.

(I have a different opinion of Larry Ellison, founder and CEO of Oracle. Not satisfied with being the third-richest person in the United States, he paid himself—excuse me, his board paid him—$96.2 million in 2012, a year in which Oracle's shares fell 23 percent. Ellison had to make do with $77 million in 2013 and a parsimonious $67.3 million in 2014, when he gave up the CEO position.)

Among great CEOs who were not founders is Jack Welch, CEO of General Electric from 1981 to 2001, though much of his success came from being in the right place at the right time. One top-level GE executive remarked, "Jack [Welch] did a good job, but everyone seems to forget that the company has been around for over 100 years . . . and he had 70,000 other people to help him." Jeffrey

Immelt, Welch's successor, commented that in the 1990s "anyone could have run GE and done well . . . Not only could anyone have run GE in the 1990s, [a] dog could have run GE. A German shepherd could have run GE." Welch himself admitted, "It was an easier time to be a CEO in the 1990s. The wind was on our backs."

At large, well-managed companies like GE, there are always many talented CEO candidates. James March, a management professor at Stanford, believes that if a company is good at training managers, its CEO candidates are so similar in education, skills, and experiences that they are virtually interchangeable. "Management may be extremely difficult and important even though managers are indistinguishable," March writes. "It is hard to tell the difference between two different light bulbs also; but if you take all the light bulbs away, it is difficult to read in the dark." What matters is that *someone* be the CEO.

There are other great CEOs and many good ones who are professional managers. But recall the bank CEOs who were hailed as extraordinary before October 2007—people like Ken Lewis at Bank of America, whose stock price had more than doubled since 2001; Kerry Killinger, who built Washington Mutual from a sleepy savings bank to a national powerhouse; and Dick Fuld at Lehman Brothers and James Cayne at Bear Stearns, whose firms' stock increased more than tenfold during their tenures.

In September 2007, Ken Lewis made a deal to buy Merrill Lynch for $50 billion. This acquisition squandered tens of billions of dollars, and might still be considered the worst deal in history had Lewis not acquired Countrywide a few months later, costing his shareholders another $20 billion-plus.

Lewis had made his reputation buying banks, and buying

banks was what he knew: FleetBoston Financial in 2004 for $48 billion, MBNA in 2006 for $35 billion, and LaSalle Bank in 2007 for $21 billion. He continued to buy banks even as Lehman Brothers was collapsing. Buying banks was what he knew. Buying banks was what he did. *Fish gotta swim, birds gotta fly, Lewis gotta buy banks 'til he die.*

Fuld, Cayne, and Killinger watched their reputations collapse as their companies disappeared in 2008. Fuld and Cayne financed themselves with overnight money and leveraged their companies 50 to 1. They kept on using accounting tricks to get to 30 to 1 on quarterly reporting dates. This was a high-wire act without a net, but they were making gobs of money—$427 million in compensation for Fuld in 2002–2007 and $155 million for Cayne in 2003–2007—so they kept on doing the same thing, always adding a bit more leverage to squeeze out a few more bucks.

None of them could see the iceberg ahead of them. They stayed on course and their ships sank. They were heroes until 2007 and bums a year later. On July 8, 2007, Citigroup chief Charles Prince famously said, "As long as the music is playing, you've got to get up and dance. We're still dancing." The music he was hearing was the overture to *The Subprime Meltdown*.

Most of a CEO's success has to do with luck or suitability. As I said, luck is simply being in the right place at the right time. Fit is when the CEO's skills fill the right need at the right time. Henry Ford was a great fit for the automobile business when price and manufacturing efficiency were most important. He was not a good fit when consumer desires moved to styling and color.

Business conditions are constantly changing. This is why CEOs often fail when called back to the job where they were once a great success. When A. G. Lafley made an unsuccessful return as CEO of Procter & Gamble in 2013, James Surowiecki wrote in *The New Yorker*:

> How could someone who, according to *Fortune*, was known as "an all-time C.E.O. hero" end up being just O.K.? Well, if commentators had looked at the track record of returning C.E.O.s—boomerang C.E.O.s, as they're sometimes called—that's precisely what they'd have predicted. A 2014 study found that profitability at companies run by boomerang C.E.O.s fell slightly, and an earlier study detected no significant difference in long-term performance between firms that reappointed a former C.E.O. and ones that hired someone new. We like triumphant comeback narratives—Jobs and, to a lesser extent, Howard Schultz, at Starbucks. But history tells us that Lafley's rather ordinary second tour of duty is the way most of these stories end.

If most CEOs were great executives, we would expect them to remain so for most of their careers, like great painters, great teachers, and great authors who may decline with age, but seldom flip from excellent to execrable in one season, as occurs often with CEOs.

Consider John Akers, Roger Smith, Ed Zander, and Steve Case. Akers and Smith became leaders of iconic American companies. Akers, CEO of IBM from 1985 to 1993, was lauded for his success with the IBM PC. Smith, CEO of GM from 1981 to 1990, was eulogized for infusing entrepreneurialism into GM when he purchased EDS and solving his labor-cost problems through robotization. But because they were unable to deal with change and industry turmoil, both Akers and Smith were fired.

Ed Zander became CEO of Motorola in 2004 and released the RAZR cellular phone. It grabbed 19 percent of the global market within a year, and he was a genius. After Apple introduced the iPhone in 2007, he became an out-of-work has-been.

Steve Case was hailed as brilliant when AOL reached a market capitalization of $222 billion in December 1999. The next year he engineered the merger of AOL and Time Warner, widely considered the most calamitous coupling in history.

Despite their supposed authority, most CEOs find their actions constrained—by the board, tradition, and internal politics. Often a CEO must fight to preserve some discretion against the force of circumstance. Perhaps the greatest constraint is the knowledge that they will be fired for failing unconventionally but keep their job by plodding conventionally.

Separating CEO luck from CEO skill and talent is difficult. I'm sticking to my belief that the CEO (excluding founders) accounts for 10 percent of a company's success or failure. Whether your competitors are even dumber than you accounts for 30 percent, nonrandom events beyond your control 35 percent, and pure randomness 25 percent.

Many academic studies support my 10 percent estimate. In "Leadership and Organizational Performance: A Study of Large Corporations," Stanley Lieberson and James O'Connor argued that CEOs had only a weak effect on company performance. Crunching a database of 167 companies, they calculated that CEO actions explained between 6.5 percent (if based on sales) and 14.5 percent (if based on profit margin) of company performance. More recent studies have found CEO effects that ranged from a low of 3.9 percent to a high of 14.7 percent.

If the CEO accounts for 10 percent of a company's success or failure, the difference between one CEO and another who might have been selected by the board is much smaller, maybe 2 percent to 3 percent.

I contend that Aaron Rodgers was more important to the success of the Packers than Hemsley, Hammergren, Souki, and Zaslav were to their organizations. The Packers paid Rodgers 10 times what his teammates averaged. Why does McKesson pay 2,000 times the average employee?

CHAPTER TWELVE

The Market Delusion

In 2016, the highest-paid baseball players were pitchers Clayton Kershaw of the Los Angeles Dodgers ($32 million) and David Price of the Boston Red Sox ($30 million). Why should we criticize Hemsley, Hammergren, Souki, and Zaslav, who run large, complex organizations, for making big money, and not guys who merely throw a baseball?

Because there is no market for CEOs. Other companies are not bidding for their services. They are not the same as athletes, movie producers, and rap artists, because CEO skills are largely company and industry specific. Kershaw and Price can take their skills to another team and immediately improve it, but a CEO's skills are seldom transferable to another company.

Negotiations between Kershaw's agent and the Los Angeles Dodgers established his compensation. Presumably, his agent calculated what competing teams might pay for his services, while the team estimated the cost of signing other free agents if they passed on Kershaw. The Dodgers could have decided to sign less-talented free agents at a lower price rather than meet Kershaw's terms. In Price's case, that is what happened. When Detroit decided not to match Boston's offer, Price moved.*

In a free market, boards would estimate the cost and value of bringing in a new CEO against retaining the existing one, and CEOs would jump ship as frequently as do baseball and football free agents. But boards rarely raid another company. The S&P 500 companies experienced only six CEO jumps in six years. Of roughly 1,800 large-company CEOs hired between 1993 and 2005, fewer than 2 percent had previously been CEOs of another public company. Contrast that with the NFL, where in 2015 more than two hundred NFL free agents switched teams.

Kershaw and Price would be superstars on any MLB team, but most CEOs would be failures if they tried to manage some other company. To succeed, a CEO needs a detailed knowledge of the organization, its culture, its products, its finances, its personnel, its customers, and its competitors. He must also command the respect of his subordinates and the board. The necessary skills, knowledge, and authority can best be obtained working within the company; they are very difficult for someone outside the company or the industry to acquire.

In a 2012 study, Charles M. Elson and Craig K. Ferrere concluded that chief executives couldn't easily move their skills from one company to another. Elson wrote that CEO compensation and peer grouping are "based on the theory of transferability of

---

* Since it imposes a luxury tax on the clubs with the highest payroll, Major League Baseball is not an absolutely free market. In 2016, this tax applied to both the Dodgers and the Red Sox. The effect of this tax is to reduce compensation for the most highly paid players. By how much in any specific case is anybody's guess.

talent. But we found that C.E.O. skills are very firm specific. C.E.O.'s don't move very often, but when they do, they're flops."

William A. Ackman's hedge fund owned 18 percent of JCPenney. In November 2011, Ackman pushed the board to recruit Ron Johnson, then the hottest person in retailing, as CEO. A Stanford grad and a Harvard MBA, Johnson had built Target and then overseen retail for Apple, where he introduced the Apple Store and the Genius Bar. JCPenney stock rose 10 percent on the news of his hire.

Seventeen months later, Johnson was fired in the wake of a disastrous 32 percent drop in fourth-quarter sales. He may have been a retailing genius, but he did not understand Penney's customers. In his effort to move the company upscale, he terminated the sales and discounts that the longtime customers loved. Because the JCPenney customers were less trendy and more price-conscious than Apple's, Johnson's skills were not transferrable.

John Sculley III rose to national prominence when he was head of Pepsi's marketing efforts and launched the "Pepsi Challenge." In 1977, at the age of thirty-eight, he became the youngest president in the company's history. In 1983, Steve Jobs hired him as the new CEO of Apple. The relationship between the founder and the CEO quickly deteriorated—to the point that in 1985 Sculley fired Jobs. In the years that followed, Sculley led Apple down a slippery slope toward bankruptcy, helped along by product flops like the Apple Newton. The board ousted him in 1993.

As CEO of the drugstore retailer CVS, Charles "Chuck" Conaway was credited with the company's expansion in stores, distribution, and Internet sales. He also engineered two large acquisitions that helped grow CVS into a nationwide chain of 4,100 stores.

At age thirty-nine, he was recruited away by Kmart, which had fallen behind its rivals, Walmart and Target. The hope was that Conaway's track record would carry over. It didn't. Kmart fired Conaway after just two years in the wake of massive layoffs and store closures that soon led to the bankruptcy and eventual sale of the company.

As Bob Nardelli rose up through the ranks at General Electric, he earned the moniker "Little Jack" after his boss and mentor, Jack Welch. In 1995, he became president and CEO of GE Power Systems and was seen as one of Welch's potential successors, but after losing out to Jeffrey Immelt in 2000, Nardelli was offered the top job at building supply retailer Home Depot.

While the hard-nosed Nardelli oversaw the growth of Home Depot over the next seven years, he also became a victim of the housing crisis and his own ego. After he reportedly refused to accept a reduction of his $32 million compensation, the board ousted him—but bestowed an incredible $210 million exit package on him as a farewell present.

I don't attribute the problems of JCPenney, Home Depot, Kmart, and Apple exclusively to Johnson, Nardelli, Conaway, and Sculley. I'm sticking to my argument—the difference between one CEO and other candidates may account for 2 to 3 percent of a company's success or failure. My point is that their skills were not transferrable. Johnson, Nardelli, Conaway, and Sculley had proven track records, but they failed because they didn't understand their new companies. JCPenney, Home Depot, Kmart, and Apple would have been better served if they had promoted an internal candidate who understood the company and its business. A CEO changing companies is almost like an athlete who switches sports.

Michael Jordan may have been the greatest basketball player ever, but he was not Major League Baseball material.

In his bestselling book *Good to Great*, Jim Collins profiled eleven companies that improved from good performers to excellent performers. The CEOs of ten out of the eleven were groomed internally. Three-quarters of corporate directors believe internal candidates are better than external ones. That is why internal promotions account for three-quarters of all new CEOs. Internal candidates of Fortune 500 companies worked an average of thirteen years at the company before becoming CEOs. They knew the company, its culture, its personnel, its customers, and its competitors. That's also one reason CEOs hired from the outside are twice as likely to be fired as internal promotions. What's more, the cost of hiring an external candidate, commonly including the cost of a search firm, is three to five times higher than the cost of hiring an internal one. Four recent studies support the conclusion that internally promoted CEOs perform better than external ones.

PEER GROUPS ASSUME A MARKET EXISTS

Hemsley's peer group included many high-paying companies that would never think of hiring him as their CEO—Amazon, American Express, and Apple, and we have not yet gotten to those that begin with B. General Electric, IBM, and Oracle were in Hammergren's peer group, though they would never bid for his services as their CEO.

The market forces of supply and demand do not determine CEO prices. Nonetheless, companies annually calculate what supposedly comparable companies—companies in their peer group—pay their CEOs. The companies that do this are all striving for external equity. Using peer groups in this way might be an effective tool for establishing fair compensation if there were a market for CEOs, but there is no such market.

In the absence of a market, there's no rationale for basing any CEO's pay on external equity. Using corporate peer groups as a basis for pay decisions is like surveying the compensation of professional golfers to determine the pay of an NFL lineman.

When a large corporation decides to replace its fleet of automobiles, it gets the best price possible through examining the market and bargaining and negotiating for the fleet that meets its needs. Here is what that corporation doesn't do:

- Hire a consultant to learn what comparable companies are paying for automobiles.
- Pay a higher price than 75 percent of those companies.
- Award the supplier a bonus of two times the purchase price if the automobiles run well.

But that is how this corporation pays its CEO.

Why don't directors do what businesses are supposed to do, control costs? Why don't they ignore what other companies do and ask if another company is likely to bid for his services? In the unlikely case that the answer is yes, the board can apply cost-benefit analysis by weighing the odds and cost of his leaving against the additional pay to keep him. This is a simple task compared to many complex business decisions.

If the answer is no, why give him more than the 3 percent increase that most other employees receive? Many directors would give the knee-jerk response of "motivation" and "pay for performance." As we will see, there is no evidence to support these claims.

Even though there's no market for CEOs, even though peer groups are nothing more than pumps for CEO pay, defenders still contend that "you get what you pay for." They argue that the skills required to successfully manage large enterprises are both rare and valuable. The market rewards them accordingly. This is how free markets work.

If you get what you pay for, the United States in 2007 would have had the best-managed banking system in history. But the billions paid to Lewis, Killinger, Fuld, Cayne, and their ilk bought disaster.

There's a variation on "you get what you pay for": the CEO's pay is a small fraction of the value he creates; it's his commission, as it were, on the increase in the company's value he created. Here's an example of this thinking: In the year when John Hammergren was paid $145 million, the market value of McKesson shares increased by over 21 percent, or $2 billion. Hammergren's take was only 7.7 percent of the value created, so he was a bargain for McKesson's shareholders.

This argument is replete with logical errors. It credits Hammergren for all of the increased value, an instance of the Importance Delusion. Over the same period, the S&P 500 was up 13.5 percent. We should credit the stock market, not Hammergren, for two-thirds of McKesson's gain.

If Hammergren deserves 7.7 percent of McKesson's gain, should Zaslav refund $138 million, which is 7.7 percent of the $1.8 billion lost by Discovery shareholders when its stock dropped 25 percent in 2014?

The argument that Hammergren was a bargain further assumes that Hammergren would have not done the same job for one penny less and that McKesson could not have hired anyone his equal for, say, a measly $130 million.

The directors of McKesson and most other big companies firmly believe the Market Delusion, so they never test it. Using the actual market would be very simple. Ask if anyone is trying to hire away your CEO. If not, why increase his pay? The answer "to keep him motivated" is another delusion.

CHAPTER THIRTEEN

The Motivation Delusion

Corporations invest immense amounts of time and money trying to inspire their employees. They turn to everything from the newest techniques and fads in sensitivity training, team building, mentoring, and coaching, to awards, vision and values statements, corporate image campaigns, supportive corporate cultures, free Cokes, and table tennis. But they seldom use money to motivate the rank and file, arguing that it is an ineffective motivator. Apparently it's only effective when it comes to CEOs, who are already highly motivated; they like to compete, and they like to win. Rather than rely on a pay system to instill motivation, companies should channel the motivation that's already there.

Studies on financial incentives have found that at the CEO level, not only is the money unnecessary, it's counterproductive. "There is no evidence that massive financial incentives attract the best talent," says one expert on this issue. "[They] fill up your entire thinking space, preventing you from focusing on other things or being open to ideas."

The Pay Machine's bonus metrics and lavish rewards concentrate a CEO's attention on what can earn him a bonus, thus restricting his creativity, curiosity, and innovation. Offer a CEO a bonus for increasing market share, and he will work like hell to achieve it, even if he has to neglect more important things such as process innovations and new products.

A meta-analysis of 128 studies of human behavior demonstrated that large monetary incentives tend to decrease motivation and performance. At least two dozen studies over the last three decades have conclusively shown that people who expect to receive a reward for successfully completing a task perform worse than those who expect no reward at all. J. Scott Armstrong, a professor at the Wharton School of the University of Pennsylvania, wrote:

> There is no evidence that higher pay produces better executive performance. Instead, there is evidence that higher compensation undermines the intrinsic motivation of executives, inhibits their learning, leads them to ignore some stakeholders, and discourages them from considering the long-term effects of their decisions.

> Monetary rewards improve performance for simple tasks but impair performance for more difficult ones; paying for inherently interesting tasks, and paying too much, can be counterproductive. Across multiple tasks, the higher the monetary incentives, the worse the performance.

> Job performance is much more closely aligned with intrinsic motivation. The more executives worry about their bonus, the less they will satisfy their intellectual curiosity and take pleasure in a job well done, the very things that make people perform at their best.

In his book *Drive*, Daniel Pink cites four decades of research to demonstrate that for all but routine mechanical work, monetary incentives hinder performance because they narrow focus and limit creativity. He concludes that the three most important human drives are far more powerful than money:

Autonomy—the desire to direct our own lives.
Mastery—the urge to get better and better at something that matters.
Purpose—the yearning to do what we do in the service of something larger than ourselves.

By emphasizing money, boards diminish these forces.

Alfie Kohn, author of *Punished by Rewards*, writes, "No controlled scientific study has ever found a long-term enhancement of the quality of work as a result of any reward system. For five years, I have challenged defenders of incentive systems to provide an example to the contrary, and I have yet to hear of such a study."

Moreover, satisfaction with compensation depends on the relative level and not the absolute level. The CEO Pay Machine with its constant leapfrogging based on external equity seems designed to deliver maximum compensation with minimum satisfaction as CEOs watch other CEOs vault over them.

John Mackey, CEO of Whole Foods, caps cash earnings for executives at 19 times that of the lowest-paid employee and claims that he's never lost a top executive. "We discover that once our basic material needs are satisfied, money becomes less important to us," he says. "In my experience, deeper purpose, personal growth, self-actualization and caring relationships provide very powerful motivations and are more important than financial compensation for creating both loyalty and a high-performing organization."

The absence of financial incentives did not hinder Aaron Rodgers's motivation, but their presence might have. Why do boards ignore the massive evidence that money is not an effective motivator for both quarterbacks and CEOs? Probably because no director ever raises the issue. When Stimson Bullitt, a very wise man, asked me to join the board of his company, Harbor Properties, I asked him what he wanted from a board member. "Prevent folly" was his answer. Instead of preventing folly, directors preserve delusion, never questioning an obviously false belief.

CHAPTER FOURTEEN

The Performance Delusion

The first principle of UnitedHealth Group's compensation philosophy was "pay for performance." Likewise, McKesson's, which stated, "Our executive compensation program is based on a philosophy of 'pay for performance,'" and Discovery's, "We continue to pay for performance through our executive compensation program design." Cheniere insisted that "We believe our executive team and all of our employees are motivated to perform at their highest levels when performance-based pay is a significant portion of their compensation." How did they implement pay for performance? UnitedHealth Group adopted misguided performance measures such as revenues and employee teamwork. McKesson used EPS, Cheniere looked at managing the capital budget, and Discovery ignored poor financial performance. All four companies set easy bogeys that ignored the performance of their peer groups. McKesson and UnitedHealth Group established bonus ranges that enabled their CEOs to make between 120 percent and 193 percent of their target bonuses. They awarded stock options for showing up. Stunningly, three of the four companies adjusted financial metrics upward to increase the CEO's bonus. The result: lavish pay and mediocre performance.

In my research, I analyzed only these four companies that produced the highest-paid CEOs from 2011 to 2014. They were all large companies with impressive boards and well-regarded management. Had I researched more companies, I am sure I could have found others that misused pay for performance even more egregiously.

Appropriately rewarding executives for their performance with cash, stock options, and restricted stock has been the first principle of executive compensation since the 1980s. But like United-Health Group, McKesson, Cheniere, and Discovery, other boards and their advisers cannot design a system that accurately measures and appropriately rewards CEO performance. The world of business is simply too complex and random. Tweaking and tinkering with pay for performance will only introduce more perverse incentives, unanticipated consequences, and higher CEO pay.

With one exception, requiring the CEO to generate long-term shareholder returns before all restricted stock vests, companies should jettison all CEO pay-for-performance plans. If a company uses specific pay-for-performance measures, it will probably get the performance it specified, but it will seldom get the performance it needs.

I don't claim that pay for performance never works, only that it never works over the long term for large, complex companies. Looking at the exceptions proves the rule.

Pay for specific performance should be used *only* when the company has a single overriding goal and achievement of that goal can be accurately and easily measured.

There is no tomorrow. The long-term consequences will be someone else's problem.

I used pay for specific performance effectively when I was selling a company. We had guaranteed the buyer that we would achieve certain earnings before closing. If we missed the guarantee, the buyer could either demand a price adjustment or walk away. I set earnings bogeys—i.e., goals—for each division and told division management they could pocket 10 percent of everything above the bogey. The results were astounding, far above my highest expectations. However, the longer-term consequences of slashing expenses and raising prices might be less rewarding.

I also have seen pay for performance work well in private equity when the equity partners buy a company with a single overriding goal—maximize return on investment either by selling the company or taking it public within a short period of time, usually less than five years. Nothing else matters, and there is no tomorrow after the sale. The partners load up management with incentives to increase the sale price. The specific structures vary, but ultimately, the sale price is the only thing that counts.

Most corporations are not for sale. They have tomorrows. Their single economic goal should be to provide the shareholders with a superior long-term, risk-adjusted return. This is not the same as maximizing share price. The latter goal is meaningless without a date attached. Once you have a date, you ignore everything after it; you can't care that there may be no sunny days from then on. When most companies set up bonus plans for CEOs, they are seldom selling the company; they have tomorrows and want them to be sunny. Lacking a single overriding measurable short-term goal, most companies should forget about CEO pay for performance. They can't make it work.

The Wall Street Journal's 2014 pay survey found that only one of the ten highest-paid CEOs ranked among the top 10 percent by investor performance. In 2013, more than 20 percent of S&P 500 CEOs got performance-based awards, totaling $1.4 billion, even though their companies showed negative returns relative to an index of all stocks. Nearly one-quarter of the twenty-five highest-paid executives between 1993 and 2012 worked for financial firms that were bailed out by the federal government. Eight percent of these CEOs led companies that paid fraud-related fines or settlements, and another 8 percent were fired.

An independent study in 2009 found that the companies with the highest-paid CEOs produced below-average stock market returns. Professors Michael J. Cooper of the University of Utah, Huseyin Gulen of Purdue University, and P. Raghavendra Rau of the University of Cambridge examined the relationship between CEO pay and stock performance at the 1,500 companies with the largest market capitalization. In the three-year periods from 1994–2013, they found the more CEOs got paid, the worse their companies did.

The top 10 percent of CEOs in pay returned 10 percent less to their shareholders than did their industry peers. While these CEOs were paid an average of $21 million a year, the shareholders of these companies received $1.4 billion less than comparable companies with lower-paid CEOs. The more CEOs were paid, the worse they performed. The companies in the top 5 percent in CEO pay did 15 percent worse, on average, than their peers.

Overconfidence may explain the CEOs' poor performance. Huge paychecks and CEO overconfidence are correlated. Cooper contends the highly paid CEOs don't subject their decisions to rigorous scrutiny. "They ignore disconfirming information and just think that they're right," he said. "That tends to result in overinvesting—investing too much and investing in bad projects that don't yield positive returns for investors."

The study also found that the longer CEOs were in place, the worse their firms performed. Cooper says this is because those CEOs are able to appoint more allies to their boards, and those board members are likely to go along with the bosses' bad decisions. "For the high-pay CEOs, with high overconfidence and high tenure, the effects are just crazy," he says. "They return 22 percent worse in shareholder value over three years as compared to their peers."

Hermann Stern, CEO of Obermatt, a financial research company, argues that at America's very largest companies (the S&P 100), CEO pay has no correlation with performance. Obermatt measured performance against a peer group and calculated the "excess pay" companies gave their CEOs between 2008 and 2010. Occidental Petroleum was by far the worst offender. Its boss, Ray Irani, who earned more than $200 million in 2008 alone, received almost eight times what Obermatt calculated to be his "deserved pay."

The poor correlation between performance and pay has been confirmed by other studies. A 2000 meta-analysis (a study of 137 prior studies) calculated that performance explained less than 5 percent of CEO pay. The most important variable was the size of the company, which accounted for 40 percent of pay differences. Harvard professors Lucian Bebchuk and Jesse Fried in their book *Pay Without Performance* and in subsequent papers have shown that CEO pay is negatively correlated with profitability and market valuation relative to book value. Firms with high CEO pay are not the best performers.

J. Scott Armstrong, a professor at the Wharton School, examined all the relevant literature on this subject and concluded:

> It is impossible to devise incentive schemes that relate executives' actions to the performance of the firm. Incentive systems in organizations can only work when an employee has full control over the outcomes, as with highly repetitive tasks that require little thinking or learning. This, of course, is not the case for top executives.

Some still argue the opposite. According to Professor Steven Kaplan of the University of Chicago Booth School of Business, "The system has worked . . . Firms with CEOs in the highest 20 percent of realized pay generated stock returns 60 percent greater than those of other firms in their industries over the previous three years. Firms with CEOs in the bottom 20 percent underperform their industries by almost 20 percent."

I could observe an evening of roulette and conclude that the best gamblers were rewarded for their performance. How do I know they were the best gamblers? Easy. They won the most money.

Professor Kaplan both endorsed the Importance Delusion and confused correlation with causation. Of course the CEOs whose stock performed the best made the most money. Given that stock options constituted the majority of CEO pay, this is a mathematical tautology that proves nothing. Load up every CEO with options, and the ones whose stock goes up the most will make the most money.

Imagine that a management consulting firm reveals that the companies with the cleanest offices make the most money. Business gurus spout that janitorial excellence is the key to profitability.

(Don't laugh. I have lived through worse. Remember matrix management? Total Quality Management? Management by Wandering Around?)

To encourage cleanliness, corporations lavish their head janitor with stock options. Five years later, a finance professor proclaims that the system works: there is a high correlation between company stock performance and janitorial compensation. Janitors working at companies whose stock rose made fortunes and those working at companies whose stock fell made nothing.

The janitor's compensation is obviously "pay for luck." With CEOs, pay for performance is also pay for luck.

Commenting on CEO pay, Thomas Piketty wrote:

> It is very difficult to explain the observed variations [in CEO pay] in terms of firm performance. If we look at various performance indicators, such as sales growth, profits, and so on, we can break down the observed variance as a sum of other variances: variance due to causes external to the firm (such as the general state of the economy, raw materials price shocks, variations in the exchange rate, average performance of other firms in the same sector, etc.) plus other "nonexternal" variances. Only the latter can be significantly affected by the decisions of the firm's managers. If executive pay were determined by marginal productivity, one would expect its variance to have little to do with external variances and to depend solely or primarily on nonexternal variances. In fact, we observe just the opposite: it is when sales and profits increase for external reasons that executive pay rises most rapidly.

Marianne Bertrand and Sendhil Mullainathan studied the role of luck in CEO pay by looking at important variables that the CEO cannot affect. For example, changes in oil prices, over which a CEO has no control, regularly affect the earnings and stock price of companies in the oil industry. The researchers found substantial pay for luck. They also concluded: "CEOs have managed to capture the pay process so that they set their own pay, constrained somewhat by the availability of cash or by a fear of drawing shareholders' attention."

John Hammergren made a fortune because of McKesson's "performance," but McKesson stock in 2011, when he made $145 million, was below its 1998 high. Maybe Hammergren was paid for "reversion to the mean," the statistical tendency for a variable such as company earnings to return to its long-term average after a large drop.

Attempting to correlate a CEO's pay with shareholder returns, many companies now base a portion of his annual bonus on the annual economic return to the shareholder, i.e., stock price appreciation plus dividends. The Conference Board reported that total economic return to shareholders was used in 54 percent of long-term pay awards in 2014. And 31 percent had long-term plans that used only this metric.

While avoiding the pitfalls of less direct measures such as EPS or meeting milestones, total economic return can encourage CEOs to do anything to goose the stock price, regardless of the long-term consequences.

As CEO of Valeant Pharmaceuticals, J. Michael Pearson received stock awards based upon the economic return to shareholders. His plan was highly leveraged, giving him increasing options and shares if total shareholder return hit certain levels. Under his 2011 compensation agreement, he did not receive "performance" shares unless Valeant's stock price increased by at least 15 percent a year over the next three years. Once he hit that threshold, he would get 120,000 shares. If the stock price rose further, he would get more shares. He could receive the plan maximum of 480,000 shares at a 60 percent annual return to shareholders. Pearson also got an outright grant of 500,000 stock options that under certain market conditions could become more lucrative than the performance shares. He could make as much as $2.66 billion if Valeant shares reached $1,182 on three specific dates.[15]

Pearson, a former McKinsey consultant, had huge incentives to increase the stock price. Traditionally, pharmaceutical firms charged high prices for drugs and spent 20 percent of their income on research and development. But R&D can take decades to pay off, so Pearson fashioned a strategy built on financial manipulation: Cut research and development, which promise no short-term benefit, and acquire drug companies with proven drugs, financing these deals by issuing junk bonds. Then raise prices, sometimes by 300 percent to 400 percent, and push sales. Between 2011 and 2014, Valeant made more than thirty acquisitions. One business reporter described the company's strategy as "buy a new company, stuff its patents and trademarks in a tax shelter, fire scientists, dispose of underperforming drugs, and dramatically jack up prices for the best sellers."

Like betting on black at roulette, Pearson's strategy was great so long as it worked: As long as Valeant's earnings increased, Wall Street would underwrite his junk bonds and bid up his stock, and Valeant could continue to acquire companies, raise prices, increase sales, and grow earnings. A perpetual-motion miracle.

This worked, for a while. Through shares and options acquired mostly from his compensation plans, the value of Mr. Pearson's 3 percent ownership swelled to over $2.5 billion by August 2015. As Pearson grew rich, his compensation plan was hailed by *The Wall Street Journal* as a sensible and successful way to motivate and compensate CEOs. Then Valeant lost 90 percent of its value in eight months, the share price plummeting from a high of 262.5 on August 5, 2015, to 26.1 as of April 4, 2016.

The house of cards began to collapse in early fall of 2015, when senators and congressmen called for an investigation of Valeant's price increases. In October, short-seller Citron Research accused them of accounting fraud and revealed Valeant's relationship with Philidor, a shady mail-order pharmacy that filled an astronomical number of prescriptions for their drugs. Citron claimed that Valeant had been using its relationship with Philidor to file fake invoices, and also appeared to control Philidor and had consolidated its financial results with its own—facts it had not disclosed to its shareholders. After Citron's report was released, Valeant's stock fell 29 percent.

In February 2016, Valeant announced it would restate its financial results for 2014 and 2015 because $58 million in revenues previously recognized in 2014 should have been booked in subsequent periods. Shortly thereafter, it announced that it was under investigation by the SEC. On March 18, 2016, Pearson sent a memo to employees reassuring them that Valeant would not go bankrupt, even though its debt was selling for 76 cents on the dollar. Three days later, Valeant announced it was looking for a new CEO.

In an exhibition of journalistic restraint, *The New York Times* ran the headline "Valeant Is a Reminder of the Peril of Outsize

Executive Pay." If you pay CEOs to make a quick buck, you will encourage them to become quick-buck artists like Mr. Pearson.

This may be one reason that there is very little use of pay for performance outside of corporate America. I have noted that generals don't get bonuses for battles won and tenors don't get a bonus that varies with the number of high notes they hit. The president of the United States gets a fixed salary. He gets no bonus for legislation passed, executive orders issued, or terrorists assassinated. Professors must publish or perish, but they do not get bonuses for publishing in elite journals. Even within the corporate world, almost all employees outside of top management and sales work for a fixed salary.

Imagine designing a corporate-like pay-for-performance plan for Aaron Rodgers. Suppose you set bonus bogeys and bonus ranges for (1) number of completed passes, (2) percentage of completed passes, and (3) average yards per attempted pass. Rodgers would quickly see that he could max out two of the three bonuses by throwing only short passes. To cure this, you add a fourth bonus for total yards passing. Rodgers then accumulates massive yardage against poor teams with a weak pass defense, but relies only on short passes against better defenses. The Packers end up losing games they would have won if they had no bonus system.*

---

* While not yet a major portion of compensation, the use of performance bonuses is increasing in major sports. Major League Baseball allows performance incentives, but a bonus cannot be based on statistical measures or where the club finishes in the standings. A performance-incentive bonus can, however, be tied to days spent on the active list during the MLB regular season, or games played, games started, etc. Incentive bonuses may also be tied to awards such as MVP, Cy Young, and Gold Glove.

The NFL allows statistical performance bonuses. For example, Elvis Dumervil of the Baltimore Ravens triggered $3 million in salary escalators and earned $1

The difficulties with specifying goals and measuring performance are not unique to capitalism. Even Joseph Stalin, with all
the powers of a totalitarian dictator, couldn't make performance
bonuses work.

From the 1930s, [Soviet] workers were paid bonuses if output levels were attained. These could be quite high—for instance, as much as 37% of the wage for management and
senior engineers. But paying such bonuses created all sorts
of disincentives to technological change. For one thing, innovation, which took resources away from current production, risked the output targets not being met and the bonuses
not being paid. For another, output targets were usually
based on previous production levels. This created a huge incentive to never expand output, since this only meant having
to produce more in the future, since future targets would be
"ratcheted up." Underachievement was always the best way
to meet targets and get the bonus.

When the plan was formulated in tons of steel sheet, the
sheet was made too heavy. When it was formulated in terms
of area of steel sheet, the sheet was made too thin. When the
plan for chandeliers was made in tons, they were so heavy,
they could hardly hang from ceilings.

---

million in incentives when he reached the 12-sack mark in 2015. Emmanuel
Sanders of the Denver Broncos received bonuses for reaching 90 pass receptions
and 1,200 receiving yards. He will not collect a potential $500,000 bonus for being
named to the NFL all-star first team.

Coaches who preach that "There is no I in team" may rue the day such individual bonuses were introduced when a receiver with only 89 receptions assaults the
quarterback and the offensive play caller.

Pay-for-performance systems cannot work in a company or a nation that has tomorrows. No plan produces more good than harm. Yet almost no one, inside or outside of corporate boards, questions the basic premise that CEO pay for performance is a good thing. Why? First, it sounds so fair and reasonable. You get rewarded for what you accomplish. Who could be against this? Second, no CEO in his right mind would question the underlying premise of the system that enriches him. Third, any admission that pay for performance is nonsense would embarrass the board by raising questions about past excesses. Fourth, boards, encouraged by their enablers in consulting and academia, believe they solved the pay-for-performance problem long ago. But they never subject this belief to a test.

Many businesses today pride themselves on being data driven. But no board is data driven when it comes to paying their CEO. There is overwhelming data that their performance plans backfire. All they have to do is look.

CHAPTER FIFTEEN

The Alignment Delusion

Our four companies cherish "alignment." In all of the proxies, this word, in all its variants, was ubiquitous. One of the primary objectives of the UnitedHealth Group compensation plan was to "align the economic interests of our executive officers with those of our shareholders." One of McKesson's three goals for compensation was "aligning management interests with those of stockholders." They claimed to have made changes that "strengthened the alignment of our executives' interests with those of our stockholders." Cheniere boasted that "Our executive compensation programs are designed to result in payouts that are closely aligned with company and shareholder," and therefore, "our executive compensation program resulted in payouts that were closely aligned with company and shareholder performance." Discovery proclaimed that their compensation program was designed to "align the interests of management with those of our stockholders."

But does anyone think that paying these CEOs an average of $153 million, rather than increasing dividends, was in the shareholders' interests? None of the incentives for these CEOS aligned their interests with those of the shareholders. Let's begin with stock options.

In the performance-pay model, stock options were seen as the panacea. Stock options would align the interests of the CEO and the shareholders while rewarding the CEO for increasing earnings and stock price.

UnitedHealth asserted that the use of SARs aligns the interests of the CEO and other executives with the shareholders' because "they have value only if the Company's stock price increases." McKesson championed the use of stock options: "since stock option awards provide value to the holder only if the Company's stock price appreciates, the use of such incentives directly aligns the interests of our executives and stockholders." Cheniere stated that "The largest component of our [CEO's] compensation, however, is paid in performance-based equity awards to incentivize our executive officers to perform at their highest levels to obtain our strategic business plan and to align management's interests with our stockholders' interests." Discovery declared that its compensation plan would "align the interests of management with those of our stockholders through equity and equity-type incentive awards and stock ownership."

Often the CEO does not need to accomplish anything to receive stock options. When McKesson awarded Hammergren stock options, he did not have to achieve anything specific to receive these. The comp committee explained that this award was "consistent with its review of stock option awards granted to similarly situated executives by companies in the Compensation Peer Group."

UnitedHealth Group took the same approach. They gave Hemsley a bunch of options "after considering competitive market data;

the desirability of utilizing a balanced system to mitigate risk, encourage superior performance, and build ownership; and the need to retain and motivate the executives to deliver sustained performance." Discovery awarded Zaslav options for signing a long-term contract.

A shareholder pays for his stock and bears downside risk. A CEO pays nothing for options awarded to him for doing nothing and has no downside risk, making him economically motivated to take more risk than the shareholder would want. This is not alignment.

The same holds for a cash bonus based on specific achievements, such as an increase in earnings per share. The shareholders want an economic return. Hitting this year's EPS bogey may contribute little or nothing to the shareholders' long-term economic return. In fact, a bonus for increasing EPS gives the CEO a powerful incentive to care more about this year's earnings than long-term success. It encourages short-term thinking, financial manipulation, and embarrassing adjustments by the board if the CEO misses the target. Similarly, a bonus for beating budgets does not align interests; it leads to bogus budgets.

UnitedHealth Group, McKesson, Cheniere, and Discovery all paid cash bonuses based on performance measures that had little or no relevance to shareholders. Shareholders want dividends and stock price appreciation, but UnitedHealth Group based Hemsley's cash bonus, in part, on doctor/patient satisfaction, employee engagement, and employee teamwork. If employee engagement and teamwork lead to higher dividends and stock price, they are in the shareholders' interests. If not, they are money wasted on feel-good initiatives. A bonus for achievements that may not help the shareholders misaligns interests.

McKesson based Hammergren's bonus on increasing EPS, which as I have pointed out, is a flawed and easily manipulated measure. All other things being equal, shareholders welcome growth in EPS, but paying Hammergren a bonus for a 5 percent EPS increase when his competitors are averaging 26 percent does not align his interests with theirs.

For misalignment, it is hard to top Cheniere. They awarded Souki a cash bonus for meeting milestones such as completing the financing for and commenced construction of Trains 3 and 4 at the Sabine Pass LNG terminal in May 2013 and initiating FERC prefiling for Trains 5 and 6 at the terminal in February 2013. These actions may produce or destroy value for the shareholders, but the odds favored "destroy" when oil prices dropped in 2015. To align interests, Cheniere should have chosen to wait to see if these actions paid off before rewarding Souki. Alternatively, they could have continued their warped logic and paid a special dividend to the shareholders to celebrate the initiation of FERC prefiling for Train 5. If you give crazy rewards to both the CEO and the shareholders, at least you have alignment.

Discovery based one-third of Zaslav's cash bonus on vague and hard-to-measure goals: manage growth, drive international growth, develop management succession plans, and develop strategies on content and distribution. How these align with shareholder interests is not immediately apparent. The remaining two-thirds depended on meeting targets for (1) net revenue, (2) adjusted free cash flow, and (3) adjusted OIBDA. These goals encouraged him to pursue acquisitions, since they would inevitably increase his chances of meeting revenue and OIBDA goals, and might help meet his free cash flow goal. Zaslav made acquisitions

in 2014, including increasing Discovery's equity stake in Euros-
port to reach a majority interest and forming a fifty-fifty joint venture with Liberty Global to acquire All3Media, a producer and
distributor of TV programming. Acquisitions helped Zaslav's bonus, but will they help the shareholders? Not if history is any guide.

CEOs are exhilarated by acquisitions that satisfy their quench
for glory and conquest. Unfortunately, for large-company shareholders, acquisitions usually destroy value. The stock of the acquiring company declines on average by 1 percent after an acquisition
is announced. The accounting firm KPMG found that 44 percent of
acquirers achieved little or none of the cost reductions they anticipated from synergies.

After a public firm is acquired, shareholders lose 5.9 cents per
dollar. The net losses for the 2,642 public companies acquiring
other public companies over a twenty-year period were $257 bil-
lion. UnitedHealth Group, McKesson, and Discovery demonstrated their hypocrisy on alignment by adjusting the numbers to
increase their CEO's bonus. When do these boards make offset-
ting adjustments that favor the shareholder?

The only way to align the interests of the shareholders and
the CEO is to terminate not only stock options but also every
other form of bonus except restricted stock. Every other CEO
performance-related bonus is a conflict of interest because the
CEO's interests are never precisely aligned with the shareholders'.
Directors of UnitedHealth Group, McKesson, Cheniere, and Discovery should ponder why it is that shareholders are voting
against compensation plans that the companies insist are aligned
with their interests.

Quarterback Aaron Rodgers, who has no bonus plan, was far

more aligned with his organization's goals than Hemsley, Hammergren, Souki, and Zaslav, who have multiple bonuses designed supposedly to align their interests with the shareholders'.

I have argued that if only one of corporate America's five delusions—importance, market, motivation, performance, and alignment—turns out to be false, the justification for the pay system collapses. If the CEO is not so important, why pay him so much? If other companies are not bidding for his services, why pay him so much? If the Pay Machine either misdirects his motivation, or cannot properly measure his performance, or does not align him with the shareholders, why use it?

Supposedly hard-nosed, cost-conscious, and data-driven corporate directors have watched CEO pay skyrocket for four decades and still clung to expensive and illogical practices and procedures that would be laughable applied to any other corporate expenditure. They have ignored all evidence that the CEO Pay Machine should be junked. The realization that all five of their delusions are false should compel them to find a better way.

CHAPTER SIXTEEN

The Fix and How to Get There

Before writing this book, I thought that corporate boards, despite dropping the ball on CEO pay, were basically honorable and responsible. Now I'm not so sure. Not only did our four companies overpay their CEOs, it appears that some misled their shareholders, most fiddled with the numbers to the benefit of the CEO and the detriment of their shareholders, and one even paid federal taxes to avoid any performance test. The boards of UnitedHealth Group and McKesson appear to have learned little from their debilitating accounting scandals. The board of Cheniere learned nothing from continued losses. Remember, I selected the four highest-paid CEOs. I was not searching for corporate malfeasance. Had I done so, I am sure I could have found more egregious examples. Before I offer a solution to this problem, let's look at reforms that should be made to corporate governance. We can start with better directors—truly independent, and not selected by the CEO and responsible to the shareholders. Scott M. Stringer, the New York City comptroller, recently demanded that shareholders who have owned at least 3 percent of a company's stock for at least three years be allowed to nominate directors for election to the board.

Boards should ask more from their directors. Attempting to govern a large company with four to six full board meetings a year is a ridiculous idea.

Boards should also prohibit the same person from being both CEO and chairman of the board, a rule that activist shareholders, institutional investors, proxy advisory firms, and regulators have demanded for years. When the CEO is also chairman, any initiatives to reform CEO pay practices are unlikely to appear high on the board's agenda. Separating the CEO and chairman roles actually saves money. One person in both roles costs 50 percent more than two people in two roles. Though this may be hard to believe, GMI, the corporate governance research firm, reported that executives who hold both jobs earn a median total compensation of slightly more than $16 million. CEOs without the top job on the board earn a median $9.8 million. When CEO and chairman roles are distinct, the two people combined earn a median $11 million. GMI found that companies that combined the roles were 86 percent more likely to be "aggressive" in accounting and governance risk. Finally, the five-year shareholder returns were nearly 28 percent higher at companies with a separate CEO and chair.

The SEC took baby steps by requiring companies to disclose their board leadership structure and explain why it's appropriate, and among S&P 500 companies, 43 percent now separate the jobs of chairman and CEO, up from 25 percent in 2002.

As a final tweak, the SEC should adopt the reforms proposed in the seventies to prevent market manipulation in corporate buybacks.*

In *Capital in the Twenty-First Century*, Thomas Piketty contends the relative equality we enjoyed between 1914 and 1973 was abnormal. While he expects inequality in America to increase, he does not think it is inevitable because "the history of the distribution of wealth has always been deeply political, and it cannot be reduced to purely economic mechanisms."

His solution for the income inequality problem is a world tax on wealth that he acknowledges is politically unlikely. I can't offer a comprehensive solution to income inequality, but reforming CEO pay is a good first step. This is the low-hanging fruit.

Start with what we want to achieve: a CEO pay system that enables companies to hire and retain talented CEOs, fully align the CEO with the shareholders, and eliminate the harm that the Pay Machine inflicts on companies, shareholders, and the economy.

Hiring and retaining a talented CEO is not difficult. Most CEO slots are filled by internal promotions, and at a large, well-run company, there is seldom a lack of candidates for the job: colonels usually want to become generals. Any pay system based on internal equity will work for internal candidates. The guy getting the job is like you before you met your fairy godmother. He's getting a great new job and a big raise. He couldn't be happier.

How much total compensation should a large-company CEO

---

* The reforms are highly technical and not the subject of this book. Therefore, readers can be thankful that I have chosen not to spell them out in detail.

be paid? Boards should ask, "Is any company likely to try to hire him away?" The highly probable answer is no. In that case, pay should be established by internal equity. Internal equity will also work for external candidates, who are almost never a sitting CEO of another large company, and as we've seen, companies are better off not trying to hire a sitting CEO. They tend not to work out. And they certainly won't work out if they flout the company's system of internal equity.

As we've seen, there's no need to award high pay to motivate a CEO. The company needs only to channel motivation. The pay system should provide strong incentives for the CEO to act at all times in the long-term interests of the shareholders. Specific pay-for-performance bonuses will always create perverse incentives and a short-term orientation.

The only way to fully align the CEO's interests with the shareholders' is to make him one. At least half his compensation should be in the form of restricted stock—ideally, two-thirds stock, one-third salary. At least half of those awards should vest over a minimum of five years and preferably longer. The CEO will get the balance when he retires or leaves, provided (1) that he has been CEO for at least five years, and (2) that the shareholders benefited while he was CEO—i.e., received a return above that of the S&P 500 over at least a five-year period. In theory, company returns should be compared with those of a "peer group" with a similar risk profile. But given how corporate boards have abused the peer group concept, I prefer an objective index like the S&P 500.

The only exception to ending all performance pay would be to tie at least half of the restricted stock to above-average long-term performance. If over an extended period, the shareholders do worse than average, the CEO forfeits half or more of his restricted stock. This is the only performance measure that perfectly aligns the CEO and the shareholders.

It's that simple—salary plus restricted stock. No pay for specific performance, no short-term bonus, no stock options, no bonus bogeys, no after-the-fact adjustments by the board, and no pay consultants—nothing except salary and restricted stock

Under my proposal, CEOs would be prohibited from selling restricted stock during their tenure at the company. If they need liquidity for some reason, they can borrow against the stock; a bank might loan them 50 percent of market value. Upon retirement or leaving the company, CEOs would be allowed to unload their shares gradually. Had such rules applied to Mr. Pearson when he was the CEO of Valeant, he might have taken a longer-term view.

Plato recommended that a community's highest wage should not exceed 5 times its lowest. In the late 1890s, J. P. Morgan set this ratio at 20 times the average. Over a hundred years later, British prime minister David Cameron considered it the maximum tolerable—in the public sector, at least. Back in 1977, business guru Peter Drucker wrote that CEO pay should be no more than 25 times an average worker's pay. In a 1984 essay, he revised the figure to no more than 20 times average worker pay. Drucker believed that a pay gap larger than that made it difficult to foster the kind of teamwork that a successful business requires. With American CEO pay now at 300 to 700 times that of the average worker, companies are not going to get to Drucker's number soon, or to Plato's number ever. But they should start. Every board should set a maximum pay ratio that's consistent with internal equity and work toward reaching this limit.

Will the same corporate boards that built the CEO Pay Machine respond to a renewed sense of responsibility, popular outrage, more SEC requirements, or additional government regulations? Left to their own devices, boards will continue to act as they have in the past. The "say-on-pay" provisions of Dodd-Frank were supposed to make boards more responsible, but in the first four years after Dodd-Frank became law, CEO pay rose on average 12 percent annually.

Shareholder indifference is the one reason "say on pay" has had little effect. By some estimates, less than 10 percent of individual shareholders bother to vote in proxy elections. Institutional shareholders, hedge funds, and brokerage houses file the most votes; they usually support management and the company on issues including "say on pay." Hedge fund managers find little reason to oppose company pay plans that would be a rounding error on their annual take. At institutional investors, executives may reason that higher CEO pay could boost their own compensation. Thus between July 2014 and June 2015, TIAA-CREF, which manages $900 billion of assets, voted in favor of company executive pay 100 percent of the time, while Vanguard ($3 trillion), Northern Trust ($900 billion), Wellington Management ($943 billion), and Fidelity ($5.1 trillion) voted in favor of at least 95 percent of company pay plans. In 2014, the median support at S&P 500 companies for company pay practices was 95 percent.

Maybe the shareholders accept the company line that their superman CEO is worth hundreds of millions. Maybe they think the game is rigged, but passively assume that nothing they do can make a difference.

How can we get boards to change?

Recall the joke:

A farmer lends a mule to a friend and advises him, "He will work hard if you just speak gently to him."

The mule won't budge for the friend. He tells the farmer, "I can't get this mule to do a damned thing."

The farmer picks up a two-by-four and whacks the mule on its head.

"I thought you told me to speak gently to him," the friend says.

"Well, first you have to get his attention," the farmer replies.

My two-by-four for corporate boards is a luxury tax on excess compensation. If it's good enough for our national pastime, Major League Baseball, it's good enough for corporate America. For every dollar above $6 million that companies pay their CEO or any other executive, they would pay a dollar in luxury tax. It would not be tax deductible. All compensation would be included—salary, bonuses, stock options, gains on stock options exercised, perks, deferred comp, the market value of restricted stock when it vests, retirement benefits, 401(k) matches, etc.*

For example, a company paying its CEO $15 million would have paid $9 million in "excess compensation." Therefore, it would have to pay an additional luxury tax of $9 million to the federal government. There are good reasons why this, unlike past government actions, will work as intended. My proposal is simple and blunt and leaves no room for interpretation. The wiliest lawyer cannot find a loophole in the rule "For every dollar over $6

---

* The value of the restricted stock at the time it vests would be included in the luxury tax. Subsequent appreciation would be excluded. Applying the luxury tax to capital gains on restricted stock would introduce perverse incentives and insane results: the higher the stock's price, the bigger the penalty for the company. Once it vests, there is no difference in stock held by the CEO and stock held by other shareholders. To maintain alignment, both should be treated the same.

million you pay your CEO, you pay a dollar to Uncle Sam as a penalty."

When restricted stock vests, the CEO would owe income tax on the total value of that stock. Tax protection payments to CEOs for stock that vested would be allowed outside the $6 million limit. I allow this exception because I want CEOs to hold a lot of stock in their companies. I don't want them selling as soon as it vests to meet tax payments.

The plan is simple and comprehensive, but would it work? If boards don't mind paying their CEOs $100 million, why would they object to $5 million or even $50 million in a luxury tax? Because today they can justify and obscure their $100 million pay levels with their accounting, consultants, peer groups, benchmarks, and PR flacks. It would be far harder to obscure and justify paying a penalty to the derided federal government. They may not admit it to researchers, but I suspect there are many directors who are embarrassed by the outrages of CEO pay and would like to change the system but don't know how. A luxury tax is precisely the blunt instrument they need to make changes.

A luxury tax would be a game changer for shareholders, institutional investors, pension funds, and proxy advisers who have largely ignored CEO pay thus far. While they have not objected to paying the CEO $20 million, coughing up an additional $14 million to the feds would be less tolerable. They would pressure boards to avoid the luxury tax.

The luxury tax would provide the excuse some directors need to smash the Pay Machine and start anew. Once a few boards capped pay at $6 million, the remainder could no longer find comfort in the conviction that "everybody does it this way."

Boards could retain any pay system, performance measures,

and bonus system they wanted. If a board honestly believes that their CEO is exceptional, they might be willing to pay the luxury tax to retain him. But the burden of proof for exceptionality would fall upon the board. However, they would be motivated to drop the pretense and nonsense of performance pay, because they would no longer be able to make excessive compensation deductible. If their performance-pay system produced pay exceeding $6 million, they would face a large tax bill and many more disgruntled shareholders than they do today.

Using their own accounting (i.e., earned compensation), large-company CEOs would see their compensation roughly halved. S&P 500 CEOs averaged under $12.6 million, with a median of $10.8 million in pay in 2015.

So no more performance pay and probably no more perks. Given a $6 million limit, most CEOs and boards would prefer cash and restricted stock to perks such as expensive home security systems; CEOs could still afford to buy less expensive ones for themselves. Stock options would disappear because the profits would be subject to the luxury tax, but appreciation in the preferred restricted stock that would align the CEO's interests with those of the shareholders would not.

There will always be a few rogue companies. Since United-Health Group paid additional taxes to avoid subjecting their CEO to performance measures, they may prefer to pay tens of millions in a luxury tax rather than reduce CEO compensation. But they might not. Evidence of any extra tax they pay today can be gleaned only by carefully scrubbing their proxy, but the tens of millions in luxury tax to the government will be obvious and highly publicized.

I expect large companies would choose to pay their CEOs

roughly one-third in cash and two-thirds in restricted stock. The days of the $100-million-plus CEO would be over. Still, a successful CEO would amass more money than anyone could possibly use. If the company's stock performed well, after ten years a CEO could amass $50 million to $100 million from restricted stock awards.

Even if you like my plan, you may question my sanity. Do I really believe a Congress that cannot tax billionaire hedge fund managers at ordinary tax rates will legislate a penalty tax on CEO pay? Yes, if it becomes a bigger political issue and opponents of the CEO Pay Machine coalesce on a compelling alternative.

Of course, I welcome all shareholders and advisers to join my campaign for salary plus restricted stock based on internal equity. With study and research, all might agree on this or even find a better solution. Then if boards refuse to change, shareholders must stand up and fight for the chosen alternative. Shareholder activism can help, but only if shareholders, unions, pension funds, and proxy advisory firms agree on a concrete alternative to the Pay Machine. They must recognize that even overwhelming no votes on a few egregious targets won't halt the CEO pay escalation. Long-accepted theories and practices can't be replaced by outrage. They can be replaced only by better theories and practices.

The elites may be apathetic, but the average voters are ready. A *New York Times*/CBS poll published in June 2015 stated, "Most Americans say that it is mainly just a few people at the top who have a chance to get ahead and that the money and wealth in this country should be more evenly distributed. The vast majority of Democrats and most independents say wealth should be more evenly distributed, but Republicans are closely split." Sixty-eight percent of the voters surveyed favored raising taxes on income of more than $1 million. Government action to reduce income inequality was favored by 57 percent and opposed by 39 percent. More to the point, 50 percent favored limiting CEO compensation, while 45 percent opposed.

And this was before Bernie Sanders made CEO pay a political issue. "Ninety-nine percent of all new income generated today goes to the top 1 percent. The top one-tenth of 1 percent owns as much wealth as the bottom 90 percent. Does anybody think that that is the kind of economy this country should have? Do we think it's moral?" he asked. He emphasized that the top 0.1 percent (my Mega Rich) now controls 21.5 percent of the nation's wealth and promised to reverse this.

Sanders has always considered CEO pay to be a big part of the problem. He introduced legislation to cap the tax deductibility of CEO pay and disallow deductions for excess salary, stock options, and perks. More recently he said, "The average chief executive in America now makes nearly 300 times more than the average worker—and the gap between the people at the top and working families is growing wider and wider. I hope that shining a spotlight on the disparity will help working families." He also wants CEOs to pay extra taxes if the gap between top and bottom salaries exceeds a certain percentage."

In December 2016, the City of Portland enacted a surtax on companies whose CEOs earn more than 100 times the median pay of their average employee. By itself this will have scant impacts. But if other cities and states pass similar legislation, it could start costing companies serious money. My plan may not appeal to the congress elected in November 2016. But remember that Donald Trump promised that the American worker would get a break and the economy would grow faster. Implementing my program is the quickest and easiest way to deliver on these promises. With CEO pay controlled, there would be more for the average worker. And unlike CEOs, who save their money, the average worker would spend it—on clothes for the kids, a new grill, or a room remodel. This spending would stimulate the economy. I remain optimistic that the reforms I advocate, or something like them, will eventually be adopted. I have faith that capitalism can coexist with democracy and each can enhance the other.

The last two times America faced such income inequality was in the age of the robber barons and the Roaring Twenties. In reaction to excesses of the Gilded Age, the reforms of the Progressive Era from 1886 to 1920 produced women's suffrage, the Sherman and Clayton antitrust acts and trust busting, the Pure Food and Drug Act, a progressive income tax,* the Federal Reserve System, direct election of senators, the Interstate Commerce Commission, the Federal Trade Commission, and Henry Ford's $5-a-day wage.

The New Deal reforms of the 1930s included the SEC, minimum wage and maximum hours for workers, Social Security, the Glass-Steagall Act to regulate banking and finance, the FDIC to guarantee individual bank accounts, and the Wagner Act, the Magna Carta for labor unions.

Today's third peak of income inequality can galvanize America to reform itself again. As Winston Churchill said, "You can always count on Americans to do the right thing—after they've tried everything else." Let's begin with CEO pay.

---

* The first income tax was enacted in 1894. The Supreme Court later ruled this income tax to be unconstitutional. In 1913, the 16th Amendment enabled an income tax.

GLOSSARY

AMORTIZATION is the expensing of the costs of intangible assets over a specific period of time, usually the useful life of the asset, for accounting and tax purposes. For example, the amounts over book value that an acquirer pays for an acquisition goes on its balance sheet as an intangible asset, such as client base and brand value. These costs are then expensed over a number of years. Since amortization does not consume cash, it is known as a non-cash expense and is excluded from certain measures of profitability such as EBITDA and OIBDA. (Amortization also refers to the repayment of loan principal over time but is not used that way in this book.)

An **AUDIT COMMITTEE** is charged with overseeing a company's financial reporting and internal financial controls. This committee, which comprises a selected number of members of a company's board of directors, retains the company's external auditors to audit and opine on the company's financial statements.

BENCHMARK, in this book, is a verb. The board benchmarks a CEO selecting a percentile within a peer group to target a CEO's pay. If the company benchmarks him at the 75th percentile, they will then set the target at the 75th percentile of the peer group.

A **BONUS BOGEY** is the goal or hurdle an executive must accomplish in order to receive a bonus. For example, having selected EPS as a performance measure, the board could set the bogey in terms of percentage increase over the previous year or a specific dollar amount.

BONUS RANGE establishes the minimum and maximum amount of a bonus within a bonus category. Often the range is set as a multiple of the base bonus rather than a specific number. For example, the range may be set at 2.5 times the base bonus. If the base bonus is $1,000,000 then the range is $1,000,000 to $2,500,000. By using a multiple, the comp committee does not have to revisit ranges every year.

BONUS TARGETS are the amounts a CEO or other executives would make if they hit but do not exceed the bonus bogey.

A **BUYBACK** is when a company purchases its own shares on an open market. This is also known as a stock repurchase. The two main reasons that companies buy back shares are:

1. To reduce the number of shares outstanding in an attempt to increase or support the current share price. By reducing the number of shares outstanding, the company should increase EPS. Then the share price will rise so long as the stock maintains the pre-buyback price-to-earnings (P/E) ratio.
2. To obtain shares to be used to reward executives when granting restricted stock or exercising stock options previously granted. By buying these shares on the open market, the company avoids diluting the existing shareholders.

CASH FLOW is the net of cash collected less cash expended. In accounting, cash flow is the difference in amount of cash available at the beginning of a period (opening balance) and the amount at the end of that period (closing balance).

COMPENSATION COMMITTEES, or comp committees, are the groups of directors who have been appointed to evaluate and set the pay rates for senior management. Comp committees are usually involved in the selection of other compensation options such as stocks, bonuses, stock options, and additional perks and establishing the parameters (performance measures, bonus bogeys, bonus ranges, etc.).

COMPENSATION CONSULTANTS, also known as executive compensation consultants, are retained by companies to advise them on the structure, systems, and amounts of executive compensation.

A **COMPENSATION TARGET**, established by the comp committee and board before or at the start of a fiscal year, is the total amount of compensation the CEO would receive if he hits, but does not exceed, all his bonus bogeys. His actual compensation may exceed or be less than the target. Often the target includes only salary and bonuses and excludes monies paid for perks and retirement benefits.

DEPRECIATION is the expensing of the costs of capital assets, such as plant and equipment, over the accounting periods that the asset is likely to be used. Like amortization, depreciation is a non-cash expense and is excluded in certain measures of profitability.

EARNED COMPENSATION, an accounting concept, is the value of compensation an executive "earns the right to keep." Under Generally Accepted Accounting Principles (GAAP), earned compensation is what corporations report to the public and their shareholders and show as an expense on their books. The major difference between the earned compensation and *realized* compensation is that the former excludes price appreciation the CEO receives when he exercises his stock options. Instead, the value of the options is estimated when the options are awarded.

EARNINGS PER SHARE (EPS) is a company's net income divided by the number of its shares outstanding. Primary earnings per share (also called fully diluted EPS) takes into account all shares currently outstanding, plus the number of shares that would be outstanding if all convertible bonds, convertible preferred stock, and stock options were converted to common stock.

EBITDA is an acronym for Earnings Before Interest, Taxes, Depreciation, and Amortization. EBITDA is a measure of the pretax earnings a firm generates before considering financing (interest) and non-cash (amortization and depreciation) charges. Many companies are valued on a multiple of EBITDA, especially in private companies' sales and in purchases by private equity firms. EBITDA does not measure cash flow, as it ignores cash required for working capital and the replacement of obsolete equipment.

EQUITY AWARDS consist of stock options, restricted stock units (RSUs), restricted stock, performance units, performance shares, deferred stock units, or stock appreciation rights (SARs). They give the holder, in one form or another, a payoff for the increase in a company's stock price.

EXTERNAL EQUITY is basing a company's CEO compensation upon what CEOs at similar or peer companies are paid.

GOLDEN PARACHUTES are large bonuses and/or lucrative contracts offered to a CEO (or other key employees) to compensate for loss of office after a takeover or merger. In theory, the parachutes protect against a CEO making a sweetheart deal to curry favor with the new owners.

INTERNAL EQUITY is basing CEO pay on how it compares with others in the company, for example, setting his pay at 50 times the compensation of the average employee or 150 percent of the next-highest-paid executive.

LONG-TERM INCENTIVE (LTI) is designed to give executives a financial interest in the long-term health of the company by bestowing equity awards that vest over time.

OIBDA, the acronym for Operating Income Before Depreciation and Amortization, is a measure of the income generated or used by a company's operations, excluding its capital spending decisions and tax structure. Like EBITDA, OIBDA does not measure cash flow. OIBDA starts out using operating income and then adds back depreciation and amortization. EBITDA starts out using earnings, i.e., net income, and adds back interest, taxes, depreciation, and amortization. OIBDA, therefore, ignores investment income, income from secondary operations, and extraordinary charges that would be included in net income and EBITDA.

P/E (PRICE-TO-EARNINGS) RATIO is the ratio of a company's share price to its per-share earnings. As the name implies, to calculate the P/E, you simply take the current stock price of a company and divide by its earnings per share (EPS). In theory, the P/E ratio reflects the market's expectation for future growth in earnings, with a high P/E indicating high growth expectations and vice versa.

PERCENTILE, as used in this book, is the percentage of the values that are smaller than that value. For example, a test score that is higher than 95 percent of the other scores is in the 95th percentile. Therefore, a CEO benchmarked at the 90th percentile will be targeted to receive total compensation that is higher than 90 percent of the CEOs in a peer group.

PERFORMANCE AWARDS, as used in this book, are bonuses granted that would meet the IRS definition of performance compensation and therefore not be taxed as excess compensation. The main requirements are: they are paid solely for attaining performance goals; the goals have been established by an independent committee consisting of two or more outside directors; the performance goals and the terms of the compensation have been disclosed to and approved by shareholders; and, before payment, the committee had to certify that the performance goals and other terms were met.

PERFORMANCE MEASURES, as used in this book, mean outcomes or results that are tied to a bonus. Where these are typically quantitative (EPS, EBITDA, stock price), they can also be qualitative.

REALIZED COMPENSATION is the total compensation received by the CEO. It's what he can spend. It includes the value received when he exercises his stock options. If the CEO holds an option with a strike price of $20 and exercises it when the stock is selling for $50 a share, he makes $30 a share. This $30 is included in realized compensation but excluded from earned compensation.

RESTRICTED STOCK is stock that cannot be sold or transferred. When granted to a CEO or other executive, the stock may vest over, say, five years. In this case, the executive receives the right to transfer or sell 20 percent in each of the next five years. Restricted stock may be forfeited if any of the SEC rules related to it are broken.

RESTRICTED STOCK UNITS (RSUS) are functionally the same as restricted stock in the normal case where one restricted stock unit equals one restricted stock share. In theory, one restricted unit could equal any number of shares, but I have never seen such a case. RSUS differ from stock options in that the company never issues new shares.

RETURN ON CAPITAL (ROC) is a company's net income divided by total capital employed (long-term debt plus equity). This is also called return on invested capital.

RETURN ON EQUITY (ROE) is a company's net income divided by the value of its equity (paid in capital plus retained earnings).

SHORT-TERM BONUS: A bonus paid for accomplishments within a single fiscal year. Usually this is paid in cash.

STOCK APPRECIATION RIGHTS (SARS) are rights to receive cash and/ or additional stock when the firm's stock price appreciates. It differs from a stock option in that the company need never issue new shares of stock and the holder can receive only cash and cannot trade in his SARs for new shares of stock.

STOCK OPTIONS give their holder the right to buy a firm's common stock at a specified price and by a specified date.

VESTING is the process by which benefits, or privileges, or rights to or interest in an asset, passes unconditionally to an executive. Restricted stock typically vests over time while performance shares would vest upon achieving certain goals.

NOTES

CHAPTER ONE

5   *37.4 percent since 2009*: Natalie Sabadish and Lawrence Mishel, "CEO Pay in 2012 Was Extraordinarily High Relative to Typical Workers and Other High Earners," Economic Policy Institute, June 26, 2013, http://www.epi.org/publication/ceo-pay-2012 -extraordinarily-high/.

8   *increase the share price*: Though not publicly traded, an independent appraisal process established the share price annually.

11   *"CEO Pay Hits 'Insane Level'"*: Mike Hall, "CEO Pay Hits 'Insane Level,'" *AFL-CIO Executive Paywatch* (blog), April 15, 2014, http://www.aflcio.org/Blog/Corporate -Greed/Paywatch-CEO-Pay-Hits-Insane-Level.

12   *bad for the economy*: Robert Reich, "Raising Taxes on Corporations That Pay Their CEOs Royally and Treat Their Workers Like Serfs," *Robert Reich* (blog), April 21, 2014, http://robertreich.org/post/83456610643.

12   *extracting vast sums*: Scott Klinger, Sam Pizzigati, and Sarah Anderson, "Executive Excess 2013: Bailed Out, Booted, Busted: A 20-Year Review of America's Top-Paid CEOs," Institute for Policy Studies, August 28, 2013, http://www.ips-dc.org/wp-content /uploads/2013/08/EE13-FINAL.pdf.

12   *everyone else has a smaller piece*: Paul Hodgson, "Top CEOs Make More than 300 Times the Average Worker," *Fortune*, June 22, 2015, http://fortune.com/2015/06/22/ceo -vs-worker-pay/.

12   *CEO pay increased by 15.6 percent*: *Executive Paywatch*, http://www.aflcio.org/Cor porate-Watch/Paywatch-2015.

12   *increase of less than half of 1 percent per year*: Lawrence Mishel and Alyssa Davis, "CEO Pay Has Grown 90 Times Faster than Typical Worker Pay Since 1978," Economic Policy Institute, July 1, 2015, http://www.epi.org/publication/ceo-pay-has -grown-90-times-faster-than-typical-worker-pay-since-1978/.

12   *CEO pay has grown 90 times faster*: Ibid.

12   *$13.5 million*: *Executive Paywatch*, http://www.aflcio.org/Corporate-Watch/Paywatch -2015.

13   *or $22.6 million*: Tim Mullaney, "Why Corporate CEO Pay Is So High, and Going Higher," CNBC.com, May 18, 2015, http://www.cnbc.com/2015/05/18/why-corporate -ceo-pay-is-so-high-and-going-higher.html.

13 *or $30 million-plus in 2014*: William Lazonick, "Taking Stock: Why Executive Pay Results in an Unstable and Inequitable Economy," Roosevelt Institute, June 5, 2014, http://www.rooseveltinstitute.net/taking-stock-executive-pay.

13 *between 300 and 700 times more*: According to the AFL-CIO, production and non-supervisory workers took home only $36,134 on average in 2014. *Executive Pay-watch,* http://www.aflcio.org/Corporate-Watch/Paywatch-2015.

This was based on CEOs of the S&P 500. I use "large-company CEOs," "Fortune 500 CEOs," and "S&P 500 CEOs" interchangeably, although the last two are not exactly the same: the Fortune 500 list is based on revenues while the S&P 500 are selected on market capitalization. Lazonick (see above) calculated S&P 500 CEOs averaged $30.3 million in total compensation in 2012, 710 times that of the average worker.

13 *only 26 times more than the average worker*: Bonnie Kavoussi, "CEO Pay Grew 127 Times Faster than Worker Pay Over Last 30 Years: Study," *Huffington Post*, May, 2, 2012, http://www.huffingtonpost.com/2012/05/02/ceo-pay-worker-pay_n_1471685.html.

13 *In 2015, CEO pay increased only modestly*: Equilar/Associated Press S&P 500 CEO Pay Study 2016, May 25, 2016, http://www.equilar.com/reports/37-associated-press -pay-study-2016.html.

The Equilar study covers the 341 CEOs who served in that role at an S&P 500 com-pany for at least two years as of fiscal year-end and whose companies filed a proxy between January 1 and April 30 of 2016.

13 *to $19.3 million in 2015*: David Gelles, "Top C.E.O. Pay Fell—Yes, Fell—in 2015," *New York Times*, May 27, 2016, http://www.nytimes.com/2016/05/29/business/top -ceo-pay-fell-yes-fell-in-2015.html?_r=0.

14 *In Japan, the ratio of CEO-to-average-worker pay*: Zaid Jilani, "Average Japanese CEO Earns One-Sixth as Much as American CEOs," ThinkProgress, July 8, 2010, http://thinkprogress.org/politics/2010/07/08/106536/japanese-ceo-american-sixth/.

14 *84 to 1 in the UK*: Gretchen Gavett," "CEOs Get Paid Too Much, According to Pretty Much Everyone in the World," *Harvard Business Review*, September 23, 2014, https:// hbr.org/2014/09/ceos-get-paid-too-much-according-to-pretty-much-everyone -in-the-world/.

CHAPTER THREE

29 *Stephen Hemsley of UnitedHealth Group*: "America's Highest Paid Chief Executives," *Forbes,* http://www.forbes.com/lists/2011/12/ceo-compensation-11_Stephen-J-Hemsley _NBHE.html.

29 *John Hammergren of McKesson*: Alain Sherter, "Highest-Paid CEOs: Top Earner Takes Home $145 Million," *CBS MoneyWatch*, December 15, 2011, http://www .cbsnews.com/8301-505123_162-57343611/highest-paid-ceos-top-earner-takes -home-$145-million/.

29 *Charif Souki of Cheniere Energy*: 2014 Equilar Top 200 Highest Paid CEO Rankings Summary, Equilar, http://www.equilar.com/nytimes.

29 *David Zaslav of Discovery Communications*: Equilar 200 Highest-Paid CEO Rankings, http://www.equilar.com/publications/51-200-highest-paid-CEO-rankings -2015.html.

31 *Hurts employee morale and productivity*: Jeffrey Pfeffer, "Human Resources from an Organizational Behavior Perspective: Some Paradoxes Explained," *Journal of Eco-nomic Perspectives* 21, no. 4 (2007), http://www.aeaweb.org/articles.php?doi=10.1257 /jep.21.4.115.

31 *lower job satisfaction*: Matt Bloom and John G. Michel, "The Relationships Among Organizational Context, Pay Dispersion, and Managerial Turnover," *The Academy of Management Journal* 45, no. 1 (2002), http://www.jstor.org/stable/3069283.

31 *low employee morale*: James B. Wade, Charles A. O'Reilly III, and Timothy G. Pollock, "Overpaid CEOs and Underpaid Managers: Fairness and Executive Compensation," *Organization Science* 17, no. 5 (2006), http://pubsonline.informs.org/doi/abs/10.1287/orsc.1060.0204.

31 *lower-quality product*: Douglas M. Cowherd and David I. Levine, "Product Quality and Pay Equity Between Lower-Level Employees and Top Management: An Investigation of Distributive Justice Theory," *Administrative Science Quarterly* 37, no. 2 (1992), http://www.questia.com/library/1G1-12729185/product-quality-and-pay-equity-between-lower-level.

31 *open and up-front with them*: American Psychological Association, "Employee Distrust Is Pervasive in U.S. Workforce," news release, April 23, 2014, https://www.apa.org/news/press/releases/2014/04/employee-distrust.aspx.

32 *cash in their stock options*: William Lazonick, "Taking Stock: Why Executive Pay Results in an Unstable and Inequitable Economy," Roosevelt Institute, June 5, 2014, http://www.rooseveltinstitute.net/taking-stock-executive-pay.

32 *exceeded net income by 16 percent*: Karen Brettell, David Gaffens, and David Rohde, "The Cannibalized Company: How the Cult of Shareholder Value Has Reshaped Corporate America," Reuters, November 16, 2015.

32 *devoted our 10 percent*: Ibid.

32 *Cisco's stock repurchases exceeded*: Cisco's stock repurchases were 118 percent of its net income during this period. Lazonick, "Taking Stock."

33 *CEO John Chambers sold more than $50 million*: "Insider Transactions: Cisco Systems, Inc.," Yahoo Finance, https://finance.yahoo.com/q/it?s=CSCO+Insider+Transactions.

33 *support for Mr. Chambers's sales*: David Eller, "Can Cisco Systems, Inc. Maintain These Massive Stock Buybacks?," *The Motley Fool,* February 25, 2014, http://www.fool.com/investing/general/2014/02/25/can-cisco-systems-inc-maintain-these-massive-stock.aspx.

33 *option awards to its executives*: Gretchen Morgenson, "Stock Buybacks That Hurt Shareholders," *New York Times,* June 5, 2015, http://www.nytimes.com/2015/06/07/business/stock-buybacks-that-hurt-shareholders.html?_r=0.

33 *announced $50 billion programs*: Ibid.

33 *170 percent of their net income on stock buybacks*: Lazonick, "Taking Stock."

33 *reduced the number of shares outstanding*: Peter Eavis, "Valeant Is a Reminder of the Peril of Outsize Executive Pay," *New York Times,* April 4, 2016, http://www.nytimes.com/2016/04/05/upshot/valeant-is-a-reminder-of-the-peril-of-outsize-executive-pay.html.

33 *Buybacks rose 9 percent to $589 billion*: Jeff Sommer, "Buybacks by Companies Like Apple May Signal Danger, Not Growth," *New York Times,* June 23, 2016, http://www.nytimes.com/2016/06/26/your-money/buybacks-by-companies-like-apple-may-signal-danger-not-growth.html.

33 *50 percent more than they paid out*: Lazonick, "Taking Stock."

34 *CEOs is only 4.6 years*: David Weidner, "Why Your CEO Could Be in Trouble," *Deal Journal* (blog), *Wall Street Journal,* September 15, 2011, http://blogs.wsj.com/deals/2011/09/15/why-your-ceo-could-be-in-trouble/.

34 *support CEO option sales*: William Lazonick, "Financialization of the U.S. Corporation: What Has Been Lost, and How It Can Be Regained," the Academic-Industry Research Network, July 17, 2012, http://mpra.ub.uni-muenchen.de/42307/.

34 *EPS would have increased more*: Gretchen Morgenson, "In Yahoo, Another Example of the Buyback Mirage," *New York Times*, March 25, 2016, http://www.nytimes.com /2016/03/27/business/in-yahoo-another-example-of-the-buyback-mirage.html.

CHAPTER FOUR

36 *lost half its value*: Jeff Sommer, "Buybacks by Companies Like Apple May Signal Danger, Not Growth," *New York Times*, June 23, 2016, http://www.nytimes.com /2016/06/26/your-money/buybacks-by-companies-like-apple-may-signal-danger -not-growth.html.

37 *19 percent above its historical average*: http://www.advisorperpectives.com/dshort/ updates/2016/12/02/market-cap-to-gdp-anupdated-look-at-thebuffett-valuation -indicator.

37 *awaiting a correction*: http://www.multipl.com/shiller-pe/.

38 *top 0.1 percent in income*: Ryan Gorman, "Wealth of Super Rich 0.1 Per Cent Is Pulling Even Further Ahead of the Rest of the Country," *Daily Mail*, April 1, 2014, http:// www.dailymail.co.uk/news/article-2593874/Super-rich-pulling-ahead-majority -one-centers.html.

38 *average real income of the Mega Rich has nearly quadrupled*: See chart on page 243. Average Income Raw Data and Footnotes.
The World Wealth and Income Database (WID), http://www.wid.world.

Source: Income
Thomas Piketty and Emmanuel Saez, "Income and Wage Inequality in the United States 1913–2002," in *Top Incomes over the Twentieth Century: A Contrast Between Continental European and English-Speaking Countries*, ed. A. B. Atkinson and T. Piketty (New York: Oxford University Press, 2007), chapter 5. Series updated by the same authors.

Source: Wealth
Thomas Piketty and Gabriel Zucman, "Capital Is Back: Wealth-Income Ratios in Rich Countries 1700–2010," *The Quarterly Journal of Economics* 129, no. 3 (2014): 1255–1310, doi:10.1093/qje/qju018. Series updated by the same authors.

WID provides average income data for separate 1–0.5 percent and 0.5–0.1 percent groups. Average income for the Top 1 percent–0.1 percent displayed in the graph was calculated using a 5:4 weighted average given the number of individuals in the separate 1–0.5 percent and 0.5–0.1 percent tiers.

38 *share of the Merely Rich rose from 6.6 percent*: See chart on page 244. Income Share Raw Data and Footnotes.
Top 0.1% Total Income Share from 1980–2013 = (Total 0.1% Aggregate Income 1980–2013)/(Total National Aggregate Income 1980–2013) = 6.33%.

38 *virtually all of the income gains*: The top 1 percent took 93 percent of all income gains during this period. Emmanuel Saez, "Striking It Richer: The Evolution of Top Incomes in the United States," UC Berkeley, January 25, 2015, https://eml.berkeley .edu/~saez/saez-UStopincomes-2013.pdf.

Weighted Avg.	Average Annual Income - Including Capital Gains (In Thousands of Real 2014 US Dollars)					
Top 1-0.1%	Bottom 90%	Top 1-0.1%	Top 1-0.5%	Top 0.5-0.1%	Top 0.1%	
$ 344.11	$ 34.02	$ 344.11	$ 269.06	$ 437.92	$ 1,597.08	1980
$ 332.00	$ 33.69	$ 332.00	$ 257.88	$ 424.65	$ 1,651.85	1981
$ 334.70	$ 32.70	$ 334.70	$ 257.62	$ 431.06	$ 1,900.11	1982
$ 352.50	$ 32.34	$ 352.50	$ 267.61	$ 458.61	$ 2,114.07	1983
$ 368.71	$ 33.28	$ 368.71	$ 279.38	$ 480.37	$ 2,358.54	1984
$ 397.43	$ 33.76	$ 397.43	$ 296.22	$ 523.95	$ 2,587.71	1985
$ 493.56	$ 34.40	$ 493.56	$ 343.61	$ 680.99	$ 3,857.37	1986
$ 428.51	$ 34.09	$ 428.51	$ 319.31	$ 565.01	$ 2,433.75	1987
$ 504.14	$ 34.43	$ 504.14	$ 355.07	$ 690.49	$ 3,548.20	1988
$ 487.90	$ 34.44	$ 487.90	$ 352.60	$ 657.02	$ 3,104.03	1989
$ 479.90	$ 33.87	$ 479.90	$ 343.83	$ 649.98	$ 2,957.79	1990
$ 449.30	$ 32.97	$ 449.30	$ 331.34	$ 596.75	$ 2,514.61	1991
$ 476.48	$ 32.64	$ 476.48	$ 344.66	$ 641.26	$ 2,993.87	1992
$ 464.98	$ 32.42	$ 464.98	$ 340.46	$ 620.62	$ 2,819.33	1993
$ 473.38	$ 32.87	$ 473.38	$ 349.48	$ 628.25	$ 2,849.61	1994
$ 517.89	$ 33.21	$ 517.89	$ 378.34	$ 692.34	$ 3,204.08	1995
$ 563.33	$ 33.70	$ 563.33	$ 405.73	$ 760.33	$ 3,885.53	1996
$ 620.07	$ 34.92	$ 620.07	$ 437.82	$ 847.89	$ 4,646.77	1997
$ 675.34	$ 36.54	$ 675.34	$ 470.85	$ 930.95	$ 5,417.97	1998
$ 730.44	$ 37.52	$ 730.44	$ 505.63	$ 1,011.45	$ 6,069.36	1999
$ 764.96	$ 37.65	$ 764.96	$ 525.99	$ 1,063.68	$ 7,035.36	2000
$ 658.89	$ 36.91	$ 658.89	$ 469.06	$ 896.19	$ 5,037.91	2001
$ 604.21	$ 35.64	$ 604.21	$ 437.01	$ 813.19	$ 4,191.44	2002
$ 609.36	$ 34.99	$ 609.36	$ 437.90	$ 823.69	$ 4,465.84	2003
$ 682.10	$ 35.54	$ 682.10	$ 478.67	$ 936.37	$ 5,647.77	2004
$ 756.60	$ 35.76	$ 756.60	$ 516.37	$ 1,056.88	$ 6,841.79	2005
$ 798.02	$ 36.00	$ 798.02	$ 538.01	$ 1,123.03	$ 7,407.84	2006
$ 826.96	$ 37.02	$ 826.96	$ 555.35	$ 1,166.48	$ 8,136.67	2007
$ 699.81	$ 34.35	$ 699.81	$ 487.21	$ 965.56	$ 6,211.09	2008
$ 597.44	$ 32.53	$ 597.44	$ 434.25	$ 801.42	$ 4,540.08	2009
$ 633.57	$ 32.26	$ 633.57	$ 450.81	$ 862.02	$ 5,396.49	2010
$ 639.63	$ 31.96	$ 639.63	$ 454.72	$ 870.77	$ 5,138.39	2011
$ 722.85	$ 32.12	$ 722.85	$ 496.18	$ 1,006.20	$ 6,854.48	2012
$ 667.71	$ 32.17	$ 667.71	$ 475.25	$ 908.29	$ 5,365.34	2013
$ 724.22	$ 33.07	$ 724.22	$ 507.88	$ 994.64	$ 6,087.11	2014

38 *their average income increased 49 percent*: World Wealth and Income Database, "Average Income Raw Data and Footnotes."

38 *made 113 times as much as the typical American household*: According to the Census ACS survey, the median household income for the United States was $53,657 in 2014, http://www.deptofnumbers.com/income/us/. As shown in note 3 above, average income for the top 0.1 percent percent was $6,087,113 in 2014.

Aggregate Income in Current Billions of US $

Year	Top 0.1% Agg. Income	Top 0.1% Income Share	Aggregate Income
1980	$ 54.12	2.23%	$ 2,426.80
1981	$ 60.70	2.23%	$ 2,722.10
1982	$ 69.59	2.45%	$ 2,840.40
1983	$ 79.88	2.61%	$ 3,060.50
1984	$ 97.47	2.83%	$ 3,444.00
1985	$ 107.21	2.91%	$ 3,684.20
1986	$ 110.44	2.87%	$ 3,848.20
1987	$ 153.65	3.73%	$ 4,119.20
1988	$ 234.11	5.21%	$ 4,493.40
1989	$ 226.68	4.74%	$ 4,782.20
1990	$ 246.77	4.90%	$ 5,036.10
1991	$ 226.11	4.36%	$ 5,186.10
1992	$ 286.53	5.21%	$ 5,499.70
1993	$ 271.63	4.72%	$ 5,754.80
1994	$ 288.59	4.70%	$ 6,140.20
1995	$ 322.68	4.98%	$ 6,479.50
1996	$ 367.74	5.33%	$ 6,899.40
1997	$ 428.80	5.81%	$ 7,380.40
1998	$ 487.15	6.20%	$ 7,857.30
1999	$ 552.74	6.64%	$ 8,324.40
2000	$ 635.07	7.13%	$ 8,907.00
2001	$ 574.96	6.26%	$ 9,184.60
2002	$ 559.60	5.93%	$ 9,436.80
2003	$ 602.70	6.11%	$ 9,864.20
2004	$ 728.38	6.91%	$ 10,540.90
2005	$ 872.21	7.76%	$ 11,239.80
2006	$ 950.78	7.92%	$ 12,004.80
2007	$ 1,005.43	8.16%	$ 12,321.40
2008	$ 971.85	7.82%	$ 12,427.80
2009	$ 853.68	7.04%	$ 12,126.10
2010	$ 958.01	7.52%	$ 12,739.50
2011	$ 985.40	7.38%	$ 13,352.30
2012	$ 1,176.21	8.36%	$ 14,069.50
2013	$ 1,074.33	7.37%	$ 14,577.10

38 *wealth as the bottom 90 percent*: Emmanuel Saez and Gabriel Zucman, "Wealth Inequality in the United States Since 1913: Evidence from Capitalized Income Tax Data," NBER Working Paper No. 20625, October 2014, http://www.nber.org/papers/w20625.

38 *hold 22 percent of the nation's wealth*: Annie Lowrey, "Even Among the Richest of the Rich, Fortunes Diverge," *New York Times*, February 10, 2014, http://www.nytimes.com/2014/02/11/your-money/even-among-the-richest-of-the-rich-fortunes-diverge.html?_r=0.

39 *They new hold 22 percent*: Nelson D. Schwartz, "In an Age of Privilege, Not Everyone Is in the Same Boat," *New York Times*, April 23, 2016, http://www.nytimes.com/2016/04/24/business/economy/velvet-rope-economy.html.

39 *constitute three-fifths of the top 0.1 percent*: Jon Bakija, Adam Cole, and Bradley T. Heim, "Jobs and Income Growth of Top Earners and the Causes of Changing Income Inequality: Evidence from U.S. Tax Return Data," April 2012, http://web.williams.edu/Economics/wp/BakijaColeHeimJobsIncomeGrowthTopEarners.pdf.

39 *accounted for about 70 percent of the increase in income*: Lowrey, "Even Among the Richest."

39 *sports and film stars thrown in*: Paul Krugman, "But the Top 0.1 Percent Isn't Diverse," The Opinion Pages, *New York Times*, January 15, 2012, http://krugman.blogs.nytimes.com/?s=but+the+top+0.1+percent+isn percent27t+diverse.

40 *"supermanagers" than with "superstars"*: Thomas Piketty, *Capital in the Twenty-First Century*, trans. Arthur Goldhammer (Cambridge, MA: Harvard University Press, 2014).

40 *among top managers of large firms*: Ibid.
Kaplan and Rauh (2007) had argued that top executives were a small part of the 0.1 percent. However, they looked at only the top five executives of public companies and were able to identify only 17 percent of the occupations of this group.

40 *CEOs use their own power*: James B. Wade, Charles A. O'Reilly III, and Timothy G. Pollock, "Overpaid CEOs and Underpaid Managers: Fairness and Executive Compensation," *Organization Science* 17, no. 5 (2006), http://pubsonline.informs.org/doi/abs/10.1287/orsc.1060.0204.

40 *5.7 million private companies*: Mary Ellen Biery, "4 Things You Don't Know About Private Companies," *Forbes*, May 26, 2013, http://www.forbes.com/sites/sageworks/2013/05/26/4-things-you-dont-know-about-private-companies/.

40   *Runaway CEO pay caused*: Compensation Ratio Raw Data and Footnotes.
The Economic Policy Institute, http://www.epi.org.

Source: Lawrence Mishel and Alyssa Davis, "Top CEOs Make 300 Times More than Typical Workers: Pay Growth Surpasses Stock Gains and Wage Growth of Top 0.1 Percent," Economic Policy Institute, June 21, 2015.

Table 1: CEO Compensation, CEO-to-Worker Compensation Ratio, and Stock Prices, 1965–2014 (2014 dollars). Source: Authors' analysis of data from Compustat's ExecuComp database, Federal Reserve Economic Data (FRED) from the Federal Reserve Bank of St. Louis, the Current Employment Statistics program, and the Bureau of Economic Analysis NIPA tables.

http://www.epi.org/publication/top-ceos-make-300-times-more-than-workers-pay-growth-surpasses-market-gains-and-the-rest-of-the-0-1-percent/.

Date Published: 6/21/2016
Notes: Including salary, bonus, stock grants, options granted, incentive payouts.

	1980	1981	1982	1983	1984	1985	1986	1987	1988	1989	1990	1991	1992	1993	1994	1995	1996	1997	1998	1999	2000	2001	2002	2003	2004	2005	2006	2007	2008	2009	2010	2011	2012	2013	2014
Salary, Bonus, Stock/Options Granted, Incentive Payouts / CEO to Worker Comp Ratio	33.8	35.9	38.2	40.6	43.2	45.9	48.9	51.9	55.2	58.7	71.2	86.2	104.4	111.8	87.3	122.6	153.8	233	321.8	286.7	376.1	214.2	188.5	227.5	256.6	308	341.4	345.3	239.3	195.8	229.7	235.5	285.3	303.1	303.4

42   *economy that is 50 percent larger*: Real per capita GDP was $50,055 in 2014, $28,133 in 1980, $28,618 in 1979, and $13,411 in 1949. http://www.multpl.com/us-real-gdp-per-capita/table/by-year.

42   *inequality curve in the form of an inverted U*: Richard B. Freeman, "Optimal Inequality for Economic Growth, Stability, and Shared Prosperity: The Economics Behind the Wall Street Occupiers Protest?," *Insights* 11 (April 2012) http://insights.unimelb.edu.au/vol11/01_Freeman.html.

43   *no one has an incentive to work*: Ibid.

44   *We've reduced our 10-year U.S. growth forecast*: "How Increasing Income Inequality Is Dampening U.S. Economic Growth, and Possible Ways to Change the Tide," Standard & Poor's, August 5, 2014, https://www.globalcreditportal.com/ratingsdirect/renderArticle.do?articleId=1351366&SctArtId=255732&from=CM&nsl_code=LIME&sourceObjectId=8741033&sourceRevId=1&fee_ind=N&exp_date=20240804-19:41:13.

44   *required for sustained economic growth*: Andrew G. Berg and Jonathan D. Ostry, "Equality and Efficiency," *Finance & Development* 48, no. 3 (2011), http://www.imf.org/external/pubs/ft/fandd/2011/09/berg.htm.

44   *experienced during growth spells*: Ibid.

45   *study by the Organisation for Economic Co-operation and Development*: OECD Directorate for Employment, Labour and Social Affairs, "Focus on Inequality and

Growth," December 2014, http://www.oecd.org/els/soc/Focus-Inequality-and-Growth
-2014.pdf.

45 *GDP loss during the Great Recession*: GDP totaled $14.96 trillion at the end of the
second quarter of 2008 and fell to $14.36 trillion one year later.

46 *policies that are more punitive*: Eduardo Porter, "In the U.S., Punishment Comes Before
the Crimes," *New York Times*, April 29, 2014, http://www.nytimes.com/2014/04/30/
business/economy/in-the-us-punishment-comes-before-the-crimes.html.

46 *finish high school*: OECD (2014), Education at a Glance 2014: OECD Indicators,
OECD Publishing, http://dx.doi.org/10.1787/eag-2014-en.

47 *household debt-to-income ratios*: Michael Kumhof and Romain Rancière, "Leverag-
ing Inequality," *Finance & Development* 47, no 4 (2010), http://www.imf.org/external
/pubs/ft/fandd/2010/12/pdf/kumhof.pdf.

47 *unequal incomes spur borrowing*: Ibid.

47 *risk of major economic crises*: Michael A. Fletcher, "Income Inequality Hurts Economic Growth, Researchers Say," *Washington Post*, January 24, 2014, http://www
.washingtonpost.com/business/economy/income-inequality-hurts-economic
-growth-researchers-say/2014/01/24/cb6e02a0-83b0-11e3-9dd4-e7278db80d86
_story.html.

47 *insufficient aggregate demand*: Lawrence H. Summers and Ed Balls, "Report of the
Commission on Inclusive Prosperity," Center for American Progress, January 15,
2015, https://www.americanprogress.org/issues/economy/report/2015/01/15/104266/
report-of-the-commission-on-inclusive-prosperity/.

47 *deter economic growth*: See Torsten Persson and Guido Tabellini, "Is Inequality
Harmful for Growth? Theory and Evidence," NBER Working Paper No. 3599, January 1991, http://www.nber.org/papers/w3599.

48 *Without trust*: Joseph E. Stiglitz, *The Great Divide: Unequal Societies and What We
Can Do About Them* (New York: W. W. Norton, 2015).

48 *a weaker economy*: Annie Lowrey, "Income Inequality May Take Toll on Growth,"
New York Times, October 16, 2012, http://www.nytimes.com/2012/10/17/business/
economy/income-inequality-may-take-toll-on-growth.html?ref=incomeinequal-
ity&_r=0.

49 *median family income was $53,306*: Federal Reserve Bank of St. Louis, Economic
Data: "Real Median Household Income in the United States," https://fred.stlouisfed
.org/series/MEHOINUSA672N.

49 *real disposable income rose*: Federal Reserve Bank of St. Louis, Economic Data: "Real
Disposable Personal Income: Per Capita," https://research.stlouisfed.org/fred2/series
/A229RX0A048NBEA.

49 *reduced US GDP by 10 percent*: The OECD average Gini index increased 3 points
from .29 to .32 between 1985 and 2011. In the United States, it increased 6 Gini
points, going from .39 to .45 over the same period. OECD, "Focus on Inequality and
Growth."

49 *additional growth been distributed equally*: The top 0.1 percent took 40 percent of all
gains since 1989. Business executives account for 70 percent of the top 0.1 percent
and therefore took 28 percent of all gains. Reallocation of two-thirds of this 28 percent means that 18.7 percent can be spread around. Real per capita income increased
by 48 percent over this period. The amount to be reallocated to the median household is the 18.7 percent x 48 percent x $53,306, the median household income in
1989. This equals $4,784. Add this to the actual household income in 2014 of $53,657

to get $58,441. If GDP decreased 10 percent, it would have been 11.1 percent higher without this decrease. 1/.9 = 1.111. Multiply $58,441 by 1.111 to obtain $64,928.

51 *Empowered elites smothering change*: This theory and examples are taken from Daron Acemoglu and James Robinson, *Why Nations Fail: The Origins of Power, Prosperity, and Poverty* (New York: Crown, 2012).

51 *they lean slightly to the right*: Lydia Saad, "U.S. '1%' Is More Republican, but Not More Conservative," Gallup, December 5, 2011, http://www.gallup.com/poll/151310 /u.s.-republican-not-conservative.aspx.

51 *Congress are millionaires*: Russ Choma, "Millionaires' Club: For First Time, Most Lawmakers Are Worth $1 Million-Plus," Opensecrets.org, January 9, 2014, http:// www.opensecrets.org/news/2014/01/millionaires-club-for-first-time-most-law makers-are-worth-1-million-plus/.

51 *cost the government $11 billion*: Lynn Forester de Rothschild, "A Costly and Unjust Perk for Financiers," *New York Times*, February 24, 2013, http://www.nytimes.com /2013/02/25/opinion/carried-interest-an-unjust-privilege-for-financiers.html?_r=0.

52 *more money than the nation's 158,000 kindergarten teachers*: Aimee Picchi, "An Eye-Popping Figure About Hedge Fund Managers," CBS MoneyWatch, May 15, 2015, http://www.cbsnews.com/news/an-eye-popping-figure-about-hedge-fund -managers/.

53 *impact of elites and interest groups on public policies*: Martin Gilens and Benjamin I. Page, "Testing Theories of American Politics: Elites, Interest Groups, and Average Citizens," *Perspectives on Politics* 12, no. 3 (2014), http://journals.cambridge.org/ action/displayAbstract?fromPage=online&aid=9354310&fileId= S1537592714001595.

54 *There is near consensus*: Joe Nocera, "Rethinking Campaign Finance," *New York Times*, May 16, 2014, http://www.nytimes.com/2014/05/17/opinion/nocera-rethinking -campaign-finance.html.

54 *middle class has shrunk*: Remarks by President Obama on the economy in Osawatomie, Kansas, The White House, December 6, 2011, https://www.whitehouse.gov/the-press-office/2011/12/06/remarks-president-economy-osawatomie-kansas.

55 *inequality reduces voting*: Frederick Solt, "Economic Inequality and Democratic Political Engagement," *American Journal of Political Science* 52, no. 1 (2008), http://online library.wiley.com/doi/10.1111/j.1540-5907.2007.00298.x/abstract.

54 *public schools eliminate art classes*: Alberto Chong and Mark Gradstein, "Inequality and Institutions," Research Department Publications 4361, Inter-American Development Bank, Research Department Working Paper 506 (April 2004), http://www.iadb .org/res/publications/pubfiles/pubWP-506.pdf.

55 *that has got to change*: https://berniesanders.com/issues/income-and-wealth-in equality/.

55 *median income for male workers*: Ibid.

56 *prekindergarten program*: Ibid.

57 *no economic gains since 1980*: Derek Thompson, "Who Are Donald Trump's Supporters, Really?" *Atlantic*, March 1, 2016, http://www.theatlantic.com/politics/archive /2016/03/who-are-donald-trumps-supporters-really/471714/.

57 *do not support capitalism*: Max Ehrenfreund, "A Majority of Millennials Now Reject Capitalism, Poll Shows," *Washington Post*, April 26, 2016, https://www.washington post.com/news/wonk/wp/2016/04/26/a-majority-of-millennials-now -reject-capitalism-poll-shows/.

CHAPTER FIVE

58 *average American CEO in the 1970s earned only about 4 percent*: Salvatore Babones, "In Corporate America, Why Greed's Never Good," Inequality.org, March 26, 2012, http://inequality.org/corporate-governance-pay-performance-greeds-good/.

59 *George Romney*: David Leonhardt, "Two Candidates, Two Fortunes, Two Distinct Views of Wealth," *New York Times*, December 23, 2007, http://www.nytimes.com /2007/12/23/business/23wealth.html?pagewanted=all&_r=0.

60 *Business Roundtable Statement*: Andrew C. Sigler, "Business Forum; Reader Comment; Roundtable Reply," *New York Times*, December 27, 1981, http://www.nytimes .com/1981/12/27/business/business-forum-reader-comment-roundtable-reply.html.

60 *the well-being of society depends upon profitable*: Jia Lynn Yang, "Maximizing Shareholder Value: The Goal That Changed Corporate America," *Washington Post*, August 26, 2013, https://www.washingtonpost.com/business/economy/maximizing -shareholder-value-the-goal-that-changed-corporate-america/2013/08/26/26e9ca8e -ed74-11e2-9008-61e94a7ea20d_story.html.

60 *as familiar around [Washington] as the Marine Band*: Jerry Useem, "Tyrants, Statesmen, and Destroyers (A Brief History of the CEO): Today's Disgraced Chieftains Are the Product of 100 Years of Evolution," *Fortune*, November 18, 2002, http://archive .fortune.com/magazines/fortune/fortune_archive/2002/11/18/332249/index.htm.

61 *Friedman wrote*: Milton Friedman, "The Social Responsibility of Business Is to Increase Its Profits," *New York Times Magazine*, September 13, 1970, http://query.nytimes.com/ mem/archive-free/pdf?res=9E05E0DA153CE531A15750C1A96F9C946190D6CF.

64 *meaningful penalties for poor performance*: Michael C. Jensen and Kevin J. Murphy, "CEO Incentives—It's Not How Much You Pay, But How," *Harvard Business Review* 68, no. 3 (May–June 1990), https://hbr.org/1990/05/ceo-incentives-its-not-how-much -you-pay-but-how.

65 *compensation was twenty times more sensitive*: Michael C. Jensen, "Eclipse of the Public Corporation," *Harvard Business Review*, September–October 1989, https:// hbr.org/1989/09/eclipse-of-the-public-corporation.

65 *hostile takeovers*: Michael C. Jensen, "Takeovers: Folklore and Science," *Harvard Business Review*, November–December 1984, https://hbr.org/1984/11/takeovers-folk lore-and-science.

66 *public confidence in big business*: "Confidence in Institutions," Gallup, June 2–7, 2015, http://www.gallup.com/poll/1597/confidence-institutions.aspx.

68 *General market conditions account*: Lucian Bebchuk and Jesse Fried, *Pay Without Performance: The Unfulfilled Promise of Executive Compensation* (Cambridge, MA: Harvard University Press, 2006).

69 *the primary way to reward executives*: Joe Nocera, "What If C.E.O. Pay Is Fair?," *New York Times*, October 13, 2007, http://www.nytimes.com/2007/10/13/business/13nocera .html?pagewanted=all.

69 *she stood to collect $214 million*: Steven Davidoff, "Yahoo Chief's Pay Tied to Another Company's Performance," *New York Times*, April 29, 2014, http://dealbook.nytimes .com/2014/04/29/yahoo-chiefs-pay-tied-to-another-companys-performance/.

70 *largest part of CEO compensation*: Andrew Ross Sorkin, "More Transparency, More Pay for C.E.O.s," *New York Times*, November 10, 2014, http://dealbook.nytimes.com /2014/11/10/more-transparency-more-pay-for-c-e-o-s/.

70 *they represented just 31 percent*: Emily Chasan, "Last Gasp for Stock Options?," *Wall Street Journal*, August 26, 2013, http://blogs.wsj.com/cfo/2013/08/26/last-gasp-for -stock-options/.

71 *why pay consultants*: Ibid.

72 *high level of their CEO pay*: Michael W. Faulkender and Jun Yang, "Inside the Black Box: The Role and Composition of Compensation Peer Groups," *Journal of Financial Economics* 96, no. 2 (May 2010), http://www.sciencedirect.com/science/journal/0304405X/96/2.

72 *structural bias*: "Compensation Peer Groups at Companies with High Pay," IRRC Institute, June 2010, http://www.irrcinstitute.org/pdf/Final-Compensation-Peer-Groups-at-Companies-with-High-Pay_June2010.pdf.

72 *highly paid peers are selected*: Ibid.

73 *broad market index such as the S&P 500*: Weighted for market capitalization.

74 *50th, 75th, or 90th percentile*: At the 50th percentile benchmark, the compensation is higher than half the peer group CEOs and lower than half. At the 75th percentile, the compensation is higher than three-quarters of the CEOs in the peer group.

74 *below the 50th percentile almost never occur*: One study concluded that the "vast majority of firms that use peer groups target pay at or above the 50th percentile of the peer group." Others found that 35 percent of surveyed firms aimed to pay at the 75th percentile, and 65 percent aimed at the 50th percentile; between 46 percent and 66 percent of firms in the S&P 100 targeted their CEO compensation at above the median of the peer group. Thomas A. DiPrete, Gregory M. Eirich, and Matthew Pittinsky, "Compensation Benchmarking, Leapfrogs, and the Surge in Executive Pay," *American Journal of Sociology* 115, no. 6 (May 2010), http://www.jstor.org/stable/10.1086/652297.

75 *Pay consultants were part of the team*: Richard E. Wood, "Compensation Committee Structure, Function and Best Practices," Kirkpatrick & Lockhart Nicholson Graham LLP, June 2004, http://www.klgates.com/files/Publication/f44a6446-4d3a-4847-a157-319c05d9667b/Presentation/PublicationAttachment/3900b2fd-2183-44e8-82d7-41bd4366f0f6/CompensationCommitteeStructure.pdf.

75 *Warren Buffett's opinion*: Josh Harkinson, "The Nation's 10 Most Overpaid CEOs," *Mother Jones*, July 12, 2012, http://www.motherjones.com/politics/2012/07/executive-pay-america-top-10-overpaid-ceo.

75 *Buffett's partner, Charles Munger*: Jason Zweig, "What Warren Buffett Wants You to Know," CNNMoney.com, May 3, 2004, http://money.cnn.com/2004/05/03/pf/buffett_qanda/index.htm.

76 *higher at companies that use compensation consultants*: Kevin J. Murphy and Tatiana Sandino, "Executive Pay and 'Independent' Compensation Consultants," *Journal of Accounting and Economics* 49, no. 3 (April 2010), http://www.sciencedirect.com/science/article/pii/S0165410109000809. Also Brian Cadman, Mary Ellen Carter, and Stephen Hillegeist, "The Incentives of Compensation Consultants and CEO Pay," *Journal of Accounting and Economics* 49, no. 3 (April 2010), http://www.sciencedirect.com/science/article/pii/S0165410109000147.

76 *compensation consultants are hired to justify higher CEO*: Ibid.

76 *likely the consultants will be rehired*: Jenny Chu, Jonathan Faasse, and P. Raghavendra Rau, "Do Compensation Consultants Enable Higher CEO Pay? New Evidence from Recent Disclosure Rule Changes," September 23, 2014, http://papers.ssrn.com/sol3/papers.cfm?abstract_id=2500054.

76 *Six major consulting firms*: Warren Buffett, "Absurd CEO Salaries," YouTube video, 3:46, May 22, 2011, https://www.youtube.com/watch?v=14dBptlmquw.

76 *A cottage industry*: Sorkin, "More Transparency."

76 *Companies that switched*: Ibid.

77 *larger and more lucrative part*: Chu, Faasse, and Rau, "Compensation Consultants."

77 *half of large companies used a compensation consultant*: United States House of Representatives, Committee on Oversight and Government Reform, Majority Staff, "Executive Pay: Conflicts of Interest Among Compensation Consultants," December 2007, http://www.erieri.com/PDF/Executive-Consultant-Conflicts.pdf.

77 *11 times greater*: Ibid.

77 *CEO's pay was substantially higher*: Ibid.

77 *A recent SEC rule*: Securities and Exchange Commission, "SEC Adopts Rule Requiring Listing Standards for Compensation Committees and Compensation Advisers," news release 2012-115, June 20, 2012, http://www.sec.gov/news/press/2012/2012-115.htm:

> The new rule, required by the Dodd-Frank Wall Street Reform and Consumer Protection Act, requires exchange listing standards to address:
> The independence of the members on a compensation committee
> The committee's authority to retain compensation advisers
> The committee's consideration of the independence of any compensation advisers and
> The committee's responsibility for the appointment, compensation, and oversight of the work of any compensation adviser.
> "Once an exchange's new listing standards are in effect, a listed company must meet the standards in order for its shares to continue trading on that exchange.
> "This rule will help to enhance the board's decision-making process on executive compensation matters, particularly the selection, engagement and oversight of compensation advisers, and will provide more transparency with respect to conflicts of interest of consultants engaged by boards," said SEC Chairman Mary L. Schapiro.
> The SEC also amended its proxy disclosure rules to require new disclosures from companies about their use of compensation consultants and conflicts of interest.

78 *compensation consultants had conflicts of interest*: Marc S. Gerber, Richard J. Grossman, Neil M. Leff, Regina Olshan, Erica Schohn, Joseph M. Yaffe, "SEC Approves NYSE and Nasdaq Compensation Committee Rules," Skadden, Arps, Slate, Meagher & Flom LLP, January 24, 2013, https://www.skadden.com/insights/sec-approves-nyse-and-nasdaq-compensation-committee-rules.

79 *Clinton proposed eliminating tax deductions*: Kevin J. Murphy, "Executive Compensation and the Modern Industrial Revolution" (based on a speech presented at the Workshop on Managerial Compensation, Strategy, and Firm Performance at Humboldt-University at Berlin), is largely excerpted from "Politics, Economics, and Executive Compensation," *University of Cincinnatti Law Review*, October 1995, unpublished manuscript, on file with the *University of Cincinnatti Law Review*, http://stockoptions.org.il/Admin/App_Upload/Executive percent20Compensation percent 20and percent20the percent20Modern percent20Industrial percent20Revolution.pdf.

79 *Business was still unhappy*: David E. Rosenbaum, "Business Leaders Urged by Clinton to Back Tax Plan," *New York Times*, February 12, 1993, http://www.nytimes.com/1993/02/12/us/business-leaders-urged-by-clinton-to-back-tax-plan.html.

79 *exempt stock options from this cap*: The Editors, "The Effects of Capping Pay," The Opinion Pages, *New York Times*, February 4, 2009, http://roomfordebate.blogs.nytimes.com/2009/02/04/the-effects-of-capping-pay/?gwh=C264E35E3EE3B091AC1F642E7D42DEFC&gwt=pay.

80 *a tie vote*: David E. Rosenbaum, "The Budget Struggle: House Passes Budget Plan, Backing Clinton by 218–216 After Hectic Maneuvering," *New York Times*, August 6, 1993, http://www.nytimes.com/1993/08/06/us/budget-struggle-house-passes-budget-plan-backing-clinton-218-216-after-hectic.html?pagewanted=all.

80 *Al Gore cast the tie-breaking vote*: David E. Rosenbaum, "The Budget Struggle: Clinton Wins Approval of His Budget Plan as Gore Votes to Break Senate Deadlock," *New York Times*, August 7, 1993, http://www.nytimes.com/1993/08/07/us/budget-struggle-clinton-wins-approval-his-budget-plan-gore-votes-break-senate.html?pagewanted=all.

80 *Pay consultants correctly predicted*: Kathryn Jones, "Tax Law Expected to Bring Little Shift in Executive Pay," *New York Times*, August 24, 1993, http://www.nytimes.com/1993/08/24/business/tax-law-expected-to-bring-little-shift-in-executive-pay.html?pagewanted=all.

81 *The immediate consequence of this legislation*: Nancy L. Rose and Catherine Wolfram, "Regulating Executive Pay: Using the Tax Code to Influence CEO Compensation," NBER Working Paper No. 7842, August 2000, http://www.nber.org/papers/w7842.

82 *more remunerative than discretionary bonuses*: Kevin J. Murphy and Paul Oyer, "Discretion in Executive Incentive Contracts," working paper, June 2003, https://faculty-gsb.stanford.edu/oyer/wp/disc.pdf.

82 *The explosion in stock options*: Kevin J. Murphy, "The Politics of Pay: A Legislative History of Executive Compensation," USC, Marshall School of Business Working Paper No. FBE 01.11, August 24, 2011, http://papers.ssrn.com/sol3/papers.cfm?abstract_id=1916358.

83 *market forces, not the SEC, should control CEO pay*: The SEC then mandated, first, that corporations make detailed disclosures about executive compensation, and second, that shareholders be permitted to offer their own opinions to the board regarding executive compensation. They also required disclosures of the number of options granted to the CEO but not the value of the options.

84 *grant them substantial raises*: Piketty, *Capital in the Twenty-First Century*.

CHAPTER SIX

87 *bonuses ranged between 15 percent*: Carola Frydman and Raven E. Saks, "Executive Compensation: A New View from a Long-Term Perspective, 1936–2005," NBER Working Paper No. 14145, June 2008, http://www.nber.org/papers/w14145.

87 *54 percent of compensation*: Tim Mullaney, "Why Corporate CEO Pay Is So High, and Going Higher," CNBC.com, May 18, 2015, http://www.cnbc.com/2015/05/18/why-corporate-ceo-pay-is-so-high-and-going-higher.html.

91 *my target performance for next year*: Kevin J. Murphy and Michael C. Jensen, "CEO Bonus Plans: And How to Fix Them," Harvard Business School NOM Unit, working paper 12-022, November 19, 2011, http://papers.ssrn.com/sol3/papers.cfm?abstract_id=1935654.

92 *big bonus for being a television studio CEO*: David Gelles, "For the Highest-Paid C.E.O.s the Party Goes On," *New York Times*, May 16, 2015, http://www.nytimes.com/2015/05/17/business/for-the-highest-paid-ceos-the-party-goes-on.html.

94 *100 percent decline in EPS*: Graef Crystal, "Countrywide's 'Mozilo Math' Simply Defies Logic," *Bloomberg*, June 14, 2005.

94   *only 4 percent of shareholders voted for it*: Linda A. Johnson, "Pfizer Shareholders Reject Activist's Proposed Ban on Exec Stock Options, Back Advisory Vote," Associated Press, April 22, 2010.

95   *the directors awarded him a $528,000 bonus*: Zachary R. Mider and Jeff Green, "Heads or Tails, Some CEOs Win the Pay Game," *BloombergBusiness*, October 4, 2012, http://www.bloomberg.com/bw/articles/2012-10-04/heads-or-tails-some-ceos-win-the-pay-game.

95   *In 2011, Mylan's board decided*: Ibid.

95   *Nationwide Mutual Insurance doubled*: Ibid.

96   *Walmart also adjusted for the costs*: Walmart 2014 proxy statement, https://www.sec.gov/Archives/edgar/data/104169/000130817914000196/lwmt2014_def14a.htm.

96   *deviate from the benchmarks*: "Compensation Peer Groups at Companies with High Pay," IRRC Institute, June 2010, http://www.irrcinstitute.org/pdf/Final-Compensation-Peer-Groups-at-Companies-with-High-Pay_June2010.pdf.

98   *average 2012 perks package was worth $320,635*: Nelson D. Schwartz, "The Infinity Pool of Executive Pay," *New York Times*, April 6, 2013, http://www.nytimes.com/2013/04/07/business/executive-pay-shows-modest-2012-gain-but-oh-those-perks.html?pagewanted=all.

99   *Steve Wynn*: Ibid.

99   *Only Ron Johnson*: Elliot Blair Smith and Phil Kuntz, "CEO Pay 1,795-to-1 Multiple of Wages Skirts U.S. Law," *BloombergBusiness*, April 30, 2013, http://www.bloomberg.com/news/articles/2013-04-30/ceo-pay-1-795-to-1-multiple-of-workers-skirts-law-as-sec-delays.

99   *Qwest also purchased a California home*: Kathy Kristof, "8 Outrageous Executive Perks," Kiplinger, April 5, 2011, http://finance.yahoo.com/news/pf_article_112473.html.

100   *kept the $4 million*: Sean Gregory, "Abercrombie's CEO Grounded—for $4 Million," *Time*, April 15, 2010, http://content.time.com/time/business/article/0,8599,1982247,00.html.

102   *CEOs were happy to be bought out*: Lucian A. Bebchuk, Alma Cohen, and Charles C. Y. Wang, "Golden Parachutes and the Wealth of Shareholders," Harvard Law School, Discussion Paper No. 683, December 2010, Revised October 2012, http://papers.ssrn.com/sol3/papers.cfm?abstract_id=1718488.

CHAPTER SEVEN

104   *one-third of 1 percent, were not approved*: James B. Stewart, "Bad Directors and Why They Aren't Thrown Out," *New York Times*, March 29, 2013, http://www.nytimes.com/2013/03/30/business/why-bad-directors-arent-thrown-out.html?pagewanted=all.

104   *but remained on the board*: James B. Stewart, "When Shareholder Democracy Is Sham Democracy," *New York Times*, April 12, 2013, http://www.nytimes.com/2013/04/13/business/sham-shareholder-democracy.html?pagewanted=all.

104   *Corporate boards typically consist*: Holly J. Gregory, "Trends in Director Elections: Key Results from the 2012 Proxy Season," *Practical Law The Journal* (September 2012), http://www.weil.com/files/upload/September2012_Opinion.pdf.

106   *two-thirds of the new appointments*: Bonnie W. Gwin and Lee Hanson, "Five Trends in Board Refreshment," Heidrick & Struggles, September 22, 2015, http://www.heidrick.com/Knowledge-Center/Publication/Five-trends-in-board-refreshment.

106 *women accounted for*: "Women in S&P 500 Companies," Catalyst.org, http://www .catalyst.org/knowledge/women-sp-500-companies.

106 *minorities about 13 percent*: "Missing Pieces: Women and Minorities on Fortune 500 Boards: 2012 Alliance for Board Diversity (ABD) Census," August 15, 2013, http:// www.catalyst.org/system/files/2012_abd_missing_pieces_final_8_15_13.pdf.

106 *reappointment rate for directors*: According to a corporate library's study, the average board size is 9.2 members. Therefore, 291 replacements in 500 companies yield a replacement rate of 6.3 percent. Gregory, "Trends in Director Elections."

107 *director compensation for public companies*: Sacha Pfeiffer and Todd Wallack, "Few Hours, Soaring Pay for Corporate Board Members," *Boston Globe*, December 2, 2015, https://www.bostonglobe.com/business/2015/12/01/good-work-you-can-get -corporate-directors-among-highest-paid-part-time-employees-america/rYHP P7ozPXU0AG8VSo37MM/story.html.

107 *among Boston-area directors*: Ibid.

108 *make unanimous decisions*: William S. Neilson and Harold Winter, "The Elimination of Hung Juries: Retrials and Nonunanimous Verdicts," *International Review of Law and Economics* 25, no. 1 (March 2005), http://www.sciencedirect.com/science/article /pii/S0144818805000219.

109 *CEO is also chairman*: Paul Hodgson, "Should the Chairman Be the CEO?," *Fortune*, October 21, 2014, http://fortune.com/2014/10/21/chairman-ceo/.

110 *compensation plans with which he disagreed*: Joe Nocera, "Buffett Punts on Pay," The Opinion Pages, *New York Times*, April 25, 2014, http://www.nytimes.com/2014 /04/26/opinion/nocera-buffett-punts-on-pay.html.

112 *they cannot be personally liable*: Board decisions on the size and structure of executive compensation deserve "great deference by the courts." *Brehm v. Eisner*, Delaware Supreme Court, 746 A.2d 244, 262-263 (2000).

113 *$130 million severance payment*: In re: Walt Disney Co. Derivative Litigation, Del., No. 411, 2005, June 6, 2006, http://caselaw.findlaw.com/de-supreme-court/1268891.html.

114 *140 other graduate degrees*: Menachem Wecker, "Where the Fortune 500 CEOs Went to School," *U.S. News & World Report*, May 14, 2012, http://www.usnews.com /education/best-graduate-schools/top-business-schools/articles/2012/05/14 /where-the-fortune-500-ceos-went-to-school.

114 *Half said they were Republican*: Brandon Gaille, "47 Interesting Fortune 500 CEO Demographics," November 21, 2014, http://brandongaille.com/47-bizarre-fortune -500-ceo-demographics/.

114 *being a Democrat*: Ibid.

114 *served in the military*: Ibid.

115 *taller than average*: Ibid.

115 *better looking than average*: Laura Brinn, "CEOs Who Look the Part Earn More," *Duke Today*, April 26, 2010, https://today.duke.edu/2010/04/CEObeauty.html.

115 *They work out*: Leslie Kwoh, "Want to Be CEO? What's Your BMI?," *Wall Street Journal*, January 16, 2013, http://www.wsj.com/articles/SB100014241278873245957045 78241573341483946.

115 *Half were promoted from chief operating officer*: Jeffrey S. Sanders, "The Path to Becoming a Fortune 500 CEO," *Forbes*, December 5, 2011, http://www.forbes.com/ sites/ciocentral/2011/12/05/the-path-to-becoming-a-fortune-500 -ceo/#1fe7872828c9.

116 *how you would cook on a wood-burning stove*: Harold Geneen, *Managing* (New York: Doubleday, 1984).

117 *The average Fortune 500 CEO spends*: Judith Aquino, "33 percent of CEOs Majored in Engineering—And Other Surprising Facts About Your Boss," *Business Insider*, March 23, 2011, http://www.businessinsider.com/ceos-majored-in-engineering-2011-3.

CHAPTER EIGHT

118 *Stephen J. Hemsley of UnitedHealth Group*: "America's Highest Paid Chief Executives," *Forbes*, http://www.forbes.com/lists/2011/12/ceo-compensation-11_Stephen-J-Hemsley_NBHE.html.

118 *John Hammergren of McKesson*: Alain Sherter, "Highest-Paid CEOs: Top Earner Takes Home $145 Million," CBS MoneyWatch, December 15, 2011, http://www.cbsnews.com/8301-505123_162-57343611/highest-paid-ceos-top-earner-takes-home-$145-million/.

120 *Charif Souki of Cheniere Energy*: 2014 Equilar Top 200 Highest Paid CEO Rankings Summary, Equilar, http://www.equilar.com/nytimes.

120 *David Zaslav of Discovery Communications*: Equilar 200 Highest-Paid CEO Rankings, http://www.equilar.com/publications/51-200-highest-paid-CEO-rankings-2015.html.

121 *It provides health care access*: The SEC requires that public companies send their shareholders a proxy statement prior to a shareholder meeting. In the proxy, the company is obliged to make extensive disclosures, including a detailed discussion of compensation objectives and policies. In this chapter, when I refer to statements or claims or assertions of UnitedHealth Group, McKesson, Cheniere, and Discovery and do not cite a source, the information was disclosed in the company proxy.

121 *It is either the largest*: Peter Dreier, "Meet UnitedHealth CEO Stephen Hemsley: Rich, Powerful, Not Yet Famous," *Huffington Post*, March 18, 2010, http://www.huffingtonpost.com/peter-dreier/meet-unitedhealth-ceo-ste_b_310674.html.

122 *The Wall Street Journal estimated*: Charles Forelle and James Bandler, "The Perfect Payday," *Wall Street Journal*, March 18, 2006, http://www.wsj.com/articles/SB114265075068802118.

122 *When the scandal broke*: Dreier, "Meet UnitedHealth CEO."

122 *this is less than one-quarter*: Securities and Exchange Commission, "Former UnitedHealth Group CEO/Chairman Settles Stock Options Backdating Case for $468 Million," news release 2007-255, December 6, 2007, https://www.sec.gov/news/press/2007/2007-255.htm.

122 *The SEC investigations forced*: Dreier, "Meet UnitedHealth CEO."

122 *unaware of how the grant dates were selected*: Eric Dash, "Old Options Still Haunt an Insurer," *New York Times*, October 17, 2006, http://www.nytimes.com/2006/10/17/business/17options.html?pagewanted=all&_r=0.

122 *approved backdated mass grants*: David Phelps, "Suit: Hemsley Had Bigger Role in UNH Backdating," *Star Tribune*, May 23, 2008, http://www.startribune.com/suit-hemsley-had-bigger-role-in-unh-backdating/19196249/.

123 *Hemsley hired William Spears*: Dash, "Old Options."

123 *he managed $55 million*: Eric Dash and Milt Freudenheim, "Chief Executive at Health Insurer Is Forced Out in Options Inquiry," *New York Times*, October 16, 2006, http://www.nytimes.com/2006/10/16/business/16united.html?pagewanted=print&_r=0.

124 *Hammergren, described as "squeaky clean"*: Gary Rivlin, "He's One of the Nation's Highest-Paid CEOs—and You've Never Heard of Him," *Daily Beast*, January 2, 2012,

http:// www.thedailybeast.com/articles/2012/01/02/he-s-one-of-the-nation
-s-highest-paid-ceos-and-you-ve-never-heard-of-him.html.

124 *Hammergren has done a topnotch*: Ibid.

125 *McKesson denied any wrongdoing*: Timothy W. Martin, "McKesson to Pay $151 Million to Settle Drug-Pricing Suit," *The Wall Street Journal*, July 27, 2012.

127 *former board member explained*: Gregory Zuckerman, "The Export King: Meet America's Unlikeliest Gas Mogul," *Foreign Affairs*, November 8, 2013, https://www.foreignaffairs.com/articles/united-states/2013-11-08/export-king.

127 *Raising money was Souki's forte*: The preceding five paragraphs of information on Souki are from Zuckerman, "The Export King."

127 *By 2014, Souki believed*: Karma Allen, "Oil has Bottomed, Worst Behind Us Now: Cheniere's Souki," CNBC, April 22, 2015, http://www.cnbc.com/2015/04/22/oil-has-bottomed-worst-behind-us-now-chenieres-souki.html.

127 *take advantage of them*: Bill Loveless, "Oil Prices Challenge Cheniere's LNG Export Plan," *USA Today*, April 19, 2015, http://www.usatoday.com/story/money/business/2015/04/19/loveless-cheniere-souki/25980327/.

127 *cumulative losses of over $3 billion*: Matthew Philips, "How One Energy CEO Came Undone Twice in the Shale Boom," *BloombergBusiness*, December 15, 2015, http://www.bloomberg.com/news/articles/2015-12-15/how-cheniere-energy-s-ceo-came-undone-twice-in-the-shale-boom.

127 *with a salary of about $300,000*: Daniel Gilbert, "Cheniere CEO Collects $142 Million Pay," *Wall Street Journal*, April 29, 2014, http://www.wsj.com/articles/SB10001424052702304163604579532160970399266.

128 *$8.6 billion*: Corinne Jurney, "Lions Gate-Starz: John Malone Is on a Roll," *Forbes*, June 4, 2015, http://www.forbes.com/sites/corinnejurney/2015/06/04/lions-gate-starz-john-malone-is-on-a-roll/#15dc395ceb89.

128 *most of its executive staff*: Jack Dickey, "David Zaslav: The Cable Boss," *Time*, April 2, 2015, http://time.com/3768613/david-zaslav-the-cable-boss/.

128 *relaunched Animal Planet*: Ibid.

129 *highest-paid opera singers*: Luiz Gazzola, "Opera Singers' Income," *Operalively*, September 2, 2012, http://operalively.com/forums/showthread.php/1190-Opera-singers-income.

130 *Alton Irby, the chair of McKesson's comp committee*: Rivlin, "Highest-Paid CEOs."

132 *inflated Hammergren's payday*: "Special Report: CEO Compensation," *Forbes*, April 28, 2010, http://www.forbes.com/lists/2010/12/boss-10_CEO-Compensation_Rank.html.

141 *The board had adjusted them upward*: Adjustments in Discovery's Net Revenue, Adjusted Free Cash Flow, and Further Adjusted OIBDA:

	ADJUSTED ($BILLION)	UNADJUSTED ($BILLION)	% INCREASE
Net revenue	6.449	6.265	2.9%
Adjusted free cash flow	1.389	1.198	15.9%
Further adjusted OIBDA	2.616	2.491	5.0%

151 *less than one-quarter of the sum he would actually have collected*: Mark Maremont, "For McKesson's CEO, a Pension of $159 Million," *Wall Street Journal*, June 24, 2013, http://online.wsj.com/article/SB10001424127887323998604578565491579124154.html.

CHAPTER NINE

155 *80 percent of total realized compensation*: William Lazonick, "Taking Stock: Why Executive Pay Results in an Unstable and Inequitable Economy," Roosevelt Institute, June 5, 2014, http://www.rooseveltinstitute.net/taking-stock-executive-pay.

158 *Black-Scholes*: Named after Myron Scholes, whose economic genius both won a Nobel Prize in 1996 and helped bankrupt Long-Term Capital Management, where he was a partner, in 1997.

158 *exercising stock options*: Technically, UnitedHealth Group granted stock appreciation rights (SARs) instead of options.

163 *his gains at $68 million*: David Zaslav Gain on 2014 Exercise of Options and Vesting of Restricted Stock

DAVID ZASLAV GAIN ON 2014 EXERCISE OF OPTIONS AND VESTING OF RESTRICTED STOCK

PLAN	DATE GRANTED	TOTAL UNITS GRANTED	TOTAL BASIS OF GRANT	2014 UNITS REDEEMED	% OF TOTAL	BASIS OF REDEMPTION	PAYOUT	GAIN
DAP	1/2/2010	1,861,473	15,412,996	465,369	25%	3,853,255	25,516,182	21,662,927
DAP	1/2/2011	2,326,841	23,873,389	581,710	25%	5,968,345	26,380,549	20,412,204
CS-SAR	1/2/2012	1,718,353	15,843,215	429,588	25%	3,960,801	19,425,969	15,465,168
CS-SAR	1/2/2013	1,848,961	22,538,835	462,240	25%	5,634,706	9,878,069	4,243,363
PRSU	3/16/2011	314,258	20,301,093	314,258	100%	20,301,093	26,023,705	5,722,612
Total							107,224,474	67,506,274

163 *more than $40 million*: Gelles, "For the Highest-Paid C.E.O.s the Party Goes On."

163 *need to be paid competitively*: Ibid.

163 *Malone is an exponent*: Ibid.

CHAPTER TEN

165 *Mr. Hemsley made $48.8 million the subsequent year*: Forbes.com, Lists: "CEO Compensation," http://www.forbes.com/lists/2012/12/ceo-compensation-12_Stephen-J-Hemsley_NBHE.html.

165 *shareholders to offer two resolutions*: Shirley Westcott, "2012 Proxy Season Review: Shareholder Resolutions," *Advisor*, September 2012, http://allianceadvisorsllc.com/wp-content/uploads/2012/09/Alliance-Advisors-Newsletter-Sept.-2012-2012-Proxy-Season-Review-Shareholder-Resolutions.pdf.

165 *persistent compensation issues*: George Stahl, "Proxy Firm Urges Vote Against 4 McKesson Directors," *Wall Street Journal*, July 14, 2013, http://www.wsj.com/articles/SB10001424127887323394504578606330928211950.

166 *voting against it in a nonbinding vote*: "McKesson Shareholders Reject CEO Pay," *Teamster Nation* (blog), August 2, 2013, http://teamsternation.blogspot.com/2013/08/McKesson-shareholders-reject-CEO-pay.html.

166 *also approved an advisory measure to recapture*: Russ Britt, "McKesson Shareholders Approve 'Clawback' on Executive Pay," *MarketWatch*, July 31, 2013, http://blogs.marketwatch.com/health-exchange/2013/07/31/mckesson-shareholders-approve-clawback-on-executive-pay/.

166 *richest pensions in corporate history*: Everdeen Mason and Michael Rapoport, "McKesson Changes Executive Compensation Program," *Wall Street Journal*, February 28, 2014, http://www.wsj.com/articles/SB10001424052702303801304579410802217819202.

166 *$131 million compensation package*: http://www.forbes.com/pictures/mef45eghm/john-hammergren/.

166 *the suit demanded that $1.6 billion*: Olivia Pulsinelli, "Shareholders Challenge Cheniere Stock Awards," *Houston Business Journal*, June 4, 2014, http://www.bizjournals.com/houston/news/2014/06/04/shareholders-challenge-cheniere-stock-awards.html?.

166 *Souki reduced his yearly salary*: Olivia Pulsinelli, "Highest-Paid CEO to Receive $1 Salary," *Houston Business Journal*, December 24, 2014, http://www.bizjournals.com/houston/morning_call/2014/12/highest-paid-ceo-to-receive-1-salary.html.

166 *rejected Discovery's pay practices*: Gretchen Morgenson, "Shareholders' Votes Have Done Little to Curb Lavish Executive Pay," *New York Times*, May 16, 2015, http://www.nytimes.com/2015/05/17/business/shareholders-votes-have-done-little-to-curb-lavish-executive-pay.html.

167 *controlled by a single shareholder or family*: Paul Hodgson, "When Will Bad Governance Affect Value at Liberty Media, Liberty Global, Virgin Media and Charter Communications?," *Forbes*, April 17, 2013, http://www.forbes.com/sites/paulhodgson/2013/04/17/when-will-bad-governance-affect-value-at-liberty-media-liberty-global-virgin-media-and-charter-communications/.

167 *the company and board refused to comment*: Ibid.

168 *Mr. Hemsley's total compensation is below*: UnitedHealth Group reported Hemsley's compensation at $9 million. See pages 158–159.

169 *$49 million the following year*: Forbes.com, Lists: "CEO Compensation."

169 *CEO made $145 million*: McKesson reported Hammergren's compensation at $46 million. See page 160 for an explanation of the difference between these two numbers.

173 *no women directors*: Caroline Fairchild, "The 23 Fortune 500 Companies with All-Male Boards," *Fortune*, January 16, 2015, http://fortune.com/2015/01/16/fortune-500-companies-with-all-male-boards/.

173 *supported by 23 percent of the shareholder vote*: "Board Diversity Coalition Continues to Push for Progress," Mercy Investment Services, August 8, 2015, http://www.mercyinvestmentservices.org/community-investing-news/responsible-governance-practices/term/summary.

CHAPTER ELEVEN

176 *"about right"*: Mary Thompson, "CEO Pay Just Right, Most Directors Say in Survey," CNBC.com, February 6, 2008, http://www.cnbc.com/id/23030424.

179 *more than they paid their shareholders in dividends*: McKesson's fiscal year begins on April 1 and ends on March 31. In their fiscal year ending March 31, 2010, McKesson paid dividends of $131 million, and the next fiscal year, Makesson paid Hammergren $145 million.

183 *underperformed the S&P 500*: Phil Rosenzweig, *The Halo Effect* (New York: Free Press, 2007).

183 *42 percent of the CEOs of the Fortune 100 had MBAs*: "Fortune 500 CEOs: Where Did They Go to B-school?" CNNMoney.com

184 *the average tenure of a Fortune 500 CEO*: Weidner, "Why Your CEO Could Be in Trouble."

184 *Page has a net worth*: Kerry A. Dolan and Luisa Kroll, "The Richest People in Tech," *Forbes*, August 5, 2015, http://www.forbes.com/richest-in-tech/.

184 *$96.2 million in 2012*: Jim Finkle, "Larry Ellison, Oracle CEO, Gets $21 Million Pay Raise Despite Company's Stock Decline," *Huffington Post*, September 21, 2012, http

://www.huffingtonpost.com/2012/09/22/larry-ellison-oracle-ceo-pay-raise_n
_1905193.html.

184 *gave up the CEO position*: Julie Bort, "Former Oracle CEO Larry Ellison Took Pay
Cut . . . to $67 Million," *BusinessInsider*, September 24, 2014, http://www.businessin
sider.com/larry-ellison-took-a-pay-cut-to-67m-2014-9.

184 *Jack [Welch] did a good job*: Jeffrey Pfeffer and Robert I. Sutton, *Hard Facts, Danger-
ous Half-Truths and Total Nonsense: Profiting from Evidence-Based Management*
(Cambridge, MA: Harvard Business Review Press, 2006).

185 *A German shepherd could have run GE*: Steve Clemons, "Financial Times: The Worst
of Times?," *Washington Note* (blog), February 18, 2009, http://washingtonnote.com/
the_best_of_tim/.

185 *the wind was on our backs*: Harris Collingwood, "Do CEOs Matter?," *The Atlantic*,
June 1, 2009, http://www.theatlantic.com/magazine/archive/2009/06/do-ceos-matter
/307437/.

185 *difficult to read in the dark*: Ibid.

187 *most of these stories end*: James Surowiecki, "The Comeback Conundrum," *The New
Yorker*, September 21, 2015, http://www.newyorker.com/magazine/2015/09/21/the
-comeback-conundrum.

188 *low of 3.9 percent*: Alan Berkeley Thomas, "Does Leadership Make a Difference to Organizational Performance?," *Administrative Science Quarterly* 33, no. 3 (September
1988), http://www.wiggo.com/mgmt8510/readings/readings11/thomas1988asq.pdf.

188 *high of 14.7 percent*: Noam Wasserman, Bharat Anand, and Nitin Nohria, "When
Does Leadership Matter? A Contingent Opportunities View of CEO Leadership," in
Handbook of Leadership Theory and Practice, ed. Nitin Nohria and Rakesh Khurana
(Cambridge, MA: Harvard Business Press, 2010), http://www.hbs.edu/faculty/Pages/
item.aspx?num=37549.

CHAPTER TWELVE

190 *highest-paid baseball players*: Thomas Barrabi, "Clayton Kershaw Tops List of MLB's
Highest-Paid Players in 2016," Fox Business, March 29, 2016. http://www.foxbusi
ness.com/features/2016/03/29/clayton-kershaw-tops-list-mlbs-highest-paid
-players-in-2016.html

191 *only six CEO jumps in six years*: C. Edward Fee and Charles J. Hadlock, "Raids, Rewards, and Reputations in the Market for Managerial Talent," *Review of Financial
Studies* 16, no. 4 (Winter 2003), http://rfs.oxfordjournals.org/content/16/4/1315.

191 *fewer than 2 percent had previously been CEOs*: Martijn Cremers and Yaniv Grin-
stein, "Does the Market for CEO Talent Explain Controversial CEO Pay Practices?,"
May 21, 2013, *Review of Finance*, http://papers.ssrn.com/sol3/papers.cfm?abstract
_id=1108761.

191 *NFL free agents switched teams*: "Every NFL Free Agent Signing This Offseason," *SB
Nation NFL News*, June 22, 2015, http://www.sbnation.com/nfl/2015/3/10/8150357
/nfl-free-agent-signings-tracker-2015-rumors.

191 *chief executives couldn't easily move their skills*: Charles M. Elson and Craig K. Fer-
rere, "Executive Superstars, Peer Groups and Overcompensation: Cause, Effect and
Solution," draft, Alfred Lerner College of Business & Economics, John L. Weinberg
Center for Corporate Governance, University of Delaware, last revised October
2012, *Journal of Corporation Law* 38, no. 3, http://sites.udel.edu/wccg/files/2012/10
/Executive-Superstars-Peer-Groups-and-Over-Compensation-10-10.pdf.

191 *when they do, they're flops*: Gretchen Morgenson, "C.E.O.'s and the Pay-'Em-or-Lose -'Em Myth," *New York Times*, September 22, 2012, http://www.nytimes.com/2012/09 /23/business/ceos-and-the-pay-em-or-lose-em-myth-fair-game.html?pagewanted= all&_r=0.

194 *ten out of the eleven were groomed internally*: Jim Collins, *Good to Great: Why Some Companies Make the Leap . . . and Others Don't* (New York: HarperCollins, 2001).

194 *internal candidates are better than external ones*: Dale S. Rose, "Five Essential Questions for Getting CEO Succession Right (#2)," *Leadership Insight* (blog), February 16, 2012, http://leadershipinsightblog.com/2012/02/16/getting-ceo-succession-right-2/.

194 *internal promotions account for three-quarters*: Kevin J. Murphy and Ján Zábojník, "Managerial Capital and the Market for CEOs," working paper, April 2007, http: //papers.ssrn.com/sol3/papers.cfm?abstract_id=984376.

194 *thirteen years at the company before becoming CEOs*: "CEO Statistics," Statisticbrain .com, http://www.statisticbrain.com/ceo-statistics/.

194 *twice as likely to be fired*: William G. Hardin III and Gregory Leo Nagel, "The Transferability of CEO Skills," working paper, October 2007, http://papers.ssrn.com/sol3 /papers.cfm?abstract_id=1019413.

194 *the cost of hiring an external candidate*: James S. Ang and Gregory Leo Nagel, "The Financial Outcome of Hiring a CEO from Outside the Firm," working paper, March 14, 2011, http://papers.ssrn.com/sol3/papers.cfm?abstract_id=1657027.

194 *internally promoted CEOs perform better*: Gretchen Morgenson, "Directors Disappoint by What They Don't Do," *New York Times*, May 11, 2013, http://www.nytimes .com/2013/05/12/business/board-directors-disappoint.html?pagewanted=all.

External CEO hires were paid on average $5.5 million more than their predecessors. Despite their bigger paychecks, they didn't take their skills with them. There was no significant correlation between their success at their prior company and their performance with their new employers. Studying 192 external successions from 1993 to 2005, Richard A. Cazier and John M. McInnis find a negative correlation between excess compensation and future performance; paradoxically, the superstars underperformed. Richard A. Cazier and John M. McInnis, "Do Firms Contract Efficiently on Past Performance When Hiring External CEO's?," working paper, December 30, 2010, http://papers.ssrn.com/sol3/papers.cfm?abstract_id=1732754.

Externally hired CEOs performed below internal hires in terms of net income as well as operating performance and investors' expectations for future performance. Hardin and Nagle, "Transferability of CEO Skills."

"Experienced" CEOs, those who were formerly chief executives, delivered lower returns to shareholders than average. Chuck Lucier, Steven Wheeler, and Rolf Habbel, "The Era of the Inclusive Leader," *Strategy+Business*, May 29, 2007, http://www .strategy-business.com/article/07205?pg=all.

Outside hires compared poorly to internal promotions in a large sample of all public company CEOs in the period from 1986 to 2005. External hires did worse 85 percent of the time. The authors wrote that "compared to outside hires, internally promoted CEOs are: 1) significantly less costly to employ, 2) less likely to leave the firm, 3) as likely to deliver top cumulative performance, and 4) have a lower probability of poor performance."

196 *S&P 500 was up 13.5 percent*: On March 31, 2010, McKesson stock closed at $65.72 and the S&P 500 at 1169.43. On March 31, 2011, closing prices were $79.05 and 1328.26, respectively.

CHAPTER THIRTEEN

198 *being open to ideas*: Ruth Sullivan, "Excessive Executive Pay 'Bad for Business,'" *Financial Times*, June 3, 2013, http://www.theglobeandmail.com/report-on-business/careers/excessive-executive-pay-bad-for-business/article12029730/.

199 *decrease motivation and performance*: Edward L. Deci, Richard Koestner, and Richard M. Ryan, "A Meta-analytic Review of Experiments Examining the Effects of Extrinsic Rewards on Intrinsic Motivation," *Psychological Bulletin* 125, no. 6 (November 1999), http://psycnet.apa.org/journals/bul/125/6/627.

199 at *least two dozen studies*: Alfie Kohn, "Why Incentive Plans Cannot Work," *Harvard Business Review*, September–October 1993, https://hbr.org/1993/09/why-incentive-plans-cannot-work.

199 *no evidence that higher pay*: J. Scott Armstrong and Philippe Jacquart, "Business School Experts: High CEO Pay Hurts American Companies, Stockholders," Fox News, April 15, 2014, http://www.foxnews.com/opinion/2014/04/15/business-school-experts-high-ceo-pay-hurts-american-companies/.

199 *can be counterproductive*: Emir Kamenica, "Behavioral Economics and Psychology of Incentives," *Annual Review of Economics* 4 (September 2012) http://www.annualreviews.org/doi/abs/10.1146/annurev-economics-080511-110909.

199 *the worse the performance*: Dan Ariely, Uri Gneezy, George Loewenstein, and Nina Mazar, "Large Stakes and Big Mistakes," *Review of Economic Studies* 76 (2009), http://people.duke.edu/~dandan/Papers/Upside/largeStakes.pdf.

199 *people perform at their best*: Tomas Chamorro-Premuzic, "Does Money Really Affect Motivation? A Review of the Research," *Harvard Business Review*, April 10, 2013, https://hbr.org/2013/04/does-money-really-affect-motiv.

200 *I have yet to hear of such a study*: Alfie Kohn, "Challenging Behaviorist Dogma: Myths About Money and Motivation," *Compensation & Benefits Review*, March/April 1998, http://www.alfiekohn.org/managing/cbdmamam.htm.

200 *not the absolute level*: Charles S. Jacobs, "Why Money Isn't a Motivator," Forbes.com, March 6, 2009, http://www.forbes.com/2009/03/06/salary-cap-ceo-pay-opinions-contributors-executive-compensation.html.

200 *more important than financial compensation*: John Mackey, "Why Sky-High CEO Pay Is Bad Business," *Harvard Business Review*, June 17, 2009, https://hbr.org/2009/06/why-high-ceo-pay-is-bad-business.

CHAPTER FOURTEEN

205 *only one of the ten highest-paid CEOs*: Joann S. Lublin, "How Much the Best-Performing and Worst-Performing CEOs Got Paid," *Wall Street Journal*, June 25, 2015, www.wsj.com/articles/how-much-the-best-and-worst-ceos-got-paid-1435104565.

205 *companies showed negative returns*: Robert Reich, "Stop Subsidizing Sky-High CEO Salaries," the *Christian Science Monitor*, July 18, 2013, http://www.csmonitor.com/Business/Robert-Reich/2013/0718/Stop-subsidizing-sky-high-CEO-salaries.

205 *one-quarter of the twenty-five highest-paid*: Scott Klinger, Sam Pizzigati, and Sarah Anderson, "Executive Excess 2013: Bailed Out, Booted, and Busted—A 20-Year Review of America's Top-Paid CEOs," Institute for Policy Studies, August 28, 2013, http://www.ips-dc.org/wp-content/uploads/2013/08/EE13-FINAL.pdf.

205 *produced below-average stock market returns*: Sarah Morgan, "10 Things CEOs Won't Tell You," MarketWatch, July 1, 2011, http://www.marketwatch.com/story/10-things-ceos-wont-tell-you-1309551879312.

206 *they ignore disconfirming information*: Michael J. Cooper, Huseyin Gulen, and P. Raghavendra Rau, "Performance for Pay? the Relation Between CEO Incentive Compensation and Future Stock Price Performance," October 1, 2014, http://papers.ssrn .com/sol3/papers.cfm?abstract_id=1572085.

206 *result in overinvesting: as compared to their peers:* Ibid.

206 *"deserved pay"*: "Executive Pay and Performance," *The Economist*, February 7, 2012, http://www.economist.com/blogs/graphicdetail/2012/02/focus-0.

206 *performance explained less than 5 percent of CEO pay*: Henry L. Tosi, Steve Werner, Jeffrey P. Katz, and Luis R. Gomez-Mejia, "How Much Does Performance Matter? A Meta-analysis of CEO Pay Studies," *Journal of Management* 26, no. 2 (April 2000), doi: 10.1177/014920630002600207.

206 *are not the best performers*: Lucian Bebchuk and Jesse Fried, *Pay Without Performance: The Unfulfilled Promise of Executive Compensation* (Cambridge, MA: Harvard University Press, 2006).

207 *It is impossible to devise incentive schemes*: Armstrong and Jacquart, "Business School Experts."

207 *The system has worked*: Steven N. Kaplan, "Executive Compensation and Corporate Governance in the U.S.: Perceptions, Facts and Challenges," NBER Working Paper No. 18395, September 2012, http://www.nber.org/papers/w18395.

208 *It is very difficult to explain the observed variations*: Piketty, *Capital in the Twenty-First Century.*

209 *CEOs have managed to capture the pay process*: Marianne Bertrand and Sendhil Mullainathan, "Do CEOs Set Their Own Pay? The Ones Without Principles Do," NBER Working Paper No. 7604, March 2000, http://www.nber.org/papers/ w7604.

209 *reported that total economic return to shareholders*: Eavis, "Valeant Is a Reminder of the Peril of Outsize Executive Pay."

210 *could receive the plan maximum*: Anders Melin, Caleb Melby, and Cynthia Koons, "Valeant CEO Michael Pearson Had Chance at $2.66 Billion Payday," Bloomberg, April 29, 2016, http://www.bloomberg.com/news/articles/2016-04-29/valeant-ceo -michael-pearson-had-chance-at-2-66-billion-payday.

210 *Valeant made more than thirty acquisitions*: Stephen Witt, "Valeant Pharmaceuticals' Novel Business Approach Made It a Wall Street Darling—Then a Pariah," *New York Magazine*, January 13, 2016, http://nymag.com/daily/intelligencer/2016/01/valeant -wall-st-darling-to-pariah.html.

210 *made more than thirty acquisitions*: Eavis, "Valeant Is a Reminder."

211 *successful way to motivate*: Joann S. Lublin, "Valeant CEO's Pay Package Draws Praise as a Model," *Wall Street Journal*, August 24, 2009, http://www.wsj.com/articles /SB125106931496352353.

211 *Valeant's stock fell 29 percent*: Linette Lopez, "Short Seller: Here's Why Pharmaceutical Company Valeant Looks Like Enron," *Business Insider*, October 21, 2015, http ://www.businessinsider.com/a-short-selling-firm-is-accusing-valeant-of-being -enron-and-it-says-it-has-proof-2015-10.

211 *looking for a new CEO*: Phil Wahba, "Valeant Is Looking for a New CEO," *Fortune*, March 21, 2016, http://fortune.com/2016/03/21/valeant-ceo/.

213 *From the 1930s, [Soviet] workers were paid bonuses*: Acemoglu and Robinson, *Why Nations Fail.*

CHAPTER FIFTEEN

219 *The stock of the acquiring company declines*: Sara B. Moeller, Frederik P. Schlingemann, and René M. Stulz, "Do Shareholders of Acquiring Firms Gain from Acquisitions?," NBER Working Paper No. 9523, February 2003, http://www.nber.org/papers/w9523.

219 *achieved little or none of the cost reductions*: Barbara Petitt and Kenneth R. Ferris, *Valuation for Mergers and Acquisitions*, 2nd ed. (Upper Saddle River, NJ: FT Press, 2013).

219 *shareholders lose 5.9 cents per dollar*: Ibid.

219 *$257 billion*: Ibid.

CHAPTER SIXTEEN

222 *be allowed to nominate directors for election*: Gretchen Morgenson, "Effort Begins for More Say on Directors," *New York Times*, November 5, 2014, http://www.nytimes.com/2014/11/06/business/effort-begins-for-more-say-on-directors.html.

222 *When CEO and chairman roles are distinct*: Jena McGregor, "A Reason to Split the Role of CEO and Chairman," on *Leadership* (blog), *Washington Post*, July 2, 2012, http://www.washingtonpost.com/blogs/post-leadership/post/a-reason-to-split-the-role-of-ceo-and-chairman/2012/07/02/gJQAewK9HW_blog.html.

222 *28 percent higher at companies with a separate CEO*: Ibid.

222 *separate the jobs of chairman and CEO*: Shelly K. Schwartz, "Tipping Point for Combined Chairman and CEO?," CNBC.com, November 15, 2012, http://www.cnbc.com/id/49829626.

225 *unload their shares gradually*: For a full discussion of how to limit the unloading of restricted stock, see Lucian A. Bebchuk and Jesse M. Fried, "Paying for Long-Term Performance," *University Pennsylvania Law Review* 158 (2010), https://www.law.upenn.edu/live/files/19-bebchuk158upalrev19152010pdf.

225 *J. P. Morgan set this ratio*: Laura Fitzpatrick, "Brief History: Executive Pay," *Time*, November 2, 2009, http://www.time.com/time/magazine/article/0,9171,1931748,00.html.

225 *David Cameron considered it the maximum*: Charles Tilley, "For Fair Pay, See Plato," *Guardian*, June 3, 2010, http://www.guardian.co.uk/commentisfree/2010/jun/03/public-sector-pay-cameron-executive-bonuses.

225 *Drucker believed that a pay gap*: Eleanor Bloxham, "How Can We Address Excessive CEO Pay?," *Fortune*, April 13, 2011, http://management.fortune.cnn.com/2011/04/13/how-can-we-address-excessive-ceo-pay/.

226 *CEO pay rose on average 12 percent annually*: Gretchen Morgenson, "Shareholders' Votes Have Done Little to Curb Lavish Executive Pay," *New York Times*, May 16, 2015, http://www.nytimes.com/2015/05/17/business/shareholders-votes-have-done-little-to-curb-lavish-executive-pay.html.

226 *less than 10 percent of individual shareholders*: Alec Foege, "Does Shareholder Activism Accomplish Anything?," CNBC.com, November 20, 2012, http://www.cnbc.com/id/49885521.

226 *Thus between July 2014*: Madison Marriage, "Executive Pay 'Rubber Stamping' Rife," *Financial Times*, May 8, 2016, http://www.ft.com/cms/s/0/be4cab34-0ba4-11e6-b0f1-61f222853ff3.html#axzz48aJqHbOP.

226 *voted in favor of at least 95 percent*: Morgenson, "Shareholders' Votes."

229 *S&P 500 CEOs averaged under $12.6 million*: Equilar/Associated Press S&P 500 CEO Pay Study 2016, http://www.equilar.com/reports/37-2-associated-press-pay-study-2016.html.

231 *50 percent favored limiting CEO compensation*: Noam Scheiber and Dalia Sussman, "Inequality Troubles Americans Across Party Lines, Times/CBS Poll Finds," *New York Times*, June 3, 2015, http://www.nytimes.com/2015/06/04/business/inequality-a-major-issue-for-americans-times-cbs-poll-finds.html.

231 *Ninety-nine percent of all new income generated today*: "Where Does Bernie Sanders Stand On the Issues," http://feelthebern.org/bernie-sanders-on-economic-inequality/.

231 *now controls 21.5 percent*: Ibid.

231 *He introduced legislation*: http://www.ontheissues.org/Archive/Outsider_House_Corporations.htm.

231 *disparity will help working families*: Senator Bernie Sanders, "Sanders Statement on CEO Pay Rule," August 5, 2015, http://www.sanders.senate.gov/newsroom/recent-business/sanders-statement-on-ceo-pay-rule.

231 *wants CEOs to pay extra taxes*: Tim Murphy, "What Would Life Under President Sanders Actually Look Like?" *Mother Jones*, September 15, 2015.

231 *the City of Portland enacted a surtax*: Gretchen Morgenson, "Portland Adopts Surcharge on C.E.O. Pay in Move vs. Income Inequality," *The New York Times*, December 7, 2016.

INDEX

ABOUT THE AUTHOR

STEVEN CLIFFORD was CEO of King Broadcasting Company and National Mobile Television. Previously he had served as the chief financial officer for King Broadcasting Company and special deputy comptroller for the City of New York during the city's financial crisis, from 1974 to 1977. He has been a director of thirteen companies and a trustee of nine nonprofit institutions.

He and his wife of forty-six years, Judith, have lived in Seattle since 1978. They have two daughters: Lee Clifford, cofounder of Altruettte, and Stephanie Clifford, author of *Everybody Rise*, a *New York Times* bestseller. Steven and Judith have four grandchildren who are all above average.

Since 2010, Clifford has written a humor blog for *The Huffington Post*, which you can find at http://www.huffingtonpost.com /author/s-clifford-658.

One of seven children, he attended public schools in Montclair, New Jersey. He holds a BA from Columbia University, where he majored in Art History, and an MBA with Distinction from Harvard Business School. He served six years in the United States Army Reserves and was justifiably promoted to private first class.

In his lifetime, retirement is the only thing he has done well.